Beginning
JBoss® Seam

From Novice to Professional

Joseph Faisal Nusairat

Apress®

Beginning JBoss® Seam: From Novice to Professional

Copyright © 2007 by Joseph Faisal Nusairat

ISBN-13 (pbk): 978-1-59059-792-7

ISBN-10 (pbk): 1-59059-792-3

Printed and bound in the United States of America 9 8 7 6 5 4 3 2 1

Lead Editor: Steve Anglin
Technical Reviewer: Floyd Carver
Editorial Board: Steve Anglin, Ewan Buckingham, Gary Cornell, Jason Gilmore, Jonathan Gennick, Jonathan Hassell, James Huddleston, Chris Mills, Matthew Moodie, Dominic Shakeshaft, Jim Sumser, Keir Thomas, Matt Wade
Project Manager: Denise Santoro Lincoln
Copy Edit Manager: Nicole Flores
Copy Editor: Sharon Wilkey
Assistant Production Director: Kari Brooks-Copony
Production Editor: Lori Bring
Compositor: Patrick Cunningham
Proofreader: Dan Shaw
Indexer: John Collin
Artist: April Milne
Cover Designer: Kurt Krames
Manufacturing Director: Tom Debolski

Distributed to the book trade worldwide by Springer-Verlag New York, Inc., 233 Spring Street, 6th Floor, New York, NY 10013. Phone 1-800-SPRINGER, fax 201-348-4505, email orders-ny@springer-sbm.com, or visit http://www.springeronline.com.

For information on translations, please contact Apress directly at 2560 Ninth Street, Suite 219, Berkeley, CA 94710. Phone 510-549-5930, fax 510-549-5939, email info@apress.com, or visit http://www.apress.com.

The source code for this book is available to readers at http://www.apress.com in the Source Code/ Download section as well as at http://www.integrallis.com.

To the memory of my grandparents, Kasim Nusair and Kurdeih Rashdan;
To my grandparents, Henry Albert Baker and Mary Baker;
To my parents, Janette Darr and AJ Nusairat;
And to all my friends and family who supported me throughout the years.

Contents at a Glance

About the Author xv

About the Technical Reviewer xvii

Acknowledgments xix

Introduction xxi

CHAPTER 1   What Is JBoss Seam? 1

CHAPTER 2   Web Applications 23

CHAPTER 3   JSF Fundamentals 47

CHAPTER 4   EJB3 Fundamentals 85

CHAPTER 5   Introduction to Seam 121

CHAPTER 6   Seam Contexts 159

CHAPTER 7   Business Process in Seam 187

CHAPTER 8   Advanced Topics 223

CHAPTER 9   Advanced Configurations 269

CHAPTER 10 Seam Tools 287

APPENDIX A JBoss AS 307

APPENDIX B JBoss IDE 315

FINAL THOUGHTS 317

INDEX 319

Contents

About the Author xv

About the Technical Reviewer xvii

Acknowledgments xix

Introduction xxi

CHAPTER 1   **What Is JBoss Seam?** 1

What Does Seam Buy You? 2

Three-Tier Architecture. 2

Three-Tier Architecture with Seam 3

Component Choices 4

Seam Environment Requirements 6

Hello World Example 7

Introduction to MVC Architecture 9

Basics of MVC Architecture 9

Frameworks 10

Java 5 11

Downloading Java 5 12

Language Features 14

POJOs 20

Annotations on POJOs. 20

Configuring Your Server 20

Summary. 21

CHAPTER 2   **Web Applications** 23

Servlets. 23

Contexts in Servlets. 24

Servlets and Frameworks. 25

Implementation Patterns 25

    Understanding the Parts of Our Examples. 26

    Displaying Dynamic Data 28

    Requesting and Saving Data 30

    Logging In 34

    Listing and Viewing a Page 37

Sample Applications 40

    Garage Sale 41

    Travel Reservations 42

    Ticketing System 44

Summary. 45

■CHAPTER 3   **JSF Fundamentals** 47

Background 48

Implementations 49

Hello World Example. 49

Configuration 51

    Using Tomahawk. 51

    Configuring XML Files 52

    Creating the WAR File 57

Rapid Application Development 59

Architecture 59

    JSF Areas 60

    Managed Beans 67

Life Cycle 68

Components 71

    Component Layout. 72

    Standard Components 73

JSF Expression Language 74

Page Flow 76

Put It All Together 78

    Add Page. 79

    List Page 81

Summary 83

CHAPTER 4   EJB3 Fundamentals 85

History of EJB3 86

    EJB 2.x 86

    EJB3 87

Configuring EJB3s for Deployment 88

    Creating XML Files 88

    Packaging 90

Session Beans 92

    Stateless Session Beans 93

    Stateful Session Beans 97

Message-Driven Beans 101

Entity Beans 102

    Basics of an Entity Bean 102

    Entity Bean Annotations 104

    Collections Annotations 107

Entity Manager 110

    Persistence Context 110

    Operations on the Entity Manager 111

    JPQL—EJB3 Query Language 113

Transactions 114

    What Is a Transaction? 114

    Transaction Processing 115

Calling EJBs 119

Testing 120

Summary 120

CHAPTER 5   Introduction to Seam 121

What Is Seam? 122

Basic Seam Configuration 123

    Downloading Seam 123

    Configuring Seam 124

First Example: Stateless Session Bean 126

Architecture 131

    POJOs and Annotations 132

    Inversion of Control and Bijection 132

    Interceptors. 134

    Seam Contexts 135

    Three-Tier Architecture with Seam 138

Components 141

    Seam Configuration Options 141

    Logging 143

    Debug Mode 144

    Data Model 147

    Validation. 151

Summary. 157

■CHAPTER 6   **Seam Contexts** 159

Stateless Context. 160

Session Context 161

Application Context 164

Event Context 165

Page Context 165

Conversation Context 166

    What the Conversation Context Brings You. 167

    How It Works 167

    Additional Configuration 172

    JSF Integration with Conversations 172

    Seam Debugging 180

More on How to Access Contexts. 180

    Using Roles 181

    Where Do Contexts Live? 182

Default Bindings 184

    Stateless Session Beans. 184

    Entity Beans 184

    Message-Driven Beans. 184

    Stateful Session Beans. 185

    JavaBeans. 185

Summary 186

CHAPTER 7   Business Process in Seam 187

What Is JBoss jBPM? 188

Process Definitions 189

How jBPM Works 190

An Example for Using jBPM: Ticketing System. 190

Creating a Workflow 191

Components Involved in Creating a Process Definition. 192

Process Definition Creation in Seam 197

Configuring jBPM with Seam 197

Creating the Process Definition. 203

Viewing Tasks 204

Creating a Task 207

Switching Process Definitions 211

Page Flow Definitions 213

Components Involved in Creating a Page Flow. 217

Page Flow Creation in Seam 220

Configuring Page Flow with Seam 220

Starting the Page Flow 220

Summary. 221

CHAPTER 8   Advanced Topics 223

Internationalization 223

Understanding Language Bundles 224

Using Language Bundles with Seam 226

Selecting a Language 231

Themes 234

Creating Themes 234

Using Themes. 236

Selecting Themes 236

Web Services 237

Types of Web Services 238

REST in Seam. 239

Ajax 240

    Seam Remoting 240

    Ajax4jsf in Seam 250

    JMS Messaging Using Ajax 255

Security 258

    Implementing Authentication 258

    The Seam Security Manager 262

    Component-Level Authentication 263

    Page-Level Authentication 263

Drools Support 264

    Configuring Drools 265

    Using Drools in a Seam Component 265

    Using Drools in jBPM 266

Summary 267

▮CHAPTER 9   **Advanced Configurations** 269

Optional Environmental Configurations 269

    Running Seam in the Embedded EJB3 Container 270

    Running Seam with Hibernate 275

Optional Component Configurations 282

    Additions to faces-config.xml 282

    Additions to web.xml 284

Portlet Support 284

Summary 285

▮CHAPTER 10   **Seam Tools** 287

Testing 288

    Unit Testing 288

    TestNG 288

    Integration Testing 292

Hibernate Console with Seam 294

    Database in Question 294

    Reverse Engineering the Database 295

jBPM Designer 303

    Starting the Process 303

    Creating a Process Definition. 304

    Creating a Page Flow 305

Summary. 306

■APPENDIX A   JBoss AS. 307

What Is JBoss?. 307

Downloading JBoss. 307

Installing JBoss 308

Using JBoss 311

    Running JBoss 311

    Deploying JBoss. 312

    Adding a Data Source 312

    Locating and Configuring Log Files 314

■APPENDIX B   JBoss IDE. 315

■FINAL THOUGHTS 317

■INDEX 319

About the Author

JOSEPH FAISAL NUSAIRAT is a software developer who has been working full-time in the Columbus, Ohio, area since 1998, primarily focused on Java development. His career has taken him into a variety of Fortune 500 industries, including military applications, data centers, banking, Internet security, pharmaceuticals, and insurance. Throughout this experience, he has worked on all varieties of application development—from design to architecture to development. Joseph, like most Java developers, is particularly fond of open source projects and tries to use as much open source software as possible when working with clients.

Joseph is a graduate of Ohio University with dual degrees in Computer Science and Microbiology and a minor in Chemistry. While at Ohio University, Joseph also dabbled in student politics and was a research assistant in the virology labs.

Currently, Joseph works as a senior partner at Integrallis Software (http://www. integrallis.com). In his off-hours he enjoys watching bodybuilding and Broadway musicals, specifically anything with Lauren Molina in them.

About the Technical Reviewer

FLOYD CARVER has been building software systems for 20 years. During this time, he has performed in many roles, from developer to architect and from student to instructor. He is currently providing consultant services as an applications architect. When not consulting, Floyd enjoys traveling, playing and coaching soccer, and coaching basketball.

Acknowledgments

As this is my first book, there are so many people to thank for helping me put this together. The order of my thanks in no way signifies importance; everyone here and even more helped in some way to get this off the ground. I would like to first thank the publisher, Apress, without whom there would be no book. Thank you to Steve Anglin for giving a starting author the opportunity to write. In addition, I would like to thank my copy editor, Sharon Wilkey, who helped me quite a bit with my writing. Denise Santoro Lincoln, my project manager, for continuously pushing me to try to meet my deadlines. Finally, my copy edit manager, Nicole Flores, and many other staff members of Apress for all the work they put into publishing the book.

And thank you to my technical reviewer Floyd Carver, who, when I asked if he would be my tech reviewer, said yes without thinking twice. I appreciate that, considering the amount of work he had in store—thanks for all your time spent. Also I would like to thank Brian Sam-Bodden, my business partner, for his mentoring and for pushing me to start writing. I would also like to thank Chris Judd for not only reviewing some of my chapters but also giving me good advice on writing early on (I actually followed some of it). Also Marie Wong, who not only helped keep me sane during this process, but also helped convert my drawings to meaningful diagrams.

Because this is a book on JBoss, I would be remiss not to thank Gavin King, JBoss, and the contributors to Seam for creating the Seam framework. Also I would like to thank all those who contributed to the Seam Forum on the JBoss site. I was a regular viewer, and I even tried to take note of items that people seemed to have trouble with in order to make this a better book.

Writing a book was one of the most pleasurable experiences I have had—well, pleasurable and stressful all in the same breath. Everyone along my school and career path helped me get where I am today. The Ohio University computer science department, and in particular Dr. Shawn Ostermann, helped inspire me not only to stick with computer science but to want to learn even more—something that I hope is with me today. In addition, Scott Carter of TSYS in Columbus, Georgia, was my first mentor as I was learning Java, and he definitely helped push me on the right path for clean, functional development practices.

Finally, my siblings, Sarah, Michael, Robert, Angela, Adam, and Ashley—you are all great, and I hope you all enjoy the book.

I am sure I left out someone, so just a general thanks to all those that helped.

And finally, you the reader, for picking this book to read out of all the Java books out there. I appreciate it and hope you come away with a better understanding of JBoss Seam.

Introduction

Agile, agile, agile, Ruby, Ruby, Ruby. It seems like every conference you go to these days talks about either agile or Ruby. Those are the big buzzwords in the industry. Everywhere you go, that's all you seem to hear. And as my friend Rob Stevenson says, that's all he wants to do. In fact, the only books he reads now are Ruby books. The real question is, why? Personally I think it's because he likes a limited selection of books. But the other reason is, Ruby is fun. It's fast, it's cool, it's new, and it makes development a pleasure. And computer-savvy developers seem to love anything new. I honestly get a bit tired of *everything* coming out calling itself agile. Its such a key word these days that I am just waiting for recruiters and sales managers of consulting companies to start telling their clients they need agile developers.

The real question has to be, what is meant by *agile*? What is needed to make something agile? Agile development keeps the ease of development while still making the code clean. And I think that's what every user is *really* looking for. It's why Ruby is popular, and it's the attraction to Trails. There is so much work going into plumbing these days that it's almost overwhelming. Every team seems to want to reinvent the wheel. Larger companies have extended frameworks such as Apache Struts and are using it for what they think are specific needs. Sometimes this is useful; other times all they have done is added a layer of confusion.

In today's business world, companies are trying to minimize cost and time while maximizing product. This often results in many shortcuts and can result in code that is even more difficult to maintain. This is where agile development comes into play. This is also where JBoss Seam comes into play. We as developers need to develop the business logic and the presentation tier as fast as possible. With agile development, this becomes possible.

I like refer to Seam as an enterprise agile framework, which to some people may seem like an oxymoron because *agile* precludes you to think something is small and easy, whereas *enterprise* often brings to mind bountiful amounts of code. However, I am hoping that is exactly what your experience will be while reading this book and using Seam.

Throughout this book, you will examine the concepts of web development, the parts of Seam, and various examples using Seam. By the end, you should have an appreciation that although Seam is complex behind the scenes, to the developer it can be fairly smooth. And although it may not have the kinks out of its armor yet, it is definitely proceeding down a path that is good for the Java community.

Items Covered in This Book

In this book, you will first learn some of the basics of web application design. You'll then learn about the JSF and EJB3 components. After that, the book will progressively move to more-advanced and interesting topics related to Seam. The following list outlines the contents of each chapter:

Chapter 1: What Is JBoss Seam?

This introductory chapter briefly explains Seam and provides an introduction to the Model View Controller (MVC) framework, Java 5, and JBoss 4. Both Java 5 and JBoss 4 are needed to run most of the applications in the book, and Java 5 is a must for Seam. If you know both of them, you can skip ahead.

Chapter 2: Web Applications

This chapter starts by covering the basics of web application design. We will step through basic design patterns when creating the presentation tier and compare and contrast them between Struts and Seam. The idea is to start the process of thinking how Seam will save you time as compared to traditional web application development. The end of the chapter presents the two basic samples we will use as the example applications throughout the book.

Chapter 3: JSF Fundamentals

Seam requires the use of JavaServer Faces (JSF) for its presentation tier component. Although you do not need the most advanced JSF knowledge to use Seam, you still need a basic understanding. This chapter provides the basic knowledge and architecture of JSF, while limiting discussion of certain topics, such as backing beans, because they do not have high reuse when using Seam.

Chapter 4: EJB3 Fundamentals

Seam requires Enterprise JavaBeans 3 (EJB3) for its business logic and persistence tiers. Although you could get away with having a limited or beginner's understanding of JSF to use Seam, an intermediate knowledge of EJB3 is more desirable. Because this is where the bulk of the coding takes place, this chapter introduces you to the three major facets of EJB3: the stateful session bean (SFSB), stateless session bean (SLSB), and entity bean (EB). I also go over the message-driven bean (MDB), but to a lesser extent. This chapter focuses more on the needs of the EB because those are radically different from the EJB 2.1 specification.

Chapter 5: Introduction to Seam

This is the first official chapter introducing you to Seam. The previous chapters presented background information required for beginners. In this chapter, you will learn how to write a basic Seam application. You will also learn the fundamentals of the Seam architecture. Near the end, you will learn about additional beginner components of Seam. By the end of this chapter, you will be able to write more-complex Seam applications.

Chapter 6: Seam Contexts

With basic Seam knowledge in hand, you will learn in this chapter more-advanced Seam topics, namely contexts. Contexts in Seam are essentially the same as they are in servlets. However, there are more of them and they have more functionality. This chapter discusses the Stateless, Event, Page, Conversation, Session, and Application contexts.

Chapter 7: Business Process in Seam

This chapter focuses on using JBoss Business Process Management (jBPM) with Seam. jBPM is JBoss's business process management system, which usually requires custom code to interact with. However, there is a Seam context specifically for Business Process components. This chapter covers the basics of jBPM and how to use it with Seam.

Chapter 8: Advanced Topics

By this point, all of the basics on using Seam and its various contexts have been covered. This chapter covers more-advanced topics, from internationalization and themes to Drools support. Although these topics may not be extremely difficult, they are necessary topics for users who want to make the most out of Seam.

Chapter 9: Advanced Configurations

Earlier I alluded to how you do not have to use EJB3 with Seam. This chapter starts by showing you how you can use EJB3 outside the application server. We will then go on to using Seam without EJB3 at all, just by using JavaBeans for our business logic and Hibernate for our persistence tier. This chapter will be especially helpful if your ability to deploy to a full application server is not quite there yet.

Chapter 10: Seam Tools

This chapter introduces you to free tools available to help create Seam applications. These are a mix of Seam-specific and non-Seam-specific tools that help make enterprise development easier. This chapter also covers how to perform testing with Seam, specifically with TestNG.

Who This Book Is For

This book is a beginner's guide to Seam. However, the book also provides details on the components used by Seam such as JSF and EJB3. Although having a Java EE client/server developer background is not an absolute must, without it the benefit of using Seam may not be 100 percent clear, because most of its functionality deals with overcoming problems developers have had in the past. That being said, at the minimum, you should have the following:

- A beginner's understanding of Java (at least Java 1.2 and preferably Java 1.4)

- An understanding of basic web application development

Downloading and Running the Source Code

I have tried to include as much of the source code as I can in this book. The source code is also available from the Source Code/Download area of the Apress website (`http://www.apress.com`) and from my Integrallis website (`http://www.integrallis.com`). From the Integrallis site, click Publications and then select Beginning JBoss Seam. From either site, you can download a zip file that includes the following:

- Source code

- Dependent library JAR files

- Apache Ant build scripts

- Database build scripts (when applicable)

You can also find any notes or updates about the book on these websites.

Contacting the Author

If you have any questions or comments about this book, you can contact me via email at `jnusairat@integrallis.com`.

CHAPTER 1

■ ■ ■

What Is JBoss Seam?

seam (sēm) *n.*

A line of junction formed by sewing together two pieces of material along their margins.

A similar line, ridge, or groove made by fitting, joining, or lapping together two sections along their edges.

The preceding definition[1] of *seam* is usually used when discussing sewing. However, this definition also fits the latest in frameworks from JBoss—JBoss Seam. *JBoss Seam* is a framework that brings together existing Java Platform, Enterprise Edition (Java EE) standards to enable them to work as an integrated solution. At its core, the Seam framework ties the Enterprise JavaBeans 3 (EJB3) and JavaServer Faces (JSF) specifications. However, Seam does not just stop there—it will also join together other component models that you may be used to, such as jBPM, Drools, and more that we will get into as the book progresses.

When I mentioned *EJB*, you may have been taken aback with fear or may have started shaking your head profusely. Although EJB 2.1 had some negative connotations, especially regarding the way it relates to stateful session beans (SFSBs) and entity beans (EBs), any negative feelings about it should be reexamined today. With the new EJB3 specification, EJBs have become lightweight plain old Java objects (POJOs) that do not require as much of the "plumbing" as before. Hopefully those of you who may harbor negative feelings toward EJB3 will review and revise those feelings as you see how Seam enables you to not only cut development time but also more clearly separate your business logic and presentation tiers by cutting out the connecting code (for example, Struts actions) normally associated with web frameworks.

For years developers realized that the JavaServer Pages (JSP)/servlets paradigm was not enough to create enterprise-level web pages. That model provided the capability for a web tier that could pass objects from the client to the server, but essentially that was it. For most developers, this simple paradigm was not enough; more-complex operations were needed, and developers found themselves writing infrastructure code to deal with

---

1. http://www.thefreedictionary.com/seam

the shortcomings of the Servlet specification. Eventually, all the ideas learned from creating custom infrastructure code resulted in the web frameworks we know today, such as Apache's Struts and Tapestry, OpenSymphony's WebWork, and so forth. The Java community also got together and through the Java Community Process (JCP) created the JSF specification to tackle some of the issues raised and deal with the shortcomings of the Servlet specification.

Even though we now have web and business tiers with improved functionality, we have still been forced to create the plumbing code needed to connect them together. With Seam, however, these two areas can now focus more exclusively on what they do best—presentation and business logic.

What Does Seam Buy You?

When picking up this book, one of your first questions should be, "Why do I even need Seam if I have EJB3 and JSF already?" After all, they were designed to simplify the process of creating web applications. What is the benefit of using the Seam framework with these components if they have already taken care of much of the plumbing that was required before?

The answer lies in what you are trying to accomplish. To be useful, your application has to be a multitiered application that uses specific components for the presentation, business, and persistence tiers. Before, you may have accomplished this with a combination of Struts (presentation), Interface21's Spring (business), and JBoss's Hibernate (persistence) frameworks. Now, following the Java EE specification, you will be using JSF (presentation), EJB3-SB (business), and EJB3-EB (persistence). As before, each of these components requires lots of glue to link them together to talk to each other. Throughout this book I will show you how Seam has transformed this messy gluing you had to do before into a now seamless process.

Three-Tier Architecture

Any beginner may ask not only, "Why do we need all this?" but also, "Where does Seam fit into the equation?" Since about 1999, standard development practice in Java EE was to divide your application into three distinct tiers: presentation, business, and persistent tiers, as illustrated in Figure 1-1. (Java EE was then known as J2EE. It became Java EE after version 1.4 of the Enterprise Edition).

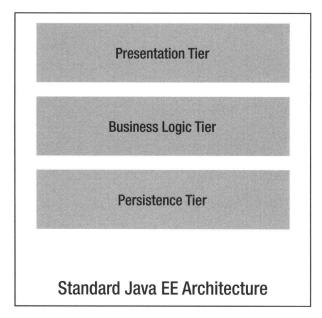

Figure 1-1. *The three-tier Java EE architecture*

These tiers are defined as follows:

Presentation tier: The presentation tier encompasses everything from the Hypertext Markup Language (HTML) page to objects controlling the request, such as Struts `Action` classes or JSF backing beans. Everything in this tier deals with communication to the client—be it a web page or BlackBerry.

Business logic tier: The business logic tier is where you make your business decisions; it contains the logic of the application. Also, this is where the business processing and (if needed) the database transactions occur.

Persistence tier: The persistence tier represents the interaction with the database. This is where you maintain data access objects (DAOs), Hibernate DAOs, or your entity beans. These classes can be either database specific or nonspecific, depending on what you need. This tier may also contain your database domain objects.

Three-Tier Architecture with Seam

Now you will take a look at the same architecture when using Seam. Figure 1-2 shows the injection points of Seam into the tiers; notice that it encompasses every tier.

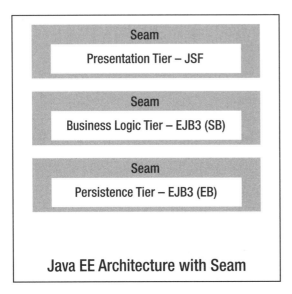

Figure 1-2. *The three-tier Java EE architecture with Seam*

In Figure 1-2, you can see that Seam wraps the components by using annotations to declare the POJOs to be wrapped. Then Seam identifies those annotated POJOs and binds the components across the tiers by using interceptors. This allows a smoother transition between tiers. Usually the binding and connecting between the tiers is much rougher in Java EE architecture without Seam. This allows you to then focus your development on the business, presentation, and persistence tiers without worrying about making them interact. Chapter 5 covers in more depth the interception of the Seam components as well as their life cycle.

Component Choices

As you know, and as I pointed out earlier, there are many different components that can work for the various tiers. So why should you use JSF + EJB3 + Seam? The simple answer is that the first two are the "new standard." However, there are additional, more-solid answers than that as well. In this section and in the following few chapters you will more closely examine the usefulness and clean implementations (due to being POJOs) of these components.

Why JSF?

JSF is now a Java standard from the JCP for presentation tier development. Now, just because something is a standard does not necessarily mean it is the best choice, but that you should factor it into the equation. JSF being part of the JCP will guarantee that there will always be support from an army of developers with skill sets specific to its implementation. Along with this support, there are also a wealth of built-in tools from vendors and third-party programs for creating robust JSF pages. Plug-ins are being created, and even more are planned to help make JSF pages as easy as possible to create by having drag-and-drop functionality for the various integrated development environments (IDEs). There are also multiple JSF implementations to choose from. Apache's MyFaces is what JBoss uses for its JSF implementation and is what we will be using throughout the book.

Another positive with JSF is its ability to handle multiple presentation tier types. Yes, many other frameworks can be hacked to do that as well, but this is out-of-the-box support. This is achieved through JSF's presentation tier component-based architecture. Although the JSF pages still use tag libraries for the display, the component orientation of the JSF components makes them more than just simple user interface (UI) pieces. The libraries are naturally then more involved with each other.

Another advantage to JSF is that it simplifies the development of code that is called from the client page. In JSF, these listeners are referred to as *backing beans*. As I said earlier, JSF is partially independent from the servlet context, so the backing beans used can be regular POJOs with no knowledge of the Servlet specification. I say *partially* because they can have access to the Servlet specification if it is directly declared.

Finally, JSF continues to make inroads into the community and with Struts. Many of the former Struts developers used their knowledge of what they did right and wrong in the past to help create the JSF specification.

Why EJB3?

EJB3 provides just about everything you could want for business logic and presentation tiers. You get enterprise-level state-managed classes, Java Message Service (JMS) listeners, and database-level objects. Now, most of you may think, "Well, so did EJB 2.1; why do I need EJB3?" Well, this is all provided without the need for Extensible Markup Language (XML), and all your classes are still POJOs. You no longer have the overhead of multiple interfaces for creation and remotes, no more convoluted deployment descriptors, and no more stub creations. Also, like JSF, this is an industry standard, so you also get the regular cadre of developers working on it as well as different implementations.

Why Seam?

The simple answer to why we are using Seam is to create simplicity from complexity. Regardless of how easy it is to implement JSF and EJB3, they still require you to create backing beans to allow your presentation tier to talk to your business logic tier. With JSF, you have to write extensive XML files telling the presentation tier what kind of domain objects to expect. By using Seam, you can remove extra coding and focus more on the parts that matter—the presentation and business logic.

Seam does this not by creating an extra class such as a JSF action listener, but by using Java annotations. Seam allows you to create a seamless transition between application tiers by utilizing metadata in the form of Java annotations to define how the presentation and business logic tiers can talk to each other. In addition, Seam also allows you to define EB domain objects to be used on the presentation tier. The question then becomes, "How are we just removing classes?" or "Were these classes really needed before?" After working with many web frameworks on many projects, I have noticed that often what your action listeners are doing is just translating presentation tier data to some business logic tier object, validating that data, and then sending it over to the business logic tier for processing. If they are doing more than that, you are often mixing business logic into your presentation tier. Seam helps you skip this step.

Of course, there are times where the presentation tier needs to do a bit more, so, if you wish, you can also use regular JavaBeans as your annotated objects as well. If you do this, note that the only reason to do so is because you need to prep the data before sending it over to the business logic tier. Based on what I have said thus far, Seam is not adding any features but just taking a few steps away—which, by itself, still makes Seam a valuable tool. However, it also does add some valuable context-management abilities, which allows you to have features such as wizards on your page without having to add a bunch of extra plumbing code. We will get into the details of this in later chapters (Chapters 5, 6, and 7). Hopefully, however, you can already start to see the value of not only Seam, but the combination of Seam, EJB3, and JSF.

Seam Environment Requirements

Because Seam is dependent on JSF and EJB3, it has a few more needs than frameworks such as Spring or Struts. Specifically, Seam requires the following:

- You have to use Java 5 or greater on the front end, because Seam relies heavily on annotations provided by Java 5 or higher implementations of Java Specification Request (JSR) 250.

- You have to use a JSF implementation for the presentation tier. This means either using an application server that supports it or using an open source provider of JSF such as Apache's MyFaces.

- For the most part, you need to have an application server that uses EJB3. Chapter 9 discusses alternatives to using EJB3. However, it is best to assume that you are either going to be able to use EJB3 now or in the near future.

Hello World Example

So before you dive into the intricate details of Seam and the functionality around it, let's take a quick look at building a simple Seam application. As I have said, it provides the glue between the presentation tier and the business logic tier, specifically EJB3. However, in reality, your business logic tier does not have to be EJBs—it can just be plain Java-Beans. So let's look at a Hello World application done with Seam. In this example, a simple JSF page will call the JavaBean to get the text of outputText that has been initialized. We will start with the Seam-annotated JavaBean in Listing 1-1.

Listing 1-1. *Our JavaBean, HelloWorldAction.java, with Seam Annotations*

```
package com.petradesigns.helloworld;

import org.jboss.seam.annotations.Create;
import org.jboss.seam.annotations.Name;

@Name("helloWorld")
public class HelloWorldAction implements IHelloWorld {

    private String outputText;

    @Create
    public void init() {
        outputText = "Hello World";
    }

    public String getOutputText() {
        return outputText;
    }
}
```

As you can see, this is a fairly straightforward Hello World JavaBean. The first @Name annotation defines for us that this is a Seam component with the name of helloWorld. You will then notice that there are two methods. The init() method has an @Create annotation signaling that this method should be called upon instantiation of the JavaBean. The public method getOutputText() can be used to retrieve the output text.

Now that we have the JavaBean, we will create the JSF page needed to retrieve it. The page is defined in Listing 1-2.

Listing 1-2. *Our JSF Page, helloWorld.jsp, to Display "Hello World"*

```
<%@ taglib uri="http://java.sun.com/jsf/html" prefix="h" %>
<%@ taglib uri="http://java.sun.com/jsf/core" prefix="f" %>

<f:view>
    <h:outputText value="#{helloWorld.outputText}"/>
</f:view>
```

This is a JSP page; more specifically, it is a JSF JSP page. The first part contains the standard tag library definitions, and the second part defines the `<f:view>` component. This is a standard component to encapsulate any JSF functionality and is required.

Finally, our #{helloWorld.outputText} references the method outputText on the Seam component helloWorld that we defined previously. When this page is run, it gives us the output shown in Figure 1-3.

Hello World

Figure 1-3. *The Hello World screen shot*

This is all the code it takes to create a Hello World example by using JSF and Seam. This small application consists of a presentation and business tier, even though our business tier is not really doing much.

■**Note** If we wanted to make the JavaBean an EJB3 object, all we would have to do is add the
@Stateless annotation to the class description of the JavaBean.

One of the first things you should notice is our JavaBean representing the business logic. Not only can it be a POJO, but there is nothing in it making it interact exclusively with the presentation tier; nor is there anything on the presentation side telling it to interact exclusively with a Seam component. Seam is handling all that messy middle work usually needed to pipe between the tiers. The end result: you are able to put the bulk of your effort in building a solid business logic tier as opposed to making those objects available to the presentation tier.

I strongly advise you to use my build script included in the source to create this code because there are some intricacies on how to create JSF + EJB3 + Seam that may not be entirely obvious to you yet. These intricacies are explained more clearly in Chapter 5. For now, this can give you a bit to play with.

Introduction to MVC Architecture

If you are familiar with web application design in Java, the MVC pattern is probably fairly well known to you. However, if this is your first time writing a web application, you should follow along closely. This is essentially the pattern that has been followed for designing most web frameworks.

This section presents the MVC architecture and gives examples of various implementations of it, including JSF. For those who are new to web applications, this should help provide some background into how it works.

Basics of MVC Architecture

If this is your first attempt at web development, the concept of Model-View-Controller (MVC) may be new to you. It is the basis for most web application development today. The core principle is to separate your business data from your view components, and then have the ability to translate the data back and forth, as illustrated in Figure 1-4.

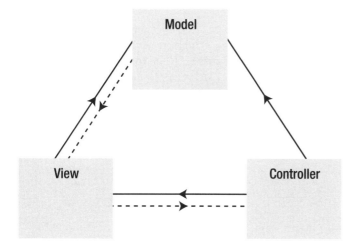

Figure 1-4. *A diagram of the MVC architecture*

The following are the definitions of the MVC parts:

Model: This represents data in the business logic tier and the business rules defining interactions with that data.

View: The view renders the contents of the model for the presentation tier.

Controller: The controller translates the model into the view. The translation will be performed by POST/GET requests from the Web.

Frameworks

A variety of web frameworks have come out over the last few years to implement MVC. For this book we will be using MyFaces, an open source implementation of the JSF specification. However, it would be handy to learn about a few of the others as well.

Fundamentally, all web frameworks work the same way. They all, in some way, extend the Servlet specification. How they usually differ is in how much you are aware that they are extending this specification. When using Struts 1.*x* and Spring MVC, you are fully aware that your classes are part of the Servlet specification. There are servlet-specific classes such as `HttpServletRequest` and `HttpServletResponse` given to you. When using frameworks such as Struts 2 and JSF, you are not as aware. In general, the servlet-specific objects are fairly well hidden and you have to explicitly ask for items such as `HttpServletRequest` and `HttpServletResponse`. Finally, with frameworks such as Tapestry, you are not really aware of the specification at all except through configuration files.

Next you will take a look at each of these frameworks. This small preview gives you an idea of what is out there and has been tried and will hopefully give you insight about why you do not have to worry about the nitty-gritty of these when using Seam.

Struts

Struts, one of the first web frameworks, has definitely proved to be the most popular one out there. It works by having a front controller servlet call action classes. The data from the screen is passed into the classes via an `ActionForm`. With Struts 1.*x* versions, the user was fully aware that they were working in a presentation tier—and the classes were concrete, not POJOs. Much of this has been redressed with Struts 2; however, Struts 2 does not have nearly the success and is not used as much as Struts 1.*x*.

Spring MVC

Spring MVC is a more recent entrant to the MVC game. Spring MVC is distributed with the regular Spring package and can perform business logic as well for a complete Java EE framework. However, Spring MVC is not as new as the rest of Spring. It does provide various ways of interacting with the presentation tier, and if you are looking for a low-key approach, this can work well. However, Spring MVC does not seem to have the robustness of the other web frameworks such as JSF, Struts, and Tapestry.

Tapestry

Tapestry is another web framework that has been around for a long time. The major recent upgrade of Tapestry 4 is powerful. One of its biggest advantages is that, contrary to JSF and most other web frameworks, your Tapestry classes have no knowledge that they are part of a web state because your controller classes (pages in Tapestry) have no knowledge of the request or the session. However, unlike Seam, these pages are not POJOs but they implement the `IPage` interface. Another advantage of Seam is the use of Object-Graph Navigation Language (OGNL) for its presentation tier. This allows HTML and Java developers to create HTML pages that can be translated to dynamic code when run in the application server, but if viewed with a standard web browser outside the application server, the pages will still be viewable. This is not normal behavior for most web application servers.

A Seam-Tapestry combination would be great. Unfortunately, there is no plan to build one at this time.

JSF

Java Server Faces (JSF) is a JSR standard for presentation tier development. Like most other frameworks, it provides a separation between the presentation tier and the action listeners. Unlike most other web frameworks, the actual presentation tier can vary—it does not have to be a JSP-type page because JSF uses a component model to display the presentation tier. Your presentation tier can therefore switch more easily between a web page, XML page, or Java Micro Edition (ME) page. Also, because this is a standard, there are a variety of implementations of vendor support for it.

Java 5

Java 5, also known as Java 1.5.0, is the latest version (at the time of this writing) released from Sun Microsystems—which many thought was a long time coming. Java 5 adds items such as annotations and generics, which many developers had wanted for years. This latest release adds 15 JSRs and about 100 other major updates. This impressive level of enhancement and change reflected such a maturity that the external release was given a Java 5 designation. Table 1-1 lists the JSR enhancements for the release of Java 5; unfortunately, I cannot list all of them within the constraints of this book. However, a few of the enhancements are good to know, and others are important in order to understand how to use EJB3 and Seam. If you want to read a complete list of features, I suggest consulting the Sun site, `http://java.sun.com/j2se/1.5.0/docs/relnotes/features.html`.

Table 1-1. *JSRs for the Java 5 Release*

JSR Number	JSR Name	URL of Specification
003	Java Management Extensions (JMX) Specification	`http://jcp.org/en/jsr/detail?id=3`
013	Decimal Arithmetic Enhancement	`http://jcp.org/en/jsr/detail?id=13`
014	Add Generic Types to the Java Programming Language	`http://jcp.org/en/jsr/detail?id=14`

Continued

Table 1-1. *Continued*

JSR Number	JSR Name	URL of Specification
028	Java SASL Specification	http://jcp.org/en/jsr/detail?id=28
114	JDBC Rowset Implementations	http://jcp.org/en/jsr/detail?id=114
133	Java Memory Model and Thread Specification Revision	http://jcp.org/en/jsr/detail?id=133
160	Java Management Extensions (JMX) Remote API 1.0	http://jcp.org/en/jsr/detail?id=160
163	Java Platform Profiling Architecture	http://jcp.org/en/jsr/detail?id=163
166	Concurrency Utilities	http://jcp.org/en/jsr/detail?id=166
174	Monitoring and Management Specification for the Java Virtual Machine	http://jcp.org/en/jsr/detail?id=174
175	A Metadata Facility for the Java Programming Language	http://jcp.org/en/jsr/detail?id=175
200	Network Transfer Format for Java Archives	http://jcp.org/en/jsr/detail?id=200
201	Extending the Java Programming Language with Enumerations, Autoboxing, Enhanced for Loops and Static Import	http://jcp.org/en/jsr/detail?id=201
204	Unicode Supplementary Character Support	http://jcp.org/en/jsr/detail?id=204
206	Java API for XML Processing (JAXP) 1.3	http://jcp.org/en/jsr/detail?id=206
250	Common Annotations for the Java Platform	http://jcp.org/en/jsr/detail?id=250

Next I will go over where to retrieve Java 5 and will discuss language features that will help you understand and use Seam.

Downloading Java 5

One of the biggest requirements for using Seam is that you have to use Java 5. This is pretty obvious when you realize that Seam is entirely implemented in your code with annotations and that Java 5 introduced us to annotations. Of course, as indicated in Table 1-1, there is a lot more to Java 5 than annotations, and I want to share some of the language features with you. However, in order to do that, you need to download and install Java 5 first.

Many computers come preinstalled with Java 5—all Apple OS X operating systems, for example, contain Java 5 by default. With Sun's relatively new installation of Java, it runs as a service and will update it for you. You can check whether you have the correct version of Java by typing `java -version` at a command prompt. If the response indicates *build 1.5* somewhere in it, you have the right version. The following is an example of a response you might receive if you ran that command on an OS X operating system:

```
Java(TM) 2 Runtime Environment, Standard Edition (build 1.5.0_06-112)
Java HotSpot(TM) Client VM (build 1.5.0_06-64, mixed mode, sharing)
```

If you do not see *build 1.5*, you will need to download the latest Java 5 Software Development Kit (JDK 5.0), formerly known as the JDK. The JDK is needed over the regular Java Runtime Environment (JRE) because we plan on actually doing development with it. You can download it at `http://java.sun.com/javase/downloads/index.jsp`. At that page, select one of the JDKs at the top. Figure 1-5 shows the download page. You can choose any of the downloads in the highlighted section to get the Java 5 installation.

Figure 1-5. *Screen showing a highlight of one of the three JDKs to download*

The installation of the software should be fairly straightforward; if you have any problems with it, consult the documentation on the Sun website.

Language Features

As I said earlier, it would be difficult to discuss all the enhancements that have come with Java 5. However, to understand certain code examples later, you need to know about the language features that have been changed or added. I will present each of the language features and provide example code so that you can successfully use the features. You will not necessarily need to understand them all to use Seam. The only items that are absolutely necessary to understand are the annotations. However, I still suggest reading all of them. Most are designed to make your life simpler and the code cleaner.

Metadata (aka Annotations)

One of the biggest additions to Java 5—and indeed what is the core to what makes Seam work—is annotations. Annotations were partially derived because of the ever-increasing amount of XML. XML was used for deployment descriptors, configuration files, and so forth, but when all was said and done, there were often too many XML files. Another problem associated with XML files was that there was no compile-time ability to check that you wrote the XML file correctly. Finally, annotations allow us to make more classes POJOs and less reliant upon implemented objects.

Now, one of the interesting things about annotations is that, more than likely, you will never actually have to write one. However, that being said, it is always good to know how to just in case.

With all the hype I have just given them, the question really should be, "What is an annotation?" Listing 1-3 provides an example of using an annotation.

Listing 1-3. *An Example of Using an Annotation*

```
import javax.ejb.Stateless;

@Stateless
public class MyStatelessBean { }
```

As you can see, this looks awfully like a Javadoc tag. However, it does much more than a Javadoc tag. Annotations do not affect the semantics of the program; they affect the way a program is treated by the tools running it. So in the preceding code, we have an example of an EJB3 stateless session bean. By using annotations, we have transformed what used to be a complex object into a POJO.

For the purpose of this discussion I am not going to describe how to design your own custom annotation. You could create one, but then you would also have to create a framework that will access it. It is something that can be valuable but out of the scope of our needs for this book.

Generics

One of the biggest headaches I had recently occurred when another team gave me an application programming interface (API) to use, and the API was full of lists with names that were not very descriptive. Furthermore, many names in the system were similar to one another, and the Javadoc was quite incomplete. As a result, I used a lot of trial and error in attempting to add the right lists and to retrieve the right lists, and I received many casting errors. I am sure just about every developer has made this mistake as well. You run your code and then up comes a `ClassCastException` because you casted the wrong type of object from the list. Having errors like this that are relatively simple to make and that pop up only at runtime is unsafe.

The good news is that we no longer have to worry about this with generics. Now we can check our collections at compile time. Listing 1-4 is an example without generics.

Listing 1-4. *An Example of Iterating Through a Collection Without Generics*

```
public void sumWOGenerics(Collection col) {
    int sum = 0;
    for (Iterator it = col.iterator(); it.hasNext() ;) {
        Integer temp = (Integer)it.next();
        sum += temp.intValue();
    }
    System.out.println(sum);
}
```

So if someone was calling the method, they would have to know the details of the method to determine what type of collections to pass through to it. However, Listing 1-5 shows an example using generics.

Listing 1-5. *An Example of Iterating Through a Collection with Generics*

```
public void sumWGenerics(Collection<Integer> col) {
    int sum = 0;
    for (Iterator<Integer> it = col.iterator(); it.hasNext() ;) {
        Integer temp = it.next();
        sum += temp.intValue();
    }
    System.out.println(sum);
}
```

As you can see, when using generics, the process is relatively simple, and the calling object knows exactly what type to put into its collection. But the method itself no longer has to worry about `ClassCastExceptions` at runtime. The preceding generic collection would be read as Collection of Integers.

Another concept associated with generics is the ability to return a class but specify it with a generic instead. For example, think of the `Class` object. There is a `newInstance()` method on the object that will create a new instance of that class. In general, you use that by writing something like the following:

```
String s = (String)String.class.newInstance();
```

However, by using generics you can eliminate the casting. This is because now the method is defined as follows:

```
T newInstance()
```

where `T` represents a generic type. Many objects built into the JDK, such as the `Class` object, have been retrofitted to support these changes. Another important concept to realize about generics is that they are implanted by erasure—meaning that, in practical terms, the check is only at compile time. They are not runtime-processed items (C++ developers might want to take note that the templating I just showed is very different from how it is implemented in C++).

Enhanced for Loop

As you saw with the generics, we were able to remove the casting and hard code we knew would work, or at the very least would give us warnings at compile time. However, looking at the code itself, it really does not look any less complicated. In fact, you might argue that it looks even more complicated. Fortunately, Java 5 also brings an enhanced `for each` loop. Listing 1-6 presents the generics example using the enhanced `for` loop.

Listing 1-6. *Our Generics Example with the Enhanced for Loop*

```
public void sumWGenericsAndForLoop(Collection<Integer> col) {
    int sum = 0;
    for (Integer i : col) {
        sum += i.intValue();
    }
    System.out.println(sum);
}
```

As you can see, this is much less complicated. This will take your collection and set it to the variable `i`, which is of type `Integer`. So on each loop it will go around storing the next value of the collection into the variable you defined. This is much simpler and much easier to use, especially if you want to use embedded for loops. You can also use this technique on arrays by replacing your collection with an array of integers (the rest of the code would look exactly the same—note that this will work with primitive data types as well).

Now, the only downside to this is that if you try to remove an element, you cannot do it because you do not have access to the iterator.

Autoboxing

One thing about the preceding code that is slightly annoying is that we had to use .intValue() to convert our value from an object to a primitive. By using autoboxing, you could leave it out as in Listing 1-7.

Listing 1-7. *Summation Method Using Autoboxing*

```
public Integer addWAutoboxing(Collection<Integer> col) {
    int sum = 0;
    for (Integer i : col) {
        sum += i;
    }
    System.out.println(sum);
    return sum;
}
```

We no longer need to convert the integer to a primitive value. In this example, the code is more readable. Imagine a line that has a mix of multiple integer objects and primitives adding and subtracting. Now the code will be much cleaner. Also, not only can we downcast, but we can also upcast. Notice in the preceding example that the second-to-last line is return sum, which is a primitive even though the method is returning an object.

As you can see, instead of having to use return new Integer(sum), the compiler will automatically box the primitive integer for you to an integer object. Now, with this ability you have to keep in mind a few things. I showed how easy it is to use autoboxing, so you should use it in places where you were originally going to do primitive-to-object transformations. However, it should not be done haphazardly, especially on a method that may be performance sensitive.

Typesafe Enums

Enumerated types have been something that many C and C++ developers have missed from Java. Well, fret no longer—they are here and have been given good support. Before (with Java), the only way to use enums was to create a class and have it contain a bunch of static variables. However, even if you are familiar with C and C++ enums, these enums are different and much more powerful. Instead of glorified integer holders, these enums are more like objects, and are even comparable and serializable. Listing 1-8 shows an example.

Listing 1-8. *An Example of an Enum in Java 5*

```
enum Week { Monday, Tuesday, Wedensday, Thursday, Friday, Saturday, Sunday};
```

Varargs

This step is designed to save you time rather than give you added functionality. One step that often occurs in development is creating object arrays. There are a variety of reasons to use arrays. A common one is to send a variable list of objects over to a method call. Take, for example, our concept of summing items. Suppose you have a method that you want to pass an unknown number of arguments to. In reality, the only way to do it is by creating an array and passing it in that way. The method signature would look like that in Listing 1-9.

Listing 1-9. *Passing an Integer Array for Our Summation*

```
public int sums(Integer[] values) {
        int sum = 0;

        for(int val : values) {
            sum += val;
        }

        return sum;
    }
```

However, there is downside to this. First of all, you may want to send only one argument to the method. In that case, you would be creating an array for nothing. Second, even if you do want to pass more than one argument to the method, it can look quite ugly. Check it out:

```
int sum = sum(new Integer[] {1,2,3});
```

This is quite difficult to look at, especially if we were passing items longer than just numbers. Fortunately, when using autoboxing, calling the method is not as complicated because we do not have to create new `Integer` objects for each. By using variable-length arguments (varargs), there is an easier way to do this. This is a way of telling the method that there is a variable number of values of a particular type. For example, in the preceding example, the method would change as shown in Listing 1-10.

Listing 1-10. *Passing the Values as Varargs for Our Summation*

```
public static int sum (Integer... values) {
        int sum = 0;

        for(int val : values) {
            sum += val;
        }

        return sum;
    }
```

As you can see, the method body stays the same, and we can simply treat the values as an array as we did before. However, the real ease comes when calling the method. Now in order to call it, all we have to do is write the following:

```
int sum = sum(1,2,3);
```

This tells the method that you can have a variable number of values. That value object inside the method itself will be treated as an array. However, now you do not have to create the array yourself; you can call the method in a much more elegant manner. Although I like this functionality, I can see it is easy to abuse. In general, most methods should know how many arguments they are passing into the method. Logging methods, however, or summation methods like those in the preceding code do not necessarily need to. Just be careful when implementing this step.

Static Import

Another new ability that you should use only on certain occasions is the ability to have static imports. *Static imports* are basically as they sound: they are the importing of static-level variables. Take, for example, `E` on the `Math` object. To call it, you would use `Math.E` in your code. With static imports, all you have to do is call `E` but then include the import of this at the top of the class:

```
import static java.lang.Math.E;
```

This can be very useful in a class that is doing a lot of calls to the import in the class, and especially in something like a `Math` class, where on one line you would have to reference static variables often. This would cut out the amount of code written so that it becomes cleaner. However, be careful in the use of static imports because tracking where this variable comes from by looking at the code can be confusing.

POJOs

Last, but definitely not least, are POJOs, a term I have used throughout this chapter and will continue to use even more throughout the book. POJOs not only are the basis for Seam, but are starting to be used by all web frameworks. *POJO*, which as I stated earlier stands for *plain old Java object*, is an acronym that was coined in 2000 by Martin Fowler, Rebecca Parsons, and Josh MacKenzie. The term describes a Java object that does not implement any framework design pattern. Often you see them used as domain objects or even business objects. Instead of having to extend objects and make the classes conform to a specification, they are looser. In fact some frameworks such as Spring wrap the transactioning and other business concepts on the object by using XML to define which POJOs are what.

Annotations on POJOs

The use of annotations is what gives POJOs their magic. As I said earlier, annotations add discrete functionality to the code without forcing the class to implement any interfaces or be subclassed. The area in which we are going to use POJOs the most is with EJB3, as you will see in Chapter 4. This can still be controversial because POJOs do exhibit framework-like definitions in the class; however, with annotations the annotated methods and classes have their business functionality invoked only if they are run in the correct container. As you will see when you read further in the book, POJOs have great functionality and flexibility for Java EE application development.

If you want to learn more about POJOs, I suggest checking out Brian Sam-Bodden's book, *Beginning POJOs* (Apress, 2006).

Configuring Your Server

To use Seam with our examples, you have to download a few resources, mainly JBoss Application Server (AS), Apache Ant, and MySQL. If you do not have these items already, I have included some information in the appendices on how to download and configure them.

Summary

This chapter introduced Seam and the underlying frameworks that it depends on—JSF and EJB3. The basic knowledge provided in this chapter will be enhanced in Chapters 3, 4, and 5. This chapter also defined what a basic MVC framework is and discussed the top frameworks used. In addition, it introduced Java 5 and POJOs, which will help you start understanding some of the concepts used by Seam. By now you should be ready to go with your development environment. The next chapter covers the basics of web design and outlines our sample applications. From there you will dive into development.

CHAPTER 2

■■■

Web Applications

Chapter 1 outlined the concepts of MVC and gave a brief discussion of web frameworks. The main reason for that discussion was to help you understand any major web framework that has come out since 2000. In this chapter, however, I want to go over two things: a more detailed review of the web server side, and an introduction to the web applications used in this book.

The fundamental component of any Java web application today is the servlet. It is the common denominator, and back in the '90s many of us wrote entire applications using only servlets. In this chapter, I will quickly cover what a servlet is and then we will get into some actual web application design. You will investigate a few implementation patterns. As I cover each of these implementation patterns used in Seam, I will highlight (when appropriate) the similarities and differences as compared to the Struts framework. This will expose you to more Seam code and should prepare you for Seam coding in Chapter 5.

Three major web applications are used in this book. In this chapter, you will learn about the main applications we are going to build throughout this book.

Servlets

Servlets are the basis for any web application written today. However, they may be one of the least known APIs for new Java developers who started their web development by using a framework such as Struts. The Java Community Process (JCP) designed the Servlet specification in 1997 as JSR 53. The most current version of it is defined by JSR 154 and was released in September 2005.

A `Servlet` object in the most basic sense allows for communication between a client and a server via the Hypertext Transfer Protocol (HTTP). The most common application of this is of course dynamic web pages, although you will find client-side applets talking to servers in the same manner as well.

The `Servlet` class file resides in the `javax.servlet` package. Because servlets are a specification and not a Sun implementation, in order to use servlets, one relies on an individual web container vendor such as JBoss (which uses Apache Tomcat) to implement the specification. The most common implementation of the `Servlet` interface is the

HttpServlet object, which is the basis for most web frameworks. HttpServlet will accept requests (HttpServletRequest), allow for a method for processing, and return a response (HttpServletResponse). In addition, it can keep track of a ServletContext and HttpSession object; I will go over that in more detail in a bit. The HttpServlet object is called by the application server and calls methods (doPost(..), doGet(..), service(..)) that then contain data to process the request.

Contexts in Servlets

A *context* represents an area where serializable objects (classes that implement java.io.Serializable) are stored. These objects differ mainly in their life cycles. Some of the objects are saved indefinitely, whereas others are around for just a short period of time. In servlets there are three contexts by default: the ServletContext context, the ServletRequest context, and the HttpSession context. Each context uses maps for storage.

ServletContext

The ServletContext context is represented by the interface javax.servlet.ServletContext, which you can retrieve with the getServletContext() method on the Servlet object A ServletContext context contains application data that is not user specific. This data can be set at any time and will be stored for as long as the server is alive. The type of data that is stored in a ServletContext context is usually something such as names of states or names of countries—items that are the same for any user and generally not too large.

ServletRequest Context

The ServletRequest context is represented by the interface javax.servlet.ServletRequest, which is passed as a parameter to the Servlet(s) processing methods. The data that is set on ServletRequest is typically tied to a response for a single round-trip to the server. A round-trip consists of a request that originates from the web page, is sent to the servlet, and is then sent back to the web page. After the web page has finished rendering, ServletRequest gets recycled. This object will store data that was sent over—for example, when you fill out a form online and submit it, the data is saved to the HttpServletRequest object.

HttpSession Context

The HttpSession context is represented by the interface javax.servlet.http.HttpSession, which is stored as a property on the HttpServletRequest interface. HttpSession is created for the user explicitly by the server-side application calling getSession() or getSession(true) on HttpServletRequest. The HttpSession data will persist across multiple requests to the server on one connection. To understand what I mean by one connection, think of opening a web browser and connecting to a server—that represents one connection to the server. Opening more browser windows will each represent new connections to the server.

The `HttpSession` data can be destroyed in one of three ways: by explicitly calling the `invalidate()` method on `HttpSession`, by shutting down the browser window, or by the connection timing out (which is a configurable option on `HttpSession`).

Closing Thoughts on Servlet Contexts

Even though all three of these contexts are extremely useful, you cannot do everything you want with them. However, they provide the basis to create other contexts that can be customized to have more functionality. Seam, in fact, uses seven contexts that are all in some ways derived from these three. I will touch on these contexts in Chapter 5 and then go into much greater depth with them in Chapters 6 and 7. For now we will stick with these three.

Servlets and Frameworks

One final thought about servlets before we go on: you can be an experienced developer and have never touched an `HttpServlet` object. This is because the servlet layer is where frameworks (in general) start their abstraction. So if you are a developer who started coding after about 2002, odds are that you have never had to write a servlet for a job. Even if you were developing before that, you probably had just one servlet sending you somewhere else (or for the most part, you should have). However, I wanted this section to give those who are not familiar with servlets a chance to review the basics.

Implementation Patterns

In this section, I am going to present some challenges that arise when designing web applications. Developers face various challenges when creating web applications. These tasks can be described through implementation patterns. For the experienced developer, these patterns will seem quite familiar—for example, displaying lists and logging on to a page. For the entry-level developer, these patterns will seem new but should seem obvious if you have spent any decent amount of time surfing the Web.

Table 2-1 summarizes the patterns discussed in this section. Most of these implementations will be used in this section for finding, updating, and viewing restaurants in a given zip code.

Table 2-1. *Presentation Implementation Patterns*

Topic	Description
Displaying dynamic data	We make a request to the server to get the best restaurant and save it to the request object to be displayed on the page.
Requesting and saving data	We make a request to the server to get the best restaurant as in the first pattern. However, the user will then be able to change the name of the best restaurant.
Logging in	The user passes in a username and password for validation. If the user is validated, the username will be saved to the `HttpSession` context.
Listing and viewing a page	We display a list of restaurants. The user can then select one restaurant to view the details of it.

For each pattern, I will explain to you the task at hand and the problem we are trying to solve. Then I will present a standard activity diagram indicating how this issue will be solved.

I will first present the Struts implementation of it and then the Seam implementation. I decided to use Struts for the examples mainly because it is simple to understand a Struts `Action` class even if you have no knowledge of Struts. Also, because Struts is so prevalent in the marketplace, it will either be familiar or provide helpful exposure to the majority of developers out there.

Now the thing to remember is that these are not 100 percent complete code samples. I have left out the JSPs (for Struts) and the JSF pages (for Seam). Also, for the Struts examples I am not actually implementing the business class created. However, the business class will get implemented for the Seam example. This is because Seam essentially skips having to write any servlet-based class and gets you directly to the EJB3 page.

The purpose of these pages is not to give you lots of code examples to learn from, but to give you an ability to compare and contrast what the code looks like in Struts as compared to Seam. My hope is that you will start to gain an appreciation for Seam and some of the benefits to using it. As you read along the rest of the book, we will use these implementation patterns at various points to cut down on coding time and increase the clarity of the code. So for right now just look at these patterns from an abstract point of view of how they could help you more.

Before diving into the patterns, you will take a look at brief explanations of the Struts and Seam pages that will be used in the examples.

Understanding the Parts of Our Examples

As I said, these examples are going to have two Java files for them: a Seam one and a Struts one. Because not everyone is going to understand each, I will present a crash course on each example setup.

Struts

For those of you who have never seen Struts, think of this as a crash course. If you understand a `Servlet` object, you will understand an `Action` class. The `Action` classes very much mimic the way a `Servlet` object looks. Listing 2-1 provides an example of an `Action` class.

Listing 2-1. *An Example of a Basic Struts Class*

```
public class GenericStrutsAction extends Action {

    public ActionForward execute(ActionMapping mapping, ActionForm form,
            HttpServletRequest request, HttpServletResponse response) {

        DynaActionForm dynaForm = (DynaActionForm) form;

        return mapping.findForward("success");
    }
}
```

A couple of these attributes should be familiar to you—`HttpServletRequest` and `HttpServletResponse`, which we have just gone over. The other two objects will take a bit more explanation.

`ActionForm` is a Struts object used to represent the request data that the user has sent over. This object allows us to have a more concrete implementation that is defined in an XML file. Notice that in the method itself, `ActionForm` is casted to `DynaActionForm`. `DynaActionForm` is a `DynaBean`, which are type-safe maps. This means that in a configuration file, you can specify that this object is being stored as a Boolean. This is useful because all objects sent over from the browser—whether numbers or letters—are strings by default.

Finally, you have `ActionMapping`, which is used to look up what page to forward the next request to. This allows the user to map names to actual JSP pages. This way, if you decide to change to a different page, you can do it in the XML file instead of changing your code.

Throughout the Struts examples, I will be referring to a business service that is a global property on the `Action` class. You can think of this as an EJB that has been injected into the `Action` class. I won't provide concrete implementation of these interfaces because what they specifically do is not important. The important thing is what the Struts page is doing and how it interacts with the business service.

Seam

Now although it may seem unfair to display a bunch of Seam pages without more explanation, the purpose is just to appreciate Seam's simplicity. However, I do want to make a few notes about these pages. The classes are all annotated with @Stateless, which indicates that these are all actual stateless session beans (SLSBs). There will be no plumbing code such as Action or Servlet classes to write; that is all handled by the framework. Also the Seam objects each implement an interface. I have not provided a concrete representation of the interface, but just assume it contains the same methods that are on the Seam component itself.

Now that you have the basics underway, I'll start showing some code.

Displaying Dynamic Data

Aside from a perfectly static page of text, a page that is generated by dynamic data is probably one of the most commonly used types of pages. In this example, we have a request made to the server to find the best restaurant for an inputted zip code.

Figure 2-1 shows an activity diagram outlining the steps to take when creating this page.

As you can see, after the request is made, the server will retrieve the name of the best restaurant for display on the page. In Struts this will happen by an Action class calling a business service. Listing 2-2 provides this code.

Listing 2-2. *The Struts Action for Retrieving the Best Restaurant*

```
public class LookupRestaurantStrutsAction extends Action {

    // Business Service
    LookupRestaurant lookup;

    public ActionForward execute(ActionMapping mapping, ActionForm form,
            HttpServletRequest request, HttpServletResponse response) {

        String zipcode = request.getParameter("zipCode");

        String restaurant = lookup.findBestRestaurant(zipcode);

        request.setAttribute("bestRestaurant", restaurant );

        return mapping.findForward("success");
    }
}
```

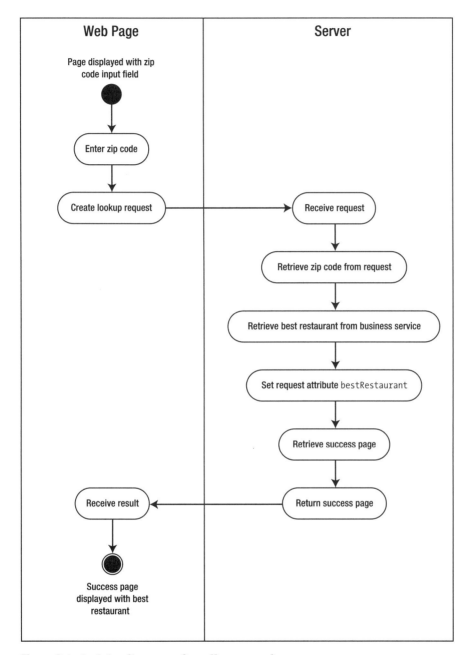

Figure 2-1. *Activity diagram of a call to a stateless page*

This code is fairly straightforward, and its steps can be outlined as follows:

1. Retrieve the zip code passed as a request parameter called `zipCode`.

2. Use our business service to look up the best restaurant by zip code.

3. Set an attribute so we can pass back the restaurant on a request attribute called `bestRestaurant`.

4. Finally, look up the success page and return to that page.

Although this is not that complex, remember that we still have to code and inject the business class for it to work, and we have basically spent this entire page setting variables to be sent over and then retrieving the variables. So now let's take a look at the Seam version of this page in Listing 2-3.

Listing 2-3. *The Seam Component for Retrieving the Best Restaurant*

```
@Stateless
@Name("restAction")
public class LookupRestaurantAction implements ILookupRestaurantAction{

    @In
    String zipCode;

    @Out
    String bestRestaurant;

    public String findBestRestaurant() {
        // do work here
        bestRestaurant = "Aladdins in " + zipCode;

        return "success";
    }
}
```

In this page we do not have to explicitly set any variables because that is done for us by Seam through injection of the variables labeled by the annotations. Additionally, we are already in our business object, so there is no need to call anything else except maybe a database. Not only does the code look cleaner now, but we do not have to worry about the `HttpRequest` and `HttpSession` data explicitly; it is handled behind the scenes by Seam.

Requesting and Saving Data

The previous example, although somewhat trivial in problem solving, hopefully exposed you a bit to the power of using Seam over traditional Struts applications. In the following example, we will still be using our restaurant, but this time we are going to save the restaurant's name. So you will first have to find the restaurant, and then the user can save it back to the page. This is drawn out for you in Figure 2-2.

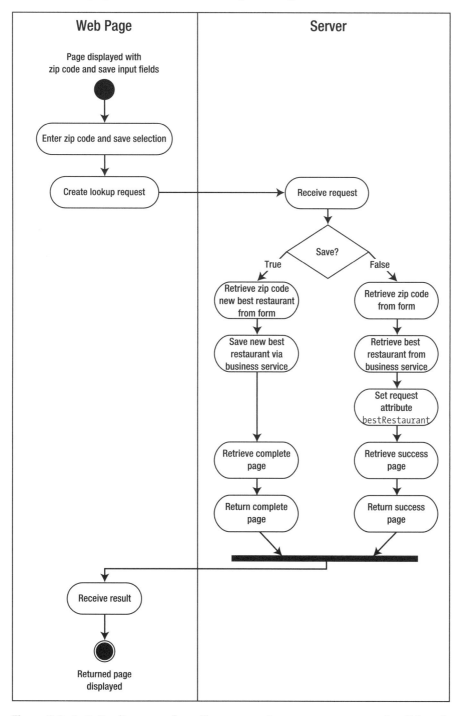

Figure 2-2. *Activity diagram of a call to a page that wants to save and validate data*

Just as before, the user makes a request to the server to find the best restaurant, which is a retrieval process. Now the user can also input data and send it back to the server to save a new restaurant. Listing 2-4 shows the Struts version of this code.

Listing 2-4. *The Struts Action for Retrieving and Saving the Best Restaurant*

```
public class ChangeRestaurantStrutsAction extends Action {

    // Business Service
    LookupRestaurant lookup;

    public ActionForward execute(ActionMapping mapping, ActionForm form,
            HttpServletRequest request, HttpServletResponse response) {

        DynaActionForm dynaForm = (DynaActionForm) form;
        boolean save = ((Boolean) dynaForm.get("save")).booleanValue();

        if (save) {
            String newBest = (String) dynaForm.get("newBestRestaurant");
            String zipCode = (String) dynaForm.get("zipCode");
            lookup.saveNewBestRestaurant(newBest, zipCode);
            return mapping.findForward("completePage");
        } else {
            String bestRestaurant
                = lookup.findBestRestaurant((String) dynaForm.get("zipCode"));
            request.setAttribute("bestRestaurant", bestRestaurant);
            return mapping.findForward("success");
        }
    }
}
```

Notice that I have introduced a Boolean to decide to save or update. We could have done this instead with two separate method calls by using DispatchAction. However, for those not too familiar with Struts, I did not want to add to the code's complexity. Also, this example introduced DynaForm. The following steps indicate what the code is doing:

1. Cast the form to its instantiated type.

2. Retrieve the Boolean value to know whether this is a save or update.

3. If it is a save, perform the following:

    a. Retrieve the new best restaurant name that we are going to save.

b. Retrieve the zip code we are going to save it to.

c. Save the new best restaurant based on the preceding two parameters.

d. Return to the `completePage` mapping.

4. If it is not a save, you request the best restaurant for the zip code by performing the following:

a. Retrieve the best restaurant by using the lookup service.

b. Save the best restaurant to the request attribute as we did before.

So as you can see, this code is a bit more complex than before, but using the form object does save some time on more-complex matters. Now let's take a look at the Seam example in Listing 2-5.

Listing 2-5. *The Seam Component for Retrieving and Changing the Best Restaurant*

```
@Stateless
@Name("changeRestAction")
public class ChangeRestaurantAction implements IChangeRestaurantAction{

    @In
    String zipCode;

    @In(required = false)
    @Out
    String bestRestaurant;

    public String findBestRestaurant() {
        // do work here
        bestRestaurant = "Aladdins in " + zipCode;

        return "success";
    }

    public String saveBestRestaurant() {
        // save restaurant code using bestRestaurant variable
        return "completePage";
    }
}
```

As you can see in this example, we only had to add another method to save the restaurant, and we had to simply add another annotation to declare that the restaurant variable can be inputted as well. Quite the minimal modifications for the performance increase.

Logging In

So now that we have covered two basic examples of retrieving and saving data, we are going to go on to another common type of code—for logging in. Now there are lots of different ways to log in to a website and many authentication models to use. In fact, Chapter 8 covers some Seam-specific ways of logging in.

For this example, however, we are going to stick to a very basic authentication process: you attempt to log in with a username and password; if you are verified, your username will be saved to the session. The HttpSession object is a common object for saving login data because it will persist the entire time that you are active on the site. When you read this, do not get too worked up about this login model, but look at it as a way of saving session-related data. Figure 2-3 shows an activity diagram of what we are going to do.

This is a simple one-request run—the user either correctly inputs the username and password and continues, or is rejected to a failure page. Listing 2-6 provides the Struts version of this code.

Listing 2-6. *The Struts Page for Logging In to a Website*

```
public class LoginStrutsAction extends Action {

    // Business Service
    LoginService service;

    public ActionForward execute(ActionMapping mapping, ActionForm form,
            HttpServletRequest request, HttpServletResponse response) {

        DynaActionForm dynaForm = (DynaActionForm) form;

        // get the variables
        String username = (String) dynaForm.get("username");
        String password = (String) dynaForm.get("password");

        // get
        boolean successful = service.login(username, password);
```

```
        if (successful) {
            request.getSession().setAttribute("loggedIn", username);
            return mapping.findForward("success");
        } else {
            return mapping.findForward("failed");
        }
    }
}
```

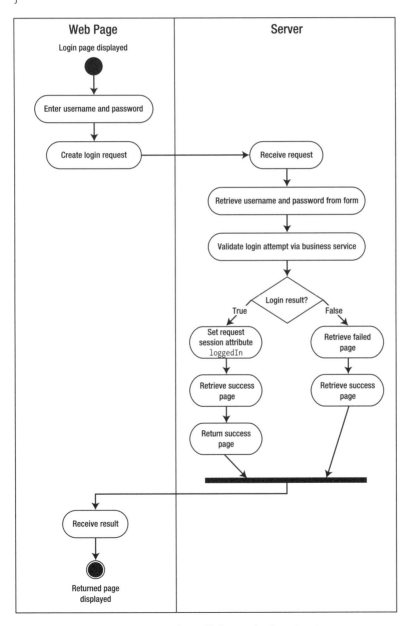

Figure 2-3. *Activity diagram of a call that is for logging in to a page*

The biggest difference between this page and the pages you have seen before is that now we are saving to the HttpSession object. Another thing to keep in mind when using Struts or any HttpSession object directly is that even if you retrieve an object from the session, you cannot just change the object but you will have to reset the attribute on the session again. The steps that this page goes through are as follows:

1. Retrieve the username.

2. Retrieve the password.

3. Call the business service to see whether this is a valid login.

4. If it is a valid login, save the username to the session and return to the "success" page.

5. If you are not successful, forward to a "failed" page.

Listing 2-7 provides the Seam version of this page.

Listing 2-7. *The Seam Page for Logging In to a Website*

```
@Stateless
@Name("loginAction")
public class LoginAction implements ILoginAction {

    @In
    String username;

    @In
    String password;

    @Out(scope = ScopeType.SESSION)
    String loggedInUser;

    public String login() {
        if (username.equals("test") && password.equals("password")) {
            loggedInUser = username;
            return "success";
        } else {
            return "failed";
        }
    }

}
```

Again, the majority of this page should seem simple, except all we have to do is label the variable to describe that the object is exposed to HttpSession. You will notice that this code is clean, and once again the amount of code is less. Furthermore, we are even in the business service already!

Listing and Viewing a Page

For our final example, I am going to show off one my favorite features with Seam: its ability to display lists and retrieve them. For this example, we are going to access a page with a list of restaurants. The user then has the ability to click on any of the restaurants and retrieve detailed information about it. Figure 2-4 shows the activity diagram for our request.

This type of request is fairly standard with web operations. Listing 2-8 shows how we perform this with Struts.

Listing 2-8. *The Struts Action for Displaying a List and Retrieving a Specific Restaurant*

```
public class ListOfRestaurantStrutsAction extends Action {

    // Business Service
    LookupRestaurant lookup;

    public ActionForward execute(ActionMapping mapping, ActionForm form,
            HttpServletRequest request, HttpServletResponse response) {

        DynaActionForm dynaForm = (DynaActionForm) form;
        long restaurantId = ((Long) dynaForm.get("restaurantId")).longValue();

        // lookup the restaurants
        List restaurants = lookup.findAllRestaurants();
        request.setAttribute("listOfRestaurants", restaurants);
        if (restaurantId == -1) {
            // delete it
            Restaurant restaurant = lookup.find(restaurantId);
            request.setAttribute("restaurant", restaurant);
        }
        return mapping.findForward("success");
    }
}
```

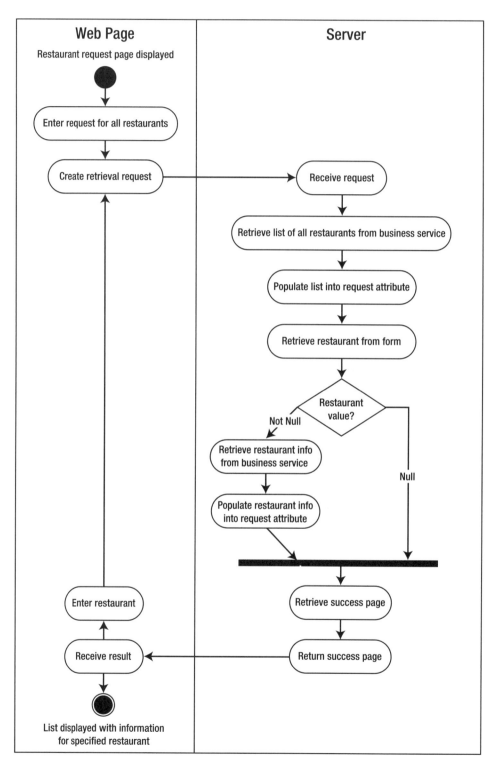

Figure 2-4. *Activity diagram showing all the hooks the user needs into the system*

Part of the complexity of this code is actually hidden from us right now because we will have to have the business service object retrieve the list. Also notice how having to retrieve the name of the restaurant can be wasteful because it requires a second call to the database. Finally, notice that we would have to keep retrieving the restaurants list each time we switch between viewing one and the list page. This could be resolved by saving the list to HttpSession, but that adds many more problems because you do not want to keep objects in the session forever and will have to determine when to destroy the session. The steps for this operation are as follows:

1. Retrieve the restaurant ID.

2. Retrieve the list of restaurants.

3. Save the list of restaurants to a request variable.

4. If the restaurant ID is populated, we want to retrieve one particular restaurant.

   a. Retrieve the restaurant from the database, based on the restaurant ID.

   b. Save the restaurant to the request.

Hopefully you can see not only the waste but the issues that can arise if you want to do anything including delete. Even if you saved the Restaurant object to the session and wanted to delete it, you would have to delete from the database and the list. This can all get complicated quickly, but fortunately Seam has a simplistic approach that takes care of all the plumbing for us. You can see this in Listing 2-9.

Listing 2-9. *The Seam Component for Displaying a List and Retrieving a Specific Restaurant*

```
@Stateless
@Name("listOfRestAction")
public class ListOfRestaurantAction implements IListOfRestaurantAction {

    @PersistenceContext(type = EXTENDED)
    EntityManager em;
    @DataModel
    List<Restaurant> restaurantList;

    @DataModelSelection
    Restaurant restaurant;

    @Factory("restaurantList")
    @SuppressWarnings("unchecked")
    public void create() {
```

```
        // This will select all from the Restaurant table
        restaurantList = em.createQuery("From Restaurant r").getResultList();
    }
}
```

Now at first glance this page may seem extremely confusing. After all, before we were defining the returns, so the page knew where to go. The multiple returns are missing; we are clearly doing two calls as before, yet only one method exists. To explain briefly, we are using annotations to define our list; we then define the selected object on the list, and finally a method to retrieve our list. Chapter 5 provides more detail. This method is where you can start to see the power of Seam. In fact, unlike the other examples that clearly required writing some database code or logic, this is all the code you would need to write on the server, assuming that the `Restaurant` object is an EB.

Sample Applications

What's a book without examples? Obviously, we need applications on which to base our code. Many books have one example throughout the whole text, and although this can be a good method, it can make it overly complex to understand the sample code when trying to do simple things. Also, Seam provides a variety of business solutions, so one sample that incorporates all of these solutions would be extremely complex.

Instead, I took the approach of giving you a few examples to base your work on. I present examples sporadically throughout the book, depending on the problem needing to be solved. Most of these examples have deployable code in the downloadable source.

However, I present three main examples that create more-robust and solid applications. These examples, more than others, will be referenced throughout the book in different parts depending on what we are doing. I will not provide complete details about each of these examples; however, the downloadable code will have complete working examples of them. The sample code will include everything you need to run the code, including Ant build scripts and database build scripts. You can either set up this code ahead of time, use the code as you go along, or wait until you are done with the book; the choice is up to you.

■**Note** Sample code can be downloaded from `http://www.integrallis.com/`.

Garage Sale

Garage Sale is our basic application for CRUD-based examples (*CRUD* stands for *create, read, update, and delete*). The Garage Sale application allows users to add, edit, search, list, and delete garage sales. Within each garage sale is a list of items that a user can view. The person who created the garage sale can add and delete items from the garage sale. These are all the basic options any normal CRUD application gives you. Figure 2-5 provides the database diagram for this application.

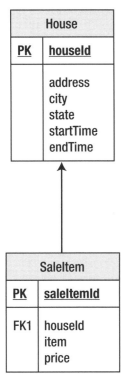

Figure 2-5. *A database diagram of our Garage Sale application*

The database has just two tables: one for the house that is having the sale, and the second for all the items they are selling. One house can therefore have multiple items for sale. Figure 2-6 provides a use case diagram of this event.

As you can see, there are two sets of paths into the application. A seller can go in, create a garage sale, and add sale items to it. The seller should also be able to delete an item after it's sold or after making a mistake. The seller will be able to get a simple list page of items back for the sale. The potential buyer has but one option, and that is to search for garage sales. After selecting a garage sale to view, the user can then see the items of the garage sale.

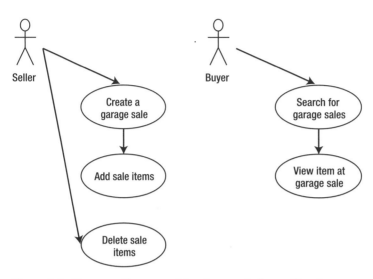

Figure 2-6. *Use case diagram of the Garage Sale application*

Travel Reservations

The Travel Reservations application is a slightly more-complex system. The goal of this system is to allow booking of flights, hotels, and cars. This system is wizard based and has previous screen items feeding into the next screen. This application allows users to create multiple travel reservations in different screens. Each screen should know its own path, but also should be able to keep track of what's going on in different screens. Figure 2-7 shows the database diagram for the travel reservations database.

The travel reservations system is a more intermediate system. You have three base database lookup tables: Flight, Car, and Hotel. These tables should be loaded dynamically when a user enters the page. The list of items is generated on the fly for each page, but on the page itself the items will stay persisted for as long as the user is on the page.

You will notice that there are not many mechanisms to determine what days are available or a subtable for different car types. The main reason for this is to keep the complexity down and not worry about fillers.

The tables above the three base tables (FlightBooked, CarBooked, and HotelBooked) will keep track of the dates booked for the user's trip. Finally, the Booking table is there to keep all the data stored for one user. Figure 2-8 shows the user flow for this application.

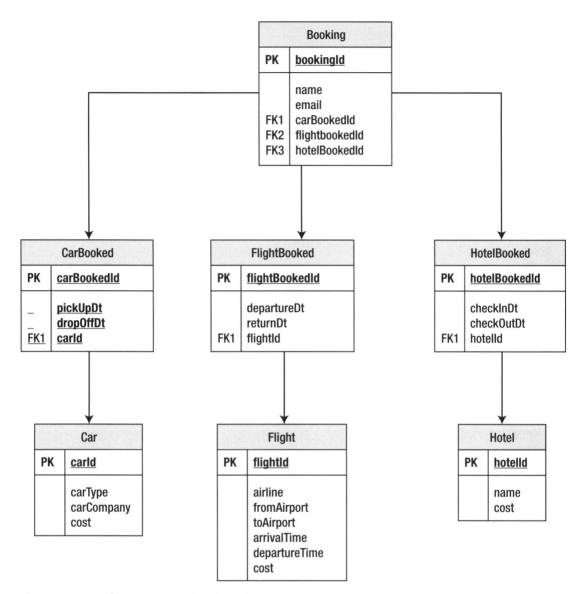

Figure 2-7. *Travel Reservations database diagram*

Figure 2-8 shows the user flow for this application.

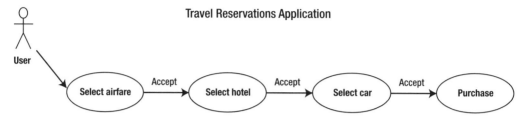

Figure 2-8. *User flow diagram for travel reservations*

Despite having a more complex database than the Garage Sale application, the system is relatively simple. The user can select airfare, hotel, and a car. The user can choose to work in order or skip certain steps and go to the end. At the end, on the purchase, the transaction is committed to the database.

Ticketing System

Our final example application is a ticketing system. This is the kind of ticketing system that has multiple users requiring input to the same object. Users can interact with the ticket, and supervisors need to approve different areas of the system that other users inputted. Figure 2-9 provides the database diagram for the ticketing system.

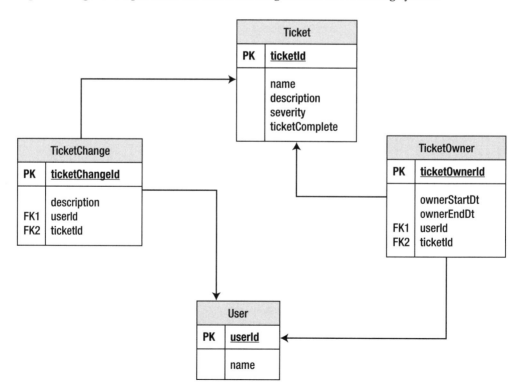

Figure 2-9. *Database diagram of the ticketing system*

This database is simpler in layout. It is for a troubleshooting ticket system. There is a name, description, and severity. You will also notice the TicketOwner table; this is actually a temporal table. The end date will be null for the entry that identifies the current owner of the ticket. This allows you to keep track of who owned the ticket and when. Figure 2-10 shows the flow for this application.

Ticketing System Application

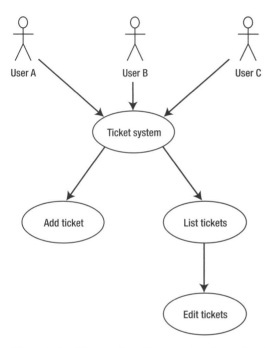

Figure 2-10. *Navigation diagram for the ticketing system*

This navigation diagram shows that there are multiple user interactions with the ticketing system. Users can access the same ticket and perform operations on the ticket within the work flow rules of the ticketing system. You will get to use this application in Chapter 7.

Summary

The goal of this chapter was to introduce you to basic web design concepts. These concepts were to make you think about the different problems you may encounter when creating web pages. I presented these problems so you can learn how Seam helps simplify handling the sometimes complex issues frequently encountered by web developers.

Even for those who are experienced developers, this chapter should have started to show you the ease that Seam brings you in designing web applications. Of course, you are going to have to wait a few more chapters before diving into full Seam development. I still need to go over the fundamentals of JSF and EJB3 to prepare you to use Seam.

I also briefly discussed the applications we are going to create. These three applications form the backbone of our examples in later chapters. These examples each represent different levels of complexity. I will refer to these in later chapters, so you may want to at least take note of the database diagrams for them.

CHAPTER 3

■■■

JSF Fundamentals

As mentioned in Chapter 1, there are two component pieces that Seam uses to provide seamless integration between frameworks. The first component that I am going to discuss is the presentation tier component. Currently the only presentation component that is supported by Seam is JavaServer Faces (JSF), so a good background and basic knowledge of it is a must. As you can see from the road map diagram in Figure 3-1, we will focus on only the presentation tier in this chapter.

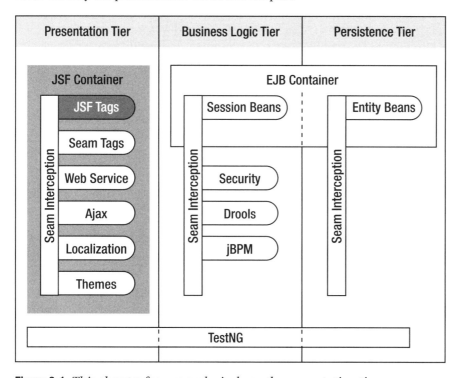

Figure 3-1. *This chapter focuses exclusively on the presentation tier.*

Because this is just a fundamentals chapter, it will not be a full how-to on JSF. What I will cover are the basics as well as the architecture of JSF. Because Seam takes over most of JSF outside of the actual JSP and page flow, I will not focus much on JSF's backing beans. I will use them only to the extent that they are needed to create the examples. But be forewarned—you can do more with them than will be covered in this chapter.

■**Note** Throughout this chapter, I will reference code from `examples/Chapter3` in the source distribution. This source code includes the basic examples as well as the more advanced example at the end of this chapter. You can find the source code at `http://www.integrallis.com`.

Background

One question that may come to mind is that with all the available Java presentation components on the market, why was JSF picked? The simple answer is that the initial purpose behind Seam was to bring the Java Sun presentation and business logic specifications together; in this case, those two are JSF and EJB3.

The JSF specification was born out of the lessons learned from other web frameworks such as Struts, Tapestry, and WebWork. The hope was to provide a specification for creation of presentation tier code, be it a web page, an applet, or an XML page.

JSF is a specification from the Java Community Process (JCP) that was created in May 2001 as JSR 1217. The final version was released in March 2004. In May of that year, a 1.1 maintenance version was released. Initially the Servlet specification was supposed to handle presentation tier development. However, the Java community quickly realized that there were major shortcomings in the specification. These shortcomings are best summed up by the first few lines of the JSR:

> *The Servlet/JSP environment provides a powerful model for creating web applications; however, it defines no APIs specifically for creating the client GUI. To build a JSP page that contains one or more HTML forms, a developer must manage the form's GUI state and build a mechanism to dispatch from incoming HTTP requests to component-specific event handling methods.*

Section 2.1 of JSR 127[1]

This in a nutshell exposes the shortcomings of the Servlet specification. Although the JSF specification addresses many items, there were two major issues that it dealt with.

First, there was no API specification for how to create a client GUI. It was up to the individual developer to implement a GUI. This resulted in multiple ways of creating the presentation tier, generally with tag libraries that differed from job to job and

---

1. `http://jcp.org/en/jsr/detail?id=127`

component to component. Not only that, but there was no clear path in the creation of components that would serve multiple types of presentation tiers (web pages, applets, and so forth).

The other major idea introduced in JSF was the mechanism to deal with incoming requests. Although the Servlet specification allowed for incoming requests, in reality it was not the best place to handle them. Unfortunately, many developers ended up using servlets to specifically interact with their business logic tier pieces. Frameworks such as Struts started this abstraction away from using servlets but still failed in that they always exposed the `HttpServletRequest` and `HttpServletSession` objects to their `Action`(s) (as you saw in the previous chapter).

The JSF specification allows you to have presentation components be POJOs. This creates a cleaner separation from the servlet layer and also makes it easier to do testing by not requiring the POJOs to be dependent on the servlet classes.

Implementations

Because JSF is a specification like EJB, you can rely on Java EE application servers to implement JSF for you. Please do not get Java EE confused with J2EE application servers, which may or may not have JSF implemented. If, however, you cannot use an application server that has JSF implemented, open source implementations of JSF are available. The main one out there is MyFaces, which is part of the Apache project. In actuality, JBoss uses MyFaces for its JSF implementation. So even though our configurations later in the chapter are referencing MyFaces classes, we will not actually be including the MyFaces JARs in the WAR, because these files are in the application server by default. However, if you are using BEA WebLogic or IBM WebSphere, some configurations may differ.

■**Note** Throughout this chapter and beyond I will use the terms *JSF* and *Faces* interchangeably.

Hello World Example

Our first example will be our basic Hello World example, to give you a taste of what you are in for with JSF. One thing that you should instantly notice is the similarity it has with our Seam example in Chapter 1. In fact, the actual JSP page is exactly the same. This should be expected, because Seam is designed to integrate between components.

Because this is our first example, I am going to introduce you to two new concepts as follows:

- Backing beans

- `faces-config.xml`

I will present a more in-depth analysis of backing beans and the `faces-config.xml` file later. But for right now I will leave it in more-simplistic terms. A *backing bean* is a POJO that has been exposed to the JSF container for either data submission or for data retrieval. The *faces-config.xml file* is a JSF-specific configuration file that configures our backing beans and a host of other components for the container. Listing 3-1 defines the JSF page for our Hello World example.

Listing 3-1. *The JSP Page with the Hello World Output*

```
<%@ taglib uri="http://java.sun.com/jsf/html" prefix="h" %>
<%@ taglib uri="http://java.sun.com/jsf/core" prefix="f" %>

<f:view>
    <h:outputText value="#{helloWorld.outputText}"/>
</f:view>
```

If this code looks familiar you, it should. It is the same code we used in Listing 1.2 of Chapter 1 (which should be expected, because Seam uses JSF pages). Next, Listing 3-2 defines the backing bean.

Listing 3-2. *The Backing Bean for the Hello World Example*

```
package com.integrallis.jsf;

public class HelloWorld {

    private String outputText = "Hello World";

    public String getOutputText() {
        return outputText;
    }
}
```

You may notice that this looks strikingly like the Seam bean we defined in Listing 1.1 of Chapter 1 (which makes sense, because they are both POJOs). The big difference is that this one does not have any Seam annotations, which means it will need additional information in order to be properly configured. This additional information will be stored in the `faces-config.xml` file defined in Listing 3-3.

Listing 3-3. *The faces-config.xml File with the HelloWorld Bean Defined*

```
<?xml version="1.0"?>
<faces-config>
    <managed-bean>
        <managed-bean-name>helloWorld</managed-bean-name>
        <managed-bean-class>com.integrallis.jsf.HelloWorld</managed-bean-class>
        <managed-bean-scope>request</managed-bean-scope>
    </managed-bean>
</faces-config>
```

This entry configures the `HelloWorld` bean we defined previously to be exposed to the JSF container as an `HttpServletRequest` scoped object.

Now keep in mind that at this point in using Seam, you get to skip the backing beans portion and go directly to the business classes. Now let's move on to configuring Faces and details of what the preceding code snippets really mean.

Configuration

Configuration of a web framework usually requires two basic parts: the configuring and addition of XML files and the addition of Java ARchive (JAR) files. Let's talk about the second part, the JAR files, and from that point of view configuration is relatively simple. In fact, there is in essence nothing to do. As mentioned, one of the pluses of Faces is that like EJB it's a specification—a specification left for individual vendors to implement. JBoss 4.0.4 provides an implementation of the JSF specification; therefore, we will not need to include JSF JAR files in our deployment because all the library files are on the server. So we will not need to add any JSF-specific library files to make the basic setup of JSF work.

However, that being said, if you decide you want to use JSF in a server environment that does not have JSF (for example, Tomcat), you will have to download a separate implementation and configure it. I am not going to describe that process here because JSF in JBoss 4.0.4 works out of the box. You can download MyFaces 1.1.4 from the Apache website at: `http://myfaces.apache.org/download.html`.

Using Tomahawk

Although the standard JSF components provide an ample number of features for your day-to-day operations, there is of course always more to want. If you have ever used Struts or any framework like it, I am sure you have come across incidents when you needed some customized components. One of the most noticeable components missing from JSF (in my humble opinion) is a date or calendar component. Tapestry has a real nice one with a pop-up calendar built in. So in JSF you have to input the date or try some other way of manipulation—yuck. Fortunately, there is an alterative: Tomahawk.

Tomahawk is actually part of the MyFaces project and gives the user extra components for JSF development. It provides, among other items, an inputDate and an inputCalendar component. We will be using the inputDate component later in this chapter when we start our Garage Sale example.

Before using Tomahawk, you need to install the Tomahawk JAR files. The JAR files are part of a zip that can be downloaded from the MyFaces home page at http://myfaces.apache.org/download.html. On that page you will see the standalone distribution. For this book we used 1.1.13. You can see a screen shot of this page in Figure 3-2.

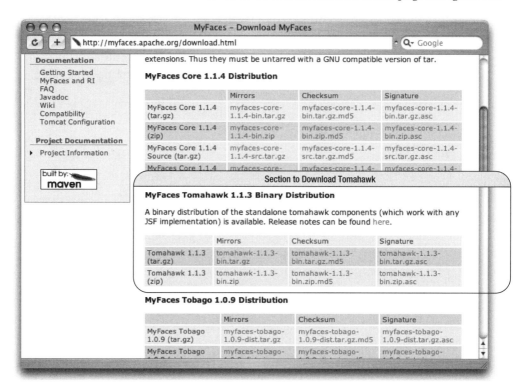

Figure 3-2. *Web page download of Tomahawk*

After you download and unzip the file, simply put the tomahawk-1.1.3.jar inside the WEB-INF/lib directory and you will be good to go. Please take note that although JBoss does use the MyFaces implementation, Tomahawk is not included with that.

Configuring XML Files

As with most frameworks, there will still be a few XML files to configure to get Faces working. There are three XML files you will have to add, depending on your demands:

web.xml, `faces-config.xml`, and `components.xml`. All of these files will reside directly under the `WEB-INF` directory.

Configuring web.xml

The `web.xml` file is a standard web deployment descriptor for any Java EE web container that defines the structure of the web application. This file defines multiple components that the application can customize, such as filters, listeners, servlets, initial parameters, tag library uniform resource identifiers (URIs), and more. These components are as follows:

Filters: Filters are designed to wrap calls to the web application, so you can intercept and perform a variety of global operations such as security.

Listeners: Listeners are what they sound like—they listen and can intercept either before or after an event.

Servlets: These are the root of the web application. The specification used in this book is Servlet 2.5. These are what you will use as an entry into your application.

Servlet mapping: These are tied to the servlet configurations and allow the servlets to be referenced with a shortcut name.

Initial parameters: These context parameters are usually picked up by the servlet for configuration.

Tag library URIs: These are used when you have a tag library stored locally that you want to be able to reference through another URI in the JSPs.

So now that we have that out of the way, let's dive into the customization of `web.xml` for JSF. Listing 3-4 defines a listener, a context parameter, and a servlet with its servlet mapping for `web.xml`.

Listing 3-4. *The web.xml File for Our Chapter 3 Example*

```
<?xml version="1.0" encoding="UTF-8"?>
<web-app version="2.4"
xmlns="http://java.sun.com/xml/ns/j2ee"
xmlns:xsi="http://www.w3.org/2001/XMLSchema-instance"
xsi:schemaLocation="http://java.sun.com/xml/ns/j2ee
        http://java.sun.com/xml/ns/j2ee/web-app_2_4.xsd">
```

```
<listener>
    <listener-class>
        org.apache.myfaces.webapp.StartupServletContextListener
    </listener-class>
</listener>

<context-param>
    <param-name>javax.faces.STATE_SAVING_METHOD</param-name>
    <param-value>client</param-value>
</context-param>

<servlet>
  <servlet-name>Faces Servlet</servlet-name>
  <servlet-class>javax.faces.webapp.FacesServlet</servlet-class>
  <load-on-startup>1</load-on-startup>
</servlet>

<servlet-mapping>
  <servlet-name>Faces Servlet</servlet-name>
  <url-pattern>*.faces</url-pattern>
</servlet-mapping>
</web-app>
```

As you can see, the configuration is quite simple and should look familiar if you have ever used any other web frameworks. The first thing we define is the listener, StartupServletContextListener. This class is needed to parse the faces-config.xml file at start-up. After that we define a context parameter to define that you must use client-side state saving. This is unfortunately due to a bug in MyFaces, so you will need to use this if you are using the MyFaces implementation (which is what JBoss uses). The final components we are implementing are for the front controller. A front controller is used to have all requests to a web application go through one servlet. This can allow for interception, processing, injection, and so forth. For JSF the front controller is javax.faces.webapp.FacesServlet, and for our example anything ending with *.faces will be mapped to our Faces servlet. This is why later in this chapter you will notice that all the uniform resource locators (URLs) end with .faces. You could have had the URL pattern end or start with whatever text you would like; however, that would also change how you reference the page on the browser.

Configuring faces-config.xml

Now that web.xml is done being configured, the web application is ready to use JSF. As I mentioned earlier, though, the JSF-specific configuration file is faces-config.xml. The configuration file in Listing 3-5 is an example of a `faces-config` configuration file. This example contains the major configuration options when creating a JSF application.

Listing 3-5. *An Example of a faces-config.xml File*

```
<?xml version="1.0"?>
<!DOCTYPE faces-config PUBLIC
  "-//Sun Microsystems, Inc.//DTD JavaServer Faces Config 1.1//EN"
  "http://java.sun.com/dtd/web-facesconfig_1_1.dtd">

<faces-config>
  <!--  Misc Navigation -->
  <navigation-rule>
   <from-view-id>/input.jsp</from-view-id>
    <navigation-case>
     <from-outcome>greeting</from-outcome>
     <to-view-id>greeting.jsp</to-view-id>
    </navigation-case>
  </navigation-rule>

  <!--  Garage Sale -->
  <managed-bean>
    <managed-bean-name>garageSale</managed-bean-name>
    <managed-bean-class>
        com.petradesigns.garageSale.backingbean.GarageSaleAction
    </managed-bean-class>
    <managed-bean-scope>session</managed-bean-scope>
  </managed-bean>

  <!--  Custom UI Components -->
    <component>
      <component-type>
        CREDIT_CARD_INPUT
      </component-type>
              <component-class>
                com.petradesigns.faces.component.CreditCardInput
              </component-class>
  </component>
```

```
<!-- Custom Renderer -->
<render-kit>

  <renderer>
    <description>
      Renderer for the credit card component.
    </description>
    <component-family>CreditCardFamily</component-family>
    <renderer-type>
            CREDIT_CARD_RENDERER
    </renderer-type>
    <renderer-class>
            com.petradesigns.faces.component.CreditCardRenderer
    </renderer-class>
  </renderer>
</render-kit>

</faces-config>
```

This configuration file has four basic sets of items you can add, each of which will be discussed in greater depth later in the chapter:

Managed bean: Also known as backing beans, these are the beans you will use to interface between the JSP and the services tier.

Navigation rule: The navigation rules define the flow between pages.

Component: These define customized components that will be used for customized UI operation.

Renderer: The renderers are used to take the custom UI components and provide classes to render them against your specific presentation tier display, such as a JSF page.

Configuring components.xml

I want you to be aware of the `components.xml` file's existence. However, we will not need it for this JSF example. It will be used more in the Seam chapters for configurations (Chapters 5, 6, 7, and 8).

Creating the WAR File

This is the first part of the book where you will actually have to develop and deploy the application to the application server. There are two basic ways of deploying an application: either to deploy it in expanded format or to deploy it in a compressed file and let the application server expand and deploy it. Often users deploying to Tomcat will use the expanded format for ease of use, and depending on your experience you may often do that. However, because that really is not a preferred way for Java EE application deployment, we will eventually be creating an Enterprise ARchive (EAR) file for deployment. In this chapter, however, we will start with the WAR file because we will not be getting into EJB3 until Chapter 4.

WAR is short for *Web ARchive* and is used to deploy web resources to an application sever. This file can be deployed either by itself or as part of an EAR file (which we will discuss in the next chapter). A WAR file is packaged in the same way as a JAR file. However, the structure is slightly different. Figure 3-3 shows the WAR structure.

Figure 3-3. *The structure layout of the WAR file*

This is the basic WAR structure. You can include the images and regular HTML files onto the root level. You then have the WEB-INF directory as you would any standard J2EE web application. Inside that directory you will have the web.xml file along with the classes and lib directory.

Compiling via Ant

As you may notice by looking at the source code, we use Apache Ant scripts for building the file. I will assume at this point that you know how to compile and move files via Ant. If you do not, take a look at the build.xml file in Listing 3-6. What I will go over here is the specific mechanism that is built into Ant to create WAR files.

Listing 3-6. *The WAR File Definition Example Used in build.xml*

```
<war warfile="${war-file}" webxml="${dd-web}/web.xml">

    <webinf dir="${dd-web}">
        <exclude name="web.xml"/>
    </webinf>

    <fileset dir="${web}">
        <include name="**/*.jsp"/>
        <include name="**/*.html"/>
    </fileset>

    <classes dir="${classes}">
        <include name="**"/>
    </classes>

    <lib dir="${lib}/tomahawk" includes="*.jar"/>
</war>
```

This WAR build should be embedded inside a target (as we have in `build.xml`). So basically, as you can see, there are a few things we need to include in our WAR file that we discussed earlier:

- XML configuration files

- HTML files, images, and so forth

- Compiled classes

- Library files

Well, fortunately, it is pretty easy to embed each one of these. The XML configuration files are done in a two-step process. Because every WAR should have a `web.xml` file, the location of the `web.xml` file is defined as a `webxml` tag on the WAR definition. The rest of the XML files are then included by writing to the `WEB-INF` directory via the `<webinf/>` directive. You will notice, however, that we have to excuse the `web.xml` or we would be attempting to write it twice.

The next two tags are specific for each item, even though you could basically do the same with `fileset` copies instead. The first one, `<classes/>`, defines all the class files to include in the `WEB-INF/classes` directory. The `<lib/>` tag defines all the JAR files to include in `WEB-INF/lib`. Now that this is done, you should be able to run it and successfully create a WAR file. Also note that you could put the JSPs under the `WEB-INF` directory for added security. If you need further information about building with Ant, Brian Sam-Bodden's *Beginning POJOs* (Apress, 2006) devotes Chapter 3 to configuring Ant.

Rapid Application Development

Rapid application development (RAD) is a term you often see thrown around these days by employers and magazines. And that is for a good reason. Proper RAD procedures can help you build web applications in a timelier manner. By using RAD development, you get predefined widgets that aid in your development process. These widgets help with the display and handling of events—all of this from within the IDE. There are generally four layers of RAD as follows:

- An underlying component architecture

- A set of standard widgets

- An application infrastructure

- The tool itself

JSF has all but the last layer, and the only reason that the last layer does not exist is because, as you recall, JSF is a specification. Of course, after you use an implementation, this becomes a moot point. Having a tool to use may seem like a minor point, but it was considered a serious implementation item missing from the Java specification. Even though many frameworks such as Struts do have plug-ins for Eclipse to help create Struts pages, there was never a standard for creating graphical user interfaces (GUIs) to design your presentation tiers.

Architecture

If you are familiar with web frameworks, the JSF architecture should be fairly easy to pick up. In this section, we are going to cover the basic architecture of JSF, how a request is created, and the various areas of a Faces application. I will go over the JSF life cycle here. Chapter 5 discusses how Seam intercepts parts of this life cycle to perform its own processing. However, before you jump into the architecture, it is useful to understand certain key components of JSF. After you understand the basic routines of JSF, you can learn how to put it all together.

The basic structure of a JSF call is actually pretty simple. From a basic point of view, you have a JSP page that controls the display on the front and controls the action a user takes to the persistence tier. It uses listeners to define the action that should be taken on the page. In fact, your presentation tier does not even have to be a JSP if you do not want it to be. JSF allows multiple presentation-tier supports. For the business logic tier object, all that is required is a simple POJO to be referenced via an XML file. This way, all of your logic and your bean references are in easy-to-use POJO classes. This allows Plug and Play capabilities of the application. This also allows for easy testing because all of the classes are simple POJOs. Figure 3-4 maps this out.

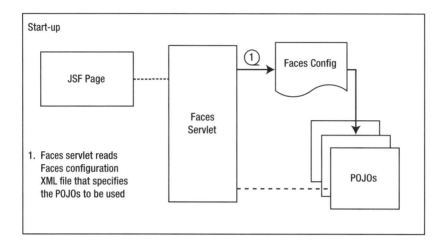

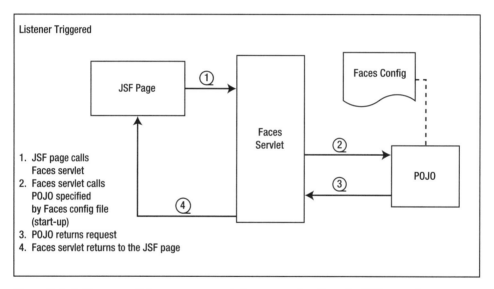

Figure 3-4. *A diagram of the start-up and the mapped call to the JSF container*

JSF Areas

Kito Mann, author of *JavaServer Faces in Action* (Manning Publications, 2005) defines the following eight core areas of JSF. This section covers each of them. However, because some of these areas are not used when using Seam with JSF, I will not go over those in very much detail.

- User interface (UI) component

- Renderer

- Validator

- Backing beans

- Converter

- Events and listeners

- Messages

- Navigation

UI Component and Renderer

The display area will be your HTML or XML or Applet output. For our examples, we will be using a standard HTML translatable presentation tier. However, this could also be Wireless Markup Language (WML), Scalable Vector Graphics (SVG), a Swing application, or something totally different.2 This poses a small problem for us. For most web applications such as Struts or Tapestry, there are built-in presentation-tier display components to use. For Struts they use JSP tag libraries, for Tapestry they use Java web component ID (JWCID) components. Now although using these built-in components exclusively is a good strategy for most web frameworks because they are in general designed to specifically serve up HTML web pages, this (as I have mentioned) is not the case with JSF. Because JSF is designed to serve up a variety of types, a much more abstract approach was needed. This is where the UI component and renderer portion come to play. In addition, you will then, if you are using a web page presentation tier, have a tag library object that will call the renderer for display.

These are the three core parts of a display component. To understand these three areas and how they work together, I am going to explain each of them in greater detail:

UI component: The UI component is the core of these three. This component itself is a basic JavaBean that extends the class `javax.faces.component.UIComponent`. After that, the class is fairly generic. This is the core to having the presentation-tier abstract. This class will then define your core functionality for the component that you are creating. This is the one class on the display side that will be reused regardless of what presentation tier you are using.

Renderer: The renderer portion is the server-side mechanism that converts the UI component into a meaningful display. In other words, if you have an HTML presentation tier, the renderer is responsible for converting it into HTML markups. Rendering can occur via two different mechanisms: direct implementation and delegated implementation:

---

2. Kito Mann, *JavaServer Faces in Action* (Greenwich, CT. Manning Publications, 2005), p 43.

- In *direct implementation*, the UI component takes care of the rendering for you. This works well with small or UI specific projects where there will never be a need to render the page in anything else. For most people this will probably be the best solution because often you are coding only for a web page.

- In *delegated implementation*, rendering is delegated to another class. The classes that are to be renderers will extend `javax.faces.render.Renderer`. The renderers will make use of the UI component properties to get the data needed for the display. It will then take that data and create the display. The renderer will be the bulk of the complexity for the presentation-tier side, and for this reason particular renderers are not part of the specification.

Tag library: The tag library creation is the final step you need for the display of your UI component. This is necessary for anyone outputting their site to a web page. This will take the renderer or UI component if you are using direct implementation and output the rendered text to the page. The tag library will extend `UIComponentTag`.

Validator

Creating a validator for validation is key to any framework, especially a web framework. (*Validator* is the term for the component that is doing the validation.) For as long as people have been writing web applications, there has been a need to validate user input. In the beginning of web applications, validation was quite a cumbersome, redundant process. Now most web frameworks have their own built-in capability to validate, so you do not have to worry about it. In Faces validation, this is accomplished by adding your validation to the component object you wish to validate, as I have done in Listing 3-7.

Listing 3-7. *An Example of a JSF Validation*

```
<h:inputText id="inputExample" value="#{example.value}">
    <f:validateLongRange minimum="1" maximum="500"/>
</h:inputText>
```

Validation in JSF is accomplished by validating on the display model. However, this being said, this is not the way validation works when using JSF with Seam. Seam has a better way of doing validation, by validating on the model object instead. This in general will work better for you, because more often than not your validation is constrained by the persistence tier rather than the presentation tier. However, you can still use this validation in Seam, which could be necessary if you are upgrading an application with existing JSF pages.

Backing Beans

Backing beans are JavaBeans that are responsible for the business logic of a JSF application. Unlike most JavaBeans, which have only private properties with getters and setters for them, in a backing bean you will also have event listener methods. On the JSF pages, submits, links, and so forth reference the event listener methods. When the submits/links are triggered, objects are set on the backing bean and the event listener method is executed. The event listeners will use model objects to call either a database or some other business process.

■**Note** Backing beans will be replaced in Seam by an actual Seam-annotated object, which will more than likely be an EJB.

I will explain how to reference backing beans in the "Managed Beans" section later in this chapter.

Converter

No matter what your presentation tier is, you will eventually have to output data other than a string. This can pose problems for a date or a number; obviously, you do not want to output a `long` for a date or all the possible digits for a float. Thankfully, JSF has built-in *converters* to convert dates and numbers into displayable items and back again. You can also add localization for help with the display of these items. Listing 3-8 shows the code to display a date object in JSF.

Listing 3-8. *Example of How to Convert a Text Value to a Date/Time Format*

```
<h:outputText value="#{user.startDate}">
    <f:convertDateTime type="date" dateStyle="medium"/>
</h:outputText>
```

In this example, we have a `User` object that had a date field on it called `startDate`. To convert the date object to readable format, we use the `convertDateTime` converter. The `dateStyle` determines the style you want for the date. By default, there are four styles you can use. Table 3-1 lists these styles.

Table 3-1. *All the Built-in Types for Converting a Date/Time*

Value	Example
short	8/24/06
medium	August 24, 2006
long	August 24, 2006
full	Thursday, August 24, 2006

You will notice that the medium and the long values look alike. In the United States, they are alike. However, the values differ in Canada. If your browser were set to Canada internationalization, you would get 24-August-2006 for medium.

Events and Listeners

In the old days of web application development, we had to worry about all the request and response objects. Even with Struts, a relatively modern web framework, you have to be concerned with the request and response objects. The purpose of newer frameworks such as JSF and Tapestry is to abstract these things away.

So obviously the next question is, well what do we do? The answer is relatively simple: use events and listeners. *Events* are items that get triggered by various presentation-tier-type requests that call upon listeners. *Listeners* are the methods that call the backing beans for processing.

Although this may seem more complicated than simply calling an execute() method on an Action class, this provides greater flexibility and makes the logic of what you are attempting more obvious. With JSF there are basically four types of events as follows:

- Value-change events

- Action events

- Data model events

- Phase events

Before discussing the various implementations of the event listener, I want to bring up a major difference between Seam and JSF. In these examples, the methods, as you will see, can take Faces-specific parameters. In Seam this is not the case; with Seam the listeners are not dependent on any framework-related object. So the following will be shown more for educational and background purposes as opposed to areas necessary for use with Seam.

Value-Change Events

Value-change events are events that occur when you change the values on a particular box on a screen. Often value-change events are triggered from the onChange events associated with form fields on the JSF page.

Action Events

Action events are probably going to be your most commonly used method of interacting with the listener. These are events that are triggered by actionable events on a page, for example, button clicks or hyperlinks—basically on any event that is used to submit data or tell the application to go to another page, that requires dynamic data. Now given the dynamic name nature, this can be extremely helpful on the front side because you can call an edit method, edit().

Also, because actionable events in general require you to make a computation and then go to another page, it is necessary for the Faces component to facilitate this. This works by having the listener return a string that references either the name of the page you want to forward to, or by referencing a page name defined in the faces-config.xml. We will discuss how the latter part works shortly when we discuss page flows. Incidentally, Seam will forward to pages in the same manner.

Data Model Events

Data model events are pretty handy components when it's necessary to display database-driven data onto a presentation tier. This allows you a fairly simple way to look up the data, determine the selected row, and use it for computations and display purposes. You then do not have to worry about figuring out what data object you are on when you have a list and want to edit or delete a particular row. Listing 3-9 provides an example of the method call needed for the backing bean.

Listing 3-9. *Example of Data Model Retrieving Code from GarageSaleAction*

```
DataModel houseDataModel = null;

public DataModel getHouseDataModel()
{
    if (houseDataModel == null)
    {
        // set the list of houses
        if (houses == null) {
            houses = retrieveHouseList();
        }
```

```
        houseDataModel = new ListDataModel(houses);
        houseDataModel.addDataModelListener(new DataModelListener()
        {
            public void rowSelected(DataModelEvent e)
            {
                FacesContext.getCurrentInstance().getExternalContext().
                log.debug("phase:"+ e.getRowIndex());
                log.debug(";row seleted:"+e.getRowIndex());
            }
        });
    }
    return houseDataModel;
}
```

Now I am not going to provide huge amounts of detail here—this is just a basic DataModel with a listener attached to it. The ListDataModel in the preceding code has multiple implementations, and we choose one for a list; however, there are ones for Arrays and ResultSets as well. Do not worry too much about this because with Seam there is a *much* simpler way of doing it. We will get to that later in Chapter 5.

Phase Events

In a bit I will talk about the JSF life cycle, which combines many of the concepts we discussed in the architecture. The life cycle basically controls changing values and updating views, and it has six phases. *Phase events* are events that can be triggered either before or after each stage in the life cycle occurs.

In all likelihood, you will probably never need to write your own phase events. Especially when using Seam, doing so could very easily complicate your application. However, there are internal parts of JSF that use these listeners to perform various functions. In fact, you will discover later that the phase events are used by Seam to intercept calls and forward them to the proper Seam components.

Messages

Messages are an integral part of any presentation-tier framework. These are used to display success or failure messages to the user. After all, you do not want to have three different ways of displaying "Please enter your name." It breaks consistency and form on a site. Throughout our application, we will use Faces messaging with our validation framework to display messages. Messages are displayed on the presentation tier by using a simple tag library reference, as in Listing 3-10.

Listing 3-10. *The Display of Errors for the Address Property*

```
<h:message id="errors" for="address"/>
```

This quite simply displays messages if an address field has not been properly validated.

Navigation

With most web applications, you will have multiple pages and the need to navigate from one page to another. Depending on the application, you will have various levels of sophistication in the flow from page to page. Faces has its own components to facilitate flow from page to page and that allow you to control the flow based on the start page and global settings. I will discuss this shortly.

Managed Beans

As you saw in the Hello World example earlier, we defined a reference to the `com.integrallis.jsf.HelloWorld` managed bean inside `faces-config.xml`. All your backing beans will be defined as *managed beans* inside the JSF. In addition, we can also initialize values of the backing beans inside the configuration file. The values you can set can be simple ones such as an `Integer`, or you can even define `java.util.List` and `java.util.Map` objects and their values. Listing 3-11 is an example of setting various objects on our backing bean.

Listing 3-11. *An Example of a Managed Bean Defined for a Make-Believe Object*

```
<managed-bean>
    <managed-bean-name>myExample</managed-bean-name>
    <managed-bean-class>com.petradesigns.jsf.MyBean</managed-bean-class>
    <managed-bean-scope>session</managed-bean-scope>
    <managed-property>
        <map-entries>
            <key-class>java.lang.Integer</key-class>
            <map-entry>
                <key>1234</key>
                 <value>A random number</value>
            </map-entry>
        </map-entries>
    </managed-property>
    <managed-property>
        <property-name>userBean</property-name>
        <value>#{otherBean}</value>
    </managed-property>
</managed-bean>
```

This is an example of a generic JavaBean called `MyBean` that we have defined as a Faces-managed bean. As you can see, we can define the scope of it, we can define initial value entries, and we can even reference other beans.

This being said, when using full-fledged Seam, you will not actually have to define managed beans at all. There are numerous reasons why the Seam team has gotten rid of defining them in Seam. The use of extensive XML files to define objects can become tedious, and can even become confusing and difficult to manage. So in Seam we do not even have to use managed beans at all; we define the necessary properties in the POJO via annotations instead.

Life Cycle

Now that you have gone through all the areas of JSF, let's put this together. The JSF life cycle is divided into six distinct phases, four of which are involved with the application itself, and two of which are used for JSF component rendering. Throughout the life cycle, the framework uses `FacesContext` to store all state information. This information includes the view and components and errors associated with it.

The six phases, shown in Figure 3-5, are as follows:

1. Restore view

2. Apply request values

3. Process validations

4. Update model values

5. Invoke application

6. Render response

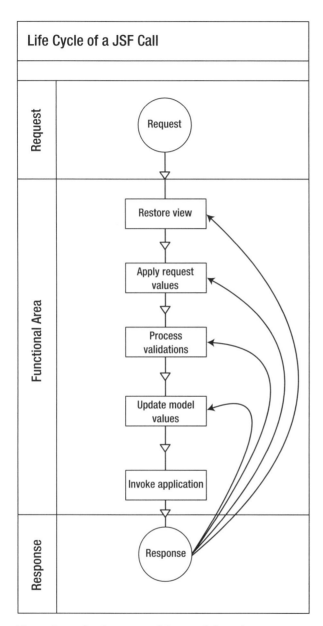

Figure 3-5. *The diagram of the JSF life cycle request*

Restore View

The Restore View phase is responsible for the initial and subsequent views of the JSP page. JSF rendering of the page is much different from something such as Struts, where the action is driving the request forward to the next page. In Struts the main ideas of "where you came from" and "what to do" are handled by the `Action` class. Then the JSP just forms to render the decisions made by that class. With JSF, the page itself in this setup is more worried about where it came from and what it has to do.

Initially, regardless of whether this is the first or a subsequent call to the page, the framework has to look up the page. The view to restore is determined by the view ID that is the name of the JSP requested. The view is represented as a `UIViewRoot` component that then can store on it a collection of components. This `UIViewRoot` is stored as a property on the `FacesContext`.

So if this is the first time that the user is going to the page, the current view will be discarded and a new one created. The view is then populated based on the events on the page. Also, if the page has components that reference backing beans, then we will have those looked up to be used to render on the page. Because this is the first view of the process, it will actually then skip the rest of the life cycle objects and go to the Render Response phase.

After the view is rendered, you have the page to be displayed. You will then have links or submits on the page to call any future pages. These links, as I explained, will reference listeners, which will then either forward you to another page or back to the same page. If they call back to the same page, they are referred to as *postbacks*. On a postback, there is no need to create the initial view because it has already been created. The JSF container will just restore the current view before moving on to the rest of the life cycle.

Apply Request Values

This phase of the life cycle takes values that have come from the request and applies them to the various components on the page. This will reference any object on the page this is of type `UIComponent`. If you look at `UIComponent`, there is an `immediate` property on it. If this value is set to `true`, it tells the system to validate immediately instead of in the next phase. If `immediate` is set to `true` on components that are buttons or hyperlinks, these will also set off action events. If at this step, you either run into a conversion-of-value error or a validation error, the error message is generated and stored on `FacesContext`.

At this point, you will proceed to the next phase unless any renderers, components, or listeners have forced the control to skip to the Render Response phase directly.

Process Validations

So after the preceding steps, we have the all the components on the page, and the values for those components on the objects. Now comes the validation of the components. Each component will be validated against predefined validation components or against custom components. Validation in JSF is designed by adding validators to the components on the presentation tier. Listing 3-12 shows an example of adding a long validator to the input text component.

Listing 3-12. *Example of Validating with a Range on Input*

```
<h:inputText id="inputExample" value="#{example.value}">
    <f:validateLongRange minimum="1" maximum="500"/>
</h:inputText>
```

As you can see, the definition of it is fairly straightforward. However, just recall that we do not do validations this way when using Seam (although this process is supported if you still want to do it). After the value is validated, the local value is set and any other value-change events will be triggered by their assigned listeners. If any of the components are marked invalid, you will be forwarded to the Render Response phase instead of continuing.

Update Model Values

Now that all the values of the components have been set and validated (both in a conversion manner and type manner), we can update the backing beans associated with them. The various backing beans are looked up via their corresponding scope.

Invoke Application

This is the point at which the listeners on the backing bean get processed. So whichever action event(s) you have triggered to run will be run at this point. This phase is where the navigation comes into effect as well. The navigation return will determine the render response.

Render Response

Now that all the properties submitted in the request have been set, all that is left to do is send the response back to the user and render. This creation of the response is the primary purpose of this phase of the life cycle; the secondary object is to save the phase. This Save phase, as you may recall, is to be used to look up the view if there is a postback to the page. Remember that in this phase there is no specific presentation tier technology that the response must incorporate, so the converters and renderers are used to convert it.

Components

The previous section defined what a UI component is. This section will go into more depth about components. You will learn how to arrange them, how to use them, and see a list of a few more common components. By the end of this section, you should be able to arrange and use your components on the page.

Component Layout

The component layout in JSF is going to be unlike any web application layouts that you are used to. In a framework such as Struts, the components create HTML tags directly. In contrast, in JSF, the server-side components generate the HTML as a direct result of the renderers used by the components. Therefore, there is no one-to-one relationship of components to output that you have with web frameworks such as Struts. The way the component-to-rendering relationship is set up is in a tree-type manner.

This can be a bit complicated to understand, so let's take a look at a somewhat simple JSP page and its output. The page in Listing 3-13 will display a table with address entries from a list object called houses. The necessary details are not important; the display is.

Listing 3-13. *The JSP Page with Faces Mock-up*

```
<%@ taglib uri="http://java.sun.com/jsf/html" prefix="h" %>
<%@ taglib uri="http://java.sun.com/jsf/core" prefix="f" %>

<f:view>
    <h:dataTable var="house" value="#{houses}" rendered="#{houses.rowCount>0}">
        <h:column>
            <f:facet name="header">
                <h:outputText value="Address"/>
            </f:facet>
            <h:outputText value="#{house.address}"/>
        </h:column>
    </h:dataTable>
</f:view>
```

Let's start by examining the page before we show the display. The first two lines are the tag library (taglib) inputs, which allow you to reference two JSF sets of tags. The http://java.sun.com/jsf/core taglib references core components for JSF. The other taglib, http://java.sun.com/jsf/html, references standard components from the HTML rendering kit.

The next tag you see is <f:view>. This is a *must-have* for the start of *any* JSF tree. This tag indicates that we are starting a set of JSF tags.

Next, the <h:dataTable> indicates the start of a data table. Basically this will output a table for us. I will discuss this tag more closely in Chapter 5 when I introduce Seam.

Now, here is where it starts to get a bit more interesting and we get some of the embedding of components to start. What is going to happen is that we are going to output the display we want for each column on a row. The number of rows is determined by the list size in houses. So to start the definition of the column, we have <h:column> define the column. The first part is the <f:facet> tag. This is a tag that is used in part of a parent-child relationship and with the name tag. We then define the name as either header or footer, and this will then define that value as part of the header. The following attribute, `<h:outputText>`, defines the dynamic value to output. All of this gives us the display in Listing 3-14.

Listing 3-14. *The Generated Output of the Code from Listing 3-13*

```
<table>
<thead>
<tr><th>Address</th></tr></thead>
<tbody id="_id0:tbody_element">
<tr><td>Our New House</td></tr>
<tr><td>Our 2nd House</td></tr></tbody></table>
```

This display of course assumes that there was a list of two objects passed through to it. As you can see, the output put what we defined with the facet tag as a header in the table header. The rest of the data was put into consecutive rows.

Standard Components

The preceding example shows the use of multiple components in conjunction with each other. Unfortunately, the scope of this book does not provide the space for a more detailed explanation of components. However, I do want to leave you with a list of commonly used components that you may need and will use for this book (see Table 3-2).

Table 3-2. *List of Standard JSF Components*

Component	Description
Button	Generates a button of type submit or reset on the page for form use
Check box	Generates a populated check box on the page
Check box list	Generates a list of check box components
Component label	Creates a label for another component
Data table	Renders a table of data
Drop-down list	Creates a drop-down select or combo box
Faces form	Creates a form tag to embed the start of a form submission
Formatted output	Formats the output of text by generating a span tag
Grid panel	Generates a table to arrange the components on a page
Group panel	Groups panels together

Continued

Table 3-2. *Continued*

Component	Description
Hidden field	Creates an input box with a type of `hidden`
Hyperlink	Generates a hyperlink for the page
Image	Generates a reference to an image for the page
Inline message	Creates a message for a single component
Link action	Creates a link with an action on the `onClick` attribute
List box	Creates a select box with a size attribute of greater than one
Message list	Displays a list of messages for the page
Multiline text area	Creates a text area on the page that spans multiple lines
Multiselect list box	Creates a select multibox that allows the selection of multiple components
Output text	Outputs text that is either static or dynamic
Radio button list	Creates a list of radio buttons for a page
Secret field	Creates an input box that is of type `password`, for use where you do not want the text displayed
Text field	Creates an input box of type `text`

JSF Expression Language

You may have noticed in the preceding "Components" section that we used expression languages to define objects inside the tag libraries (that is, `#{houses.rowCount>0}`) The JSF expression language (EL) is based on JSP 2 and uses concepts from ECMAScript (JavaScript) and XPath. This being said, if you have any experience using expression languages in XPath or using the JavaServer Pages Standard Tag Library (JSTL) with Struts, then the rest of this should come pretty easy for you.

There are only a few key differences between the JSF EL and JSP 2's EL; so make sure to pay attention to the few differences. Most of these have to do with using # instead of $ to indicate the start of an expression language. This will really only have to trouble you if you are used to JSP EL.

An expression language allows you to access and manipulate implicit objects inside a JSF page.[3] As you have seen, this allows you to not only reference the methods on an object but also express simple conditional statements.

---

3. `http://today.java.net/pub/a/today/2006/03/07/unified-jsp-jsf-expression-language.html`

So now that you have a grasp on what you use expression languages for, let's dive into a step-by-step example on how to use one.

This example uses `#{houses.rowCount>0}` from the preceding section and explains what it is and how to set it up. The following are a few guidelines to follow when creating an EL markup in JSF:

1. Use the object name that is referenced via a managed bean—or in the case of Seam, the Seam name. So `houses` is a managed bean object.

2. You have to be able to tell the container that this is an expression language, as opposed to a normal string that you want to use for a value. To do that with JSF, you surround the value with `#{ }`. You will notice this is different from regular JSP 2, in which a `$` is used instead.

3. From this point, you have a few options to choose from. If it were an array, you could surround the object with an array value or reference another component for the value—for example, `#{houses[3]` or `#{houses[num.val]}`. In our example, we are using neither.

■**Note** When referencing properties on the beans, they must be JavaBean-style properties (that is, setName/getName).

One interesting thing to realize when writing this is that you are supplying the expression to an input box, so it will be in the format `value="#{houses.rowCount}"`. Note that we surround it with double parentheses. This is a fairly common phenomenon for any developer. So what happens when you want to use an actual string value in there? You have two options: you can either surround the value with single quotations, or you can surround the whole object with a single quotation and the parameter with double quotations, as in Listing 3-15.

Listing 3-15. *An Example Using Quotations*

```
value = "#{houses.name.equals('test')}"
or
value = '#{houses.name.equals("test")}'
```

Personally, I prefer the first way. It conforms to more-standard methods. Also, as you have seen, you can use a conditional statement such as the `rowCount > 0`. However, you can also use primitive conditional statements as well—for example, `condition ? trueReturn : falseReturn`.

Page Flow

Being able to navigate from page to page is a key to any application. After all, it would be pretty boring to stay on the same page all the time. JSF has multiple options for navigation that we will get into later in this book. In this section, I will present the standard JSF navigation. Navigation in JSF is accomplished in a stateless way via page flow navigation defined in `faces-config.xml`.

In the previous "Events and Listeners" section, I mentioned how with listener methods the string return type was in reference to a page. Here is where we make that string have a meaning. The page flow is rather simple. You simply define the page that you are going to and then give options for pages to go to. Let's start with a simple example in Listing 3-16 and then we will move on to a more complex example.

Listing 3-16. *A Simple Navigation Rule*

```
<navigation-rule>
    <from-view-id>/pages/startPage.jsp</from-view-id>
    <navigation-case>
      <from-outcome>outcome1</from-outcome>
      <to-view-id>/pages/firstOutcome.jsp</to-view-id>
    </navigation-case>
    <navigation-case>
      <from-outcome>outcome2</from-outcome>
      <to-view-id>/pages/secondOutcome.jsp</to-view-id>
    </navigation-case>
  </navigation-rule>
```

As mentioned, this XML block will be located in your `faces-config.xml` file, with the navigation rules coming before the managed bean definitions. Each navigation rule is used to encapsulate the rules for one page. The `<from-view-id>` tag defines the page we are initially on when making the action request. So in this case we started on `/pages/startPage.jsp` before making the call to our backing bean. The listener on the backing bean then has three options of return values. It can return a string of `outcome1` or `outcome2`, or return a null object. The null return will return you back to the page you are already on, in this case `/pages/startPage.jsp`. If you return `outcome1` or `outcome2`, however, the server will forward you to `pages/firstOutcome.jsp` or `/pages/secondOutcome.jsp`, respectively. This makes your page navigation extremely easy.

Now what if you have some global links on the page? You obviously do not want to have to define them for every single page. Listing 3-17 provides an example of some global navigation rules.

Listing 3-17. *A Navigation Rule for Global Pages*

```
<navigation-rule>
    <from-view-id>/pages/*</from-view-id>
    <navigation-case>
      <from-outcome>defaultOutcome1</from-outcome>
      <to-view-id>/pages/defaultOutcomeOne.jsp</to-view-id>
    </navigation-case>
</navigation-rule>
<navigation-rule>
    <from-view-id>*</from-view-id>
    <navigation-case>
      <from-outcome>defaultOutcome2</from-outcome>
      <to-view-id>/pages/defaultOutcomeTwo.jsp</to-view-id>
    </navigation-case>
</navigation-rule>
```

This code defines two types of global pages. The first one, /pages/*, says for any page that the user is on that is in the pages directory, that if your listener returns a string of defaultOutcome1, forward the user to /pages/defautOutcome.jsp. This is useful for submenus and so forth. Now what if you have something more global, such as a logout? That is when the second case comes into play. For the second case, if you have any backing bean listener that returns defaultOutcome2, the server will forward the user to /pages/defaultOutcomeTwo.jsp. Now when using global froms, you can easily get into a situation where the global defines something the page defines, or multiple globals define the same thing. Listing 3-18 provides an example of navigation rules that will return the same name, defaultOutcome.

Listing 3-18. *A Navigation Rule for the Same Name Returns*

```
<navigation-rule>
    <from-view-id>/pages/startPage.jsp</from-view-id>
    <navigation-case>
      <from-outcome>defaultOutcome</from-outcome>
      <to-view-id>/pages/page1.jsp</to-view-id>
    </navigation-case>
</navigation-rule>
<navigation-rule>
    <from-view-id>*</from-view-id>
    <navigation-case>
      <from-outcome>defaultOutcome</from-outcome>
      <to-view-id>/pages/page2.jsp</to-view-id>
    </navigation-case>
```

```
<navigation-rule>
    <from-view-id>*</from-view-id>
    <navigation-case>
      <from-outcome>defaultOutcome</from-outcome>
      <to-view-id>/pages/page3.jsp</to-view-id>
    </navigation-case>
</navigation-rule>
```

In this case, you see that there are three options when returning the string
`defaultOutcome`. If you are on the page `/pages/startPage.jsp`, then the server will forward
you to `/pages/page1.jsp`. Basically, the JSF framework will default to the outcome that
best matches `<from-view-id>`. In our first case, the return string obviously matched the
first one best. Now what happens if there are two rules that match the outcome? As
in the preceding example, what if the page we were on was `/pages/otherPage.jsp`
instead, and our listener-returned `defaultOutcome`? At that point, we would match both
scenarios. The answer is, we would forward to `/pages/page3.jsp`. In these cases, the
default behavior is to go to the last one defined.

One final situation we can look for deals with `<from-view-id/>`. Suppose you want
navigation rules not based on the page you are on but based on what method on a backing bean you called. This is useful if you have a page that can have multiple returns
based on the method but you just want to return the word *success* instead. Well, fortunately, this is easy. Let's start with using the `from` action in Listing 3-19.

Listing 3-19. *Navigation Rules Based on the from Action*

```
<navigation-rule>
    <from-action>#{startBean.nextPage}</from-action>
    <navigation-case>
      <from-outcome>defaultOutcome</from-outcome>
      <to-view-id>/pages/page2.jsp</to-view-id>
    </navigation-case>
</navigation-rule>
```

In this example, you have a backing bean called `startBean` and have called the
`nextPage` method on it. If you return `defaultOutcome` from it, it will forward to `page2.jsp`.

Put It All Together

In the previous chapter, I started to present examples that I said I would use throughout
the book. It is important to be able to understand how all these components go together
and create a workable application.

This chapter marks the start of our Garage Sale application, which we will be using through this chapter and the next two chapters. This application, as I said before, is a simple CRUD application. The goal for this chapter is to create the JSP components that will be used throughout the next two chapters. These components for the most part will remain largely untouched, and this is part of the goal of Seam—to allow people who want to go from JSF to Seam to make the cost low.

So in this section, I am going to explain the creation of two pages and their corresponding backing beans. I will discuss the Add and List pages, and the List page itself will have a link for deleting and editing the page.

These examples use one backing bean called `GarageSaleAction` in `faces-config.xml`. The definition for it is quite simple:

```
<managed-bean>
    <managed-bean-name>garageSale</managed-bean-name>
    <managed-bean-class>
        com.petradesigns.garageSale.backingbean.GarageSaleAction
    </managed-bean-class>
    <managed-bean-scope>session</managed-bean-scope>
</managed-bean>
```

This defines our bean named `garageSale` for the class `GarageSaleAction`, and we have scoped it to the session. The main reason we did that was because the list objects will need the lists stored to the session.

Add Page

Let's start with the simplest piece, the Add page, in Listing 3-20.

Listing 3-20. *The JSP for the Add Page*

```
<%@ taglib uri="http://java.sun.com/jsf/html" prefix="h" %>
<%@ taglib uri="http://java.sun.com/jsf/core" prefix="f" %>
<%@ taglib uri="http://myfaces.apache.org/tomahawk" prefix="t" %>


<f:view>
<h1>Add a garage sale to your area</h1>
<div class="entry errors"><h:messages globalOnly="true"/></div>

<h:form>
<h:panelGrid columns="2" cellpadding="5" border="0">
<h:outputText value="Address:"/>
<h:inputText value="#{garageSale.house.address}" size="25"/>
```

```
<h:outputText value="City:"/>
<h:inputText value="#{garageSale.house.city}" size="25"/>

<h:outputText value="State:"/>
<h:inputText value="#{garageSale.house.state}" size="25"/>

<h:outputText value="Start Time:"/>
<t:inputDate value="#{garageSale.house.startTime}" type="both"/>

<h:outputText value="End Time:"/>
<t:inputDate value="#{garageSale.house.endTime}" type="both"/>

<f:facet name="footer">
<h:commandButton type="submit" value="Add House" action="#{garageSale.addHouse}"/>
</f:facet>
</h:panelGrid>
</h:form>
</f:view>
```

Hopefully you recognize a lot of these components. As you see, we start with the customary f:view and an f:form tag. This allows the start of the application for a form input. Now check out the panelGrid tag. As I said before, JSF is designed to allow users to create pages without having to knowingly create specific HTML tags, and that is exactly what the panelGrid tag is for. We have defined two columns on it, and so what will be outputted is a table that has every two HTML entries in a row. The output of that code appears in Figure 3-6.

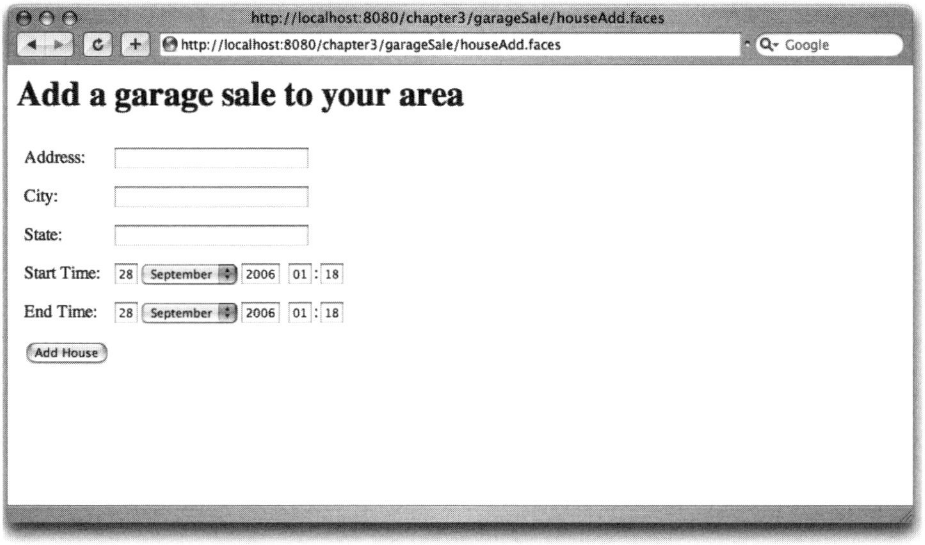

Figure 3-6. *The Add page of our Garage Sale application*

As you see, this creates a nice little form tag. The `t:inputDate` at the bottom references the Tomahawk inputs I mentioned earlier. This is one of the specific tags to help us create a date more easily.

The last part of this is the action that calls `addHouse` on our backing bean. So now let's take a look at the part of the backing bean that deals with this Add page in Listing 3-21.

Listing 3-21. *A Fragment of the GarageSaleAction That Deals with Saving the House*

```
House house = new House();


    public String addHouse() {
        // Persist it to the database
        // via an injection from EJB

        return "edit";
    }
```

The backing bean here is quite simple. You will have the `house` object set because it was referenced in the preceding JSP, so all you have to do is save it. Essentially, all this bean is doing is acting as a pass-through, taking the `house` object and sending it to a business logic tier. In this example, we do not have the backing bean persisting yet. We will add that functionality in the next chapter.

List Page

Now moving on to the List page, I am going to present a more complicated example. In this example, we are going to have to do a few things. As shown in Listing 3-22, we will have to use `HtmlDataTable` to print out the table, load up this table from the backing bean, and be able to delete parts of it.

Listing 3-22. *The JSP Page for Displaying a List of Houses Having Garage Sales*

```
<%@ taglib uri="http://java.sun.com/jsf/html" prefix="h" %>
<%@ taglib uri="http://java.sun.com/jsf/core" prefix="f" %>

<f:view>

<h:dataTable var="house" value="#{garageSale.houseDataModel}">
```

```
      <h:column>
        <f:facet name="header">
          <h:outputText value="Address"/>
        </f:facet>
        <h:outputText value="#{house.address}"/>
      </h:column>

. . .

      <h:column>
        <h:commandLink actionListener="#{garageSale.deleteHouse}">
          <h:outputText value="Delete"/>
        </h:commandLink>
      </h:column>

      <h:column>
        <h:commandLink actionListener="#{garageSale.editHouse}">
          <h:outputText value="Edit"/>
        </h:commandLink>
      </h:column>
    </h:dataTable>


</f:view>
```

For brevity, I did not list all the columns that are being outputted for display. You can find the rest in the source code. After our usual `f:view`, there is the `h:dataTable` component. This, as you may recall, is used to display the data table discussed earlier. The value here is referencing not a list, but a `DataModel`, the same `Data Model` in Listing 3-9. The output of this display is shown in Figure 3-7.

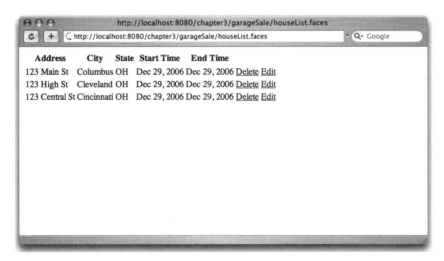

Figure 3-7. *The List page of our Garage Sale application*

This is the output of the display resulting from the execution. The deleting of an entry is where the code starts to get a bit interesting. Listing 3-23 defines a method to delete an entry.

Listing 3-23. *A Fragment of the GarageSaleAction That Deals with Deleting the House*

```
public String deleteHouse(ActionEvent e) {
        House house = (House)houseDataModel.getRowData();
        houses.remove(house);
        // TODO - remove from service

        return SUCCESS;
}
```

Here you are using the data model to retrieve the row data. This corresponds to the row you have just selected.

This concludes the explanation of our example. More details of the page flows are in the Chapter 3 section of the source code if you want to analyze it further.

Summary

The goal of this chapter was to introduce you to JSF and creating a web application using JSF. First, I presented a standard Hello World example to introduce you to the framework and its capabilities. After that you learned about the configuration of the framework, including where to get the necessary JAR files and how to configure, compile, and package your application into a WAR file in order to use JSF.

Then we moved on to the architecture of JSF. This exposed you to the various areas of JSF, from managed beans to components to event handling. You then saw how it is all put together in the life cycle and where each area is instantiated.

Afterward we went into more depth about JSF—mainly about the presentation-tier modules. This is the portion of JSF that Seam makes the most use of. You learned about components, including how to use built-in components and how to create a customized component if you need to. This lead to the use of the JSF expression language, because this becomes handy when you want to embed managed beans into a component. Finally, you read about the use of page flows, which we will get into even more in Chapter 5.

The last section allowed us to put all these parts together in the creation of the Garage Sale application. I covered specifically the List and Add pages, although the example source code that comes with the book has the complete functionality for you. You will notice that the only piece really missing here is tying this to the business tier. This will be left for us to do in the next chapter.

CHAPTER 4

■■■

EJB3 Fundamentals

This begins the second and final of our "fundamental" chapters, and if you are not famil-iar with Enterprise JavaBeans (EJBs) at all, then definitely take a close look at this chapter. Because Seam applications rely almost exclusively on EJBs to provide the domain and business logic, this chapter is important in understanding how to implement a Seam-based application. This chapter focuses almost exclusively on the Entity JavaBeans 3 specification (EJB3) but will touch on how to call EJBs from the client. The road map in Figure 4-1 shows where the focus of this chapter lies.

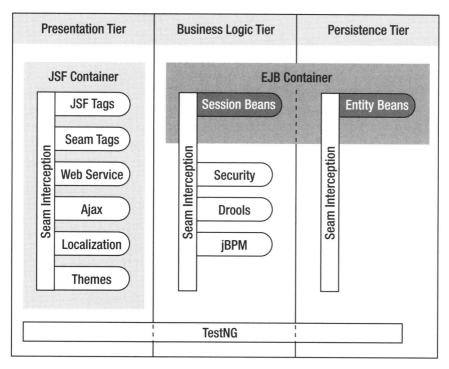

Figure 4-1. *The road map showing we will focus on mainly EJB3 for this chapter*

This chapter introduces you to the three types of EJBs: session beans, entity beans, and message-driven beans. You need to understand at least session and entity beans in order to write full web application frameworks with Seam. This is necessary because the purpose of Seam is to allow us to skip the backing beans we discussed in Chapter 3 and jump right into the creation of our business logic.

If you are familiar with the EJB 2.1 specification, you will find that EJB3 is radically different—in a good way, though. This chapter covers EJB3, how to use the various components, and at the same time shows you how this is a much more agile version of EJB than EJB 2.1. For those of you who are Spring fans, you should be pleasantly surprised by the upgrades that have taken place, but that is for you to decide.

History of EJB3

During the mid '90s, enterprise computing was in disarray—yes, even more so than it is today. During that time, Common Object Request Broker Architecture (CORBA) and Distributed Component Object Model (DCOM) were the two competing technologies, and they were everywhere. Neither technology provided us much insulation from the underlying plumbing. This made our business logic tightly coupled to the underlying technologies.

Note I will use the term *EJB* somewhat generically in this chapter, in that EJBs are derived from a JSR specification, the result of which is EJB code. However, so as not confuse you with JSR numbers, I will often just say *EJB specification* when referring to the JSR specifications for EJB.

EJB 2.*x*

Then in the late '90s, Sun Microsystems came out with a specification that was an attempt at simplifying distributed computing. Sun provided a component model that developers could use to avoid dealing with the more complex plumbing issues such as multithreading, caching, session management, and so forth. This specification, a beacon of light at the end of a long tunnel, became known as Enterprise JavaBeans (EJB). Unfortunately, as many of you know, this beacon was not a bright light but thousands of matches burning. The EJB model, although allowing us to be separated from many of the plumbing issues, still required much coding and configuring to get working. The implemented EJBs, although effective, were bloated objects that were not really portable, and the tooling mechanisms were substandard. All of this required developers to write most of the Java classes and XML configurations by hand. The configurations would start to get confusing and harder to follow with the more EJBs that were added.

After a few years of using EJB 2.1, the Java community discovered that EJB solved many problems. However, it created just as many problems as it solved.

Writing an EJB required creating quite a bit of code. Not only did developers have to write the bean itself, but also local and home interfaces as well as remote interfaces at times. That alone probably could have been overcome, but the code for the bean required implementing so many extra methods, and now that bean was dependent on those methods. This complexity seemed to obscure the intent of the code, which was to create business logic.

In addition, the mantra that EJBs could be reused within a company and easily accessed by other development silos never seemed to happen. It was never clear whether developers should look up the EJBs at runtime or just reuse the code. Even reuse was cumbersome, especially from environment to environment and from application server to application server.

Another source of endless confusion were entity beans (EBs). It was never clear by early adopters whether EBs were to be used as simple domain-DAO objects or as full-fledged business and service objects. Hence many clients either never implemented them or implemented them inconsistently. This lack of direction and consistency gave far too many developers too much power, and this ended up creating a mess that we still live with today.

EJB3

The difficulty people had with EJB 2.1 and the lack of developers using it led to the creation of EJB3. The big theme with EJB3 has been "ease of development"—this idea to make it easier to create EJB3 code and to tackle some of the major problems in the preceding version. These main problems were as follows:

- The inability to work without an application server.

- The inability to run quick tests.

- The code-compile-package-deploy cycle was too long.

- The lack of direction in how developers should use EJB3.

These issues have all been tackled with EJB3, and only time will tell whether the ideas that were implemented will catch on. Fortunately, many of the solutions are based on new common practices within the Java community.

Although EJB 2.1 led people down a road map of clear separation of their business tier, it was never a clear-enough road map to sustain its use. Therefore, many developers sought other ways to create business logic and persistent tiers. Two of the more appealing ones that have come along in the last couple of years are Spring and Hibernate. Hibernate gave us a better way to manage database SQL queries and tables via object relational mapping. Spring (and a few other frameworks) presented the idea of injection and wrapping the methods in transactions without having to code them explicitly. Using components such as Spring allowed us to have clean business objects without the plumbing of EJB 2.1. This exposed new ways of solving old problems. The other major item that helped in creating EJB3 was brought about by the advent of Java 5—the introduction of annotations for use in POJOs.

So you may ask yourself, "If we already have technologies out there that give us enterprise-level architecture without some of the drawbacks of EJB 2.*x*, why do we even need EJB3?" The main reason is for standardization. Having a standard way to solve problems provides a more universal approach for creating business tier logic and database logic. This also means that multiple vendors are creating the implementations, so you do not have to constantly worry about tracking and updating individual JAR files. The result, hopefully, is that having one standard way to create business logic and persistent tiers eases the burden—whether you are a large corporation and want a standard for your business, or you are an individual developer who wants to start a new job without having to learn completely new technologies.

Configuring EJB3s for Deployment

In the preceding chapter, I went over how to create a WAR file, which was necessary to deploy a web application. Now that we are moving up in the world to EJBs, it is going to become necessary to deploy an Enterprise ARchive (EAR) file. An EAR file is a more complex way to deploy enterprise applications by allowing the deployment of multiple modules in just one archived file. In our examples, we will only have two: the web archive and the EJB archive. However, before we create the EAR, we first need to configure the XML files for the EJB and the EAR.

Creating XML Files

The EJB 2.*x* spec was plagued with potentially long XML descriptor files, which were necessary back then because there really was no other way to configure an application. We had to define the bean's name to be stored in the Java Naming and Directory Interface (JNDI) for our presentation tier to look up. We also had to define the transactioning inside the XML file. This led to exorbitant XML files that were difficult to manage. With EJB3, most of the XML configurations have been relegated to annotations. That being said, you can still define your transactioning and other items in the XML file, but I don't recommend it and won't be covering that here.

Data Source Descriptor—persistence.xml

There are two major solutions that EJB originally provided: a mechanism for your business layer and a mechanism for database persistence. The part that deals with database persistence are the entity beans, which I will explain shortly. These will be used to interact with our database. It would be rather cumbersome and silly for us to have to write a connection script in each of our classes. So we define it rather simply in an XML file packaged with the EJB, as in Listing 4-1.

Listing 4-1. *Our persistence.xml File with the Database Defined*

```
<persistence>
    <persistence-unit name="garageSaleDatabase">
        <provider>org.hibernate.ejb.HibernatePersistence</provider>
        <jta-data-source>java:/GarageSaleDS</jta-data-source>
        <properties>
            <property name="hibernate.hbm2ddl.auto" value="update"/>
        </properties>
    </persistence-unit>
</persistence>
```

The persistence.xml file here defines the provider for the data source. In this case, because we are using JBoss as the container, we will be using the Hibernate persistence provider. Then we provide the JNDI name so that the application server can provide a name to the associated data source instance. As you may remember from Chapter 1, we deployed a database xml file that contained a JNDI name, the same one we are going to be using here. The next part allows us to actually build the database based on the EBs we provide to it.

There are a few more configuration options that are not covered in this book. However, one that may be of interest is that you can use <non-jta-data-source/> to provide a reference to your non-JTA data sources.

EJB Descriptors—ejb-jar.xml

The other EJB-specific XML file that should be quite familiar to those who have developed EJB 2.1 classes is ejb-jar.xml. For this chapter, though, we will not be using this file at all. As I mentioned earlier, annotations allow us to no longer need ejb-jar.xml to define our EJBs or transactions. There is some life cycle interception that you can define in ejb-jar.xml, which we will use in the next chapter when integrating Seam into the application. However, nothing needs to be configured for this chapter.

Application Descriptors—application.xml

Finally, let's configure the EAR itself. The EAR needs to know what it is deploying and where those deployments should live. Each compressed file (JAR) that is deployed is called a *module*. Multiple modules make up an EAR. Traditionally the EAR consists of at least one web archive and one enterprise archive. Also, you can then deploy multiple shared files in a common JAR. So let's define the `application.xml` file in Listing 4-2 that we are deploying.

Listing 4-2. *Our application.xml File Defining the Modules for the EAR*

```
<application>
    <display-name>Garage Sale</display-name>

    <module>
        <web>
            <web-uri>chapter4.war</web-uri>
            <context-root>/chapter4</context-root>
        </web>
    </module>

    <module>
        <ejb>chapter4-business.ejb3</ejb>
    </module>
</application>
```

The main tags to examine here are the `<module>` tags. These are going to define the modules you want to add. You can add EJBs, web contexts, or even JARs that you want to share across applications. This example defines our web module and the context root that our application server will bind the web application to. As you may recall, in the previous chapter the context root simply defaulted to the name of the WAR. Here, though, you can define a name different from your WAR name. Next, you will notice that we define the EJB module. You will also notice that we ended the file with `ejb3`. This is not something you have to do, because there is no set standard of how to end the EJB file. However, doing so makes it easier to tell this compressed file apart from a standard JAR when you are looking at all your build artifacts. In the next chapter, we will add to this a Seam Java module necessary for the web and EJB code.

Packaging

Now that we have all of our XML files, we should be ready to package our code together. We will still be using our WAR packaging that we created before. However, now we will also be creating a JAR package for our EJB. Finally, we will wrap them both up into the EAR.

Packaging the EJB

Unlike for the WAR file, there are no specific Ant tasks to create an EJB. This is because the EJB is essentially a JAR with a few XML files. So in Listing 4-3 we are going to package the EJB with the regular JAR builder.

Listing 4-3. *Building of the EJB JAR File*

```
<jar jarfile="${ejb3-file}">
    <metainf dir="${dd-ejb}" includes="*.xml"/>
    <!-- include all but the web classes -->
      <fileset dir="${classes}">
          <include name="**/service/**"/>
          <include name="**/domain/**"/>
          <include name="**/ejb/**"/>
      </fileset>
</jar>
```

This is a rather simple way to build JAR files, and there are only two things to watch out for. First, we do not include any of the web archive into our classes directory. In theory, you could—it will not hurt anything—but in practice it is better to keep those objects separated. Also, we store persistence.xml and ejb-jar.xml (if you have one) inside the manifest directory.

Packaging the EAR

Now that we have our WAR from the previous chapter, our EJB3 JAR from this chapter, and our application.xml configured, we are ready to combine these into our deployable EAR file. Listing 4-4 creates a specific Ant markup for the creation of the EAR, marked appropriately ear.

Listing 4-4. *Our Ant Configuration for the EAR Build*

```
<patternset id="ear.set">
    <include name="${ejb3-filename}" />
    <include name="${war-filename}" />
</patternset>

<ear destfile="${ear-file}" appxml="${dd-app-normal}/application.xml">
      <!-- you want to grab all but that application.xml we just defined -->
      <metainf dir="${dd-app-normal}" excludes="application.xml"/>
      <!-- include our ear and war file -->
```

```
        <fileset dir="${dist}">
                <patternset refid="ear.set"/>
        </fileset>
</ear>
```

We start by defining a set of JARs to deploy in the application. By using the `ear` tag on the Ant script, we define the location of the `application.xml` file. Then we go on to add everything else in our deployment directory minus `application.xml`. This call is optional and required only if you need to define anything else that is server specific for the EAR. (We will put `jboss-app.xml` into it in the next chapter). Finally, we add our suite of compressed files to the EAR for packaging.

After you have done all this, you now have a file that you can drop into the deployment directory and start using.

Session Beans

Now that you have gotten a taste of EJBs and have an Ant script configured, you're ready to start learning how to develop the EJBs that will be used as the basis for business logic for the rest of the book. Session beans (SBs) are further broken down into two types: stateless and stateful—the difference being that one maintains state and one does not.

Before I delve into the details of stateless and stateful beans, I should probably answer a bigger question: why are SBs used for our business logic tier? In theory, your business logic tier does just that, business logic. And as I have said, we should use POJOs wherever possible. So what makes SBs optimal as the wrapper for business logic? Well, there are many reasons, but two big reasons that both stateless and stateful session beans share.

First, because this is a business logic tier, it is reasonable to assume that session beans will be heavily utilized objects. Just about any request to the server or any operation you do will require some kind of business logic, or at least should. Although it is not obvious on a small-scale system, on a larger scale you are going to want to minimize the time to process whenever possible. One of those areas is the instantiation time of an object. If you have to create and then destroy an object for every single request to a server, you will waste processing time. With SBs, the objects are in a scalable pool. This means that the EJB3 container will maintain these objects, and when the presentation tier needs them, it can take the object from the pool and serve it to the user. The biggest difference between SFSBs and SLSBs lies in how their pooling mechanisms work; I will discuss each of those shortly.

The second aspect deals with transactions. For the majority of your applications, the business logic is going to have to deal with some sort of persistent tier. The ability to manage database transactions in the business logic is a fairly fundamental requirement, and you will notice most enterprise-level frameworks do the same (for example, Spring).

In this section, you will learn how to use stateful and stateless session beans and how they are pooled. The transactioning portion I will save for later because it is the same for both, and you will need to have some more information before it will make sense.

Stateless Session Beans

Stateless session beans (SLSBs) are by far the more simplistic of the two SBs, and this is why I am going to present them first. Traditionally this has been the area where Java developers have programmed the majority of their business logic. Of course, this as a statistic is a bit skewed because most developers cringed at SFSB use. With EJB3 I believe it remains to be seen whether this paradigm holds true. It will depend largely on the needs of your application.

Life Cycle

SLSBs are used when you have logic that is not state specific. SLSB are in a pool, and the pool is available for nonexclusive use by the clients. When a request is made to the container for a particular SLSB, the application server will retrieve a SLSB without regard to the user. After the SLSB is given to the client, this client holds it for the length of the request. After the client request is finished, the object is released and returned to the pool. You can see a diagram of this pool in Figure 4-2.

The diagram represents a user requesting an EJB. The container allocates the bean from the free pool, the user acts on it, and then the bean is returned back to the pool for reuse.

In actuality, the programming of the destruction and creation, even though they were often blank methods, was a requirement for EJB 2.1. Fortunately, with EJB3 we are using POJOs and by default are no longer implementing interfaces, so this once-annoying requirement has been removed.

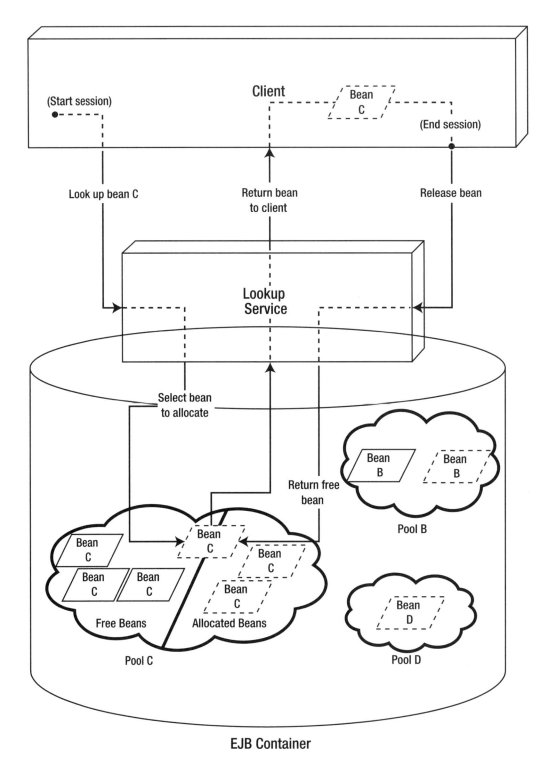

Figure 4-2. *The pooling and retrieval diagram of a SLSB*

Creating a SLSB

So what do we need to create a SLSB in EJB3? The answer is, not much—especially if you compare it to yesteryear. As mentioned earlier, part of the new use of EJB3 is the way the SLSBs are defined. No longer do you have complex XMLs nor will you have to extend EJB-specific base classes. Instead, you use an annotation to define that this is a SLSB, as shown in Listing 4-5.

Listing 4-5. *The HelloWorld POJO and Interface Defined As a SLSB*

```
import javax.ejb.Stateless;

@Stateless
public class HelloWorldAction implements HelloWorld {
}
```

```
import javax.ejb.Local;

@Local
public interface HelloWorld {
}
```

That is all that is needed to initially define our SLSB—no extra XML or extension of base classes. Of course, remember that an actual call would have methods defined in both. We have two major things here: the interface (a local interface, in this example) that we have defined for this class, and the SLSB that implements that interface. Having a local interface means that the methods defined here are available only to clients who have called for this EJB on the Java EE container itself. This interface is the equivalent of the local interfaces used with EJB 2.*x*. The @Local annotation is optional and is used only for clarification that this really is a local interface; for all intents and purposes, it will default to being local. Conversely, there is an @Remote annotation that is used when you want to define the SLSB as a remote call. However, make sure to use this sparingly because there are lots of performance costs when having to use Remote Method Invocation (RMI) to access the bean, and the parameters will now be passed by value instead of reference in a remote invocation.

On the bean itself, all that is needed is for the annotation @Stateless to be defined. Now as long as this bean is packaged properly into an EAR, the container will know that this is an EJB. Using annotations eliminates the need for stub artifact creation as before.

Life Cycle Annotations

The server manages the complete life cycle of the EJB by keeping a pool of stateless beans available when asked. The caller has no control over the number of beans in that pool. The application also has no control over initialization of that bean, which is again the job of the application server.

So what happens if you need to initialize objects such as a log factory or if you want to do simple logging when the EJB is instantiated or destroyed? In EJB 2.1, you may recall that we had a create method we had to define for the SB. As I said before, these methods are no longer required and because we no longer implement EJB-specific interfaces, the methods are not even there to implement, so now we use annotations as shown in Listing 4-6.

Listing 4-6. *The HelloWorld Defined as a SLSB*

```
import javax.ejb.Stateless;

import javax.annotation.PostConstruct;
import javax.annotation.PreDestroy;

@Stateless
public class HelloWorldAction implements HelloWorld {

@PostConstruct
public void init() {
    // call anything needed upon bean creation.
}

@PreDestroy
public void recycle() {
    // call anything upon bean destruction.
}
```

The beautiful thing about this solution is that it is *optional*. In the past, many times people were forced to write these items even though they were never implementing them. Now you have to create them only if you need them. So as you can see, there are two extra annotations that you can call on the server: @PostConstruct and @PreDestroy. The @PostConstruct annotation is called after the beans have been constructed and it has initialized all the container services for the bean. The @PreDestroy annotation is called right before the server releases the bean for garbage collection. Please remember, though, that you should use the annotations sparingly with the understanding of when these events will occur. Holding a resource for the lifetime of a SLSB instance is controlled by the user, not the application, so this resource may be held longer than you initially planned.

If you have any degree of experience with EJB 2.1, I hope you can see not only how easy it is to create a SLSB but how much less code or configurations you will need to do it. In addition, having EJBs be strict POJOs will make it much easier to wrap the EJB code into a test harness.

Stateful Session Beans

Stateful session beans (SFSBs) have always been the red-headed stepchild of SBs (no offense to any red-headed stepchildren reading this book). However, all the hype says that they work much faster than SFSBs of old and are much easier to use. Although I have not run any speed or memory tests to prove their speed, I can say they are much easier to use than before.

Life Cycle

The major difference between SFSBs and SLSBs relates to the first word, *state*. SFSBs are objects that maintain state for a client. Instead of having a nonexclusive call to a bean, SFSBs maintain an exclusive call to the bean until the client decides it no longer needs the SFSB. Pooling works differently for a SFSB than for a SLSB, in that because the object is stored, there is a chance we are going to have to persist the data. The actual lookup mechanism of it is similar to that of the SLSB. However, with a SLSB we are going to have to be able retrieve and store the data state. Fortunately, you do not have to worry about the retrieval and storage, better known as *activation* and *passivation*, because the EJB container takes care of it for you. I will, however, go over what the EJB container does do in its life cycle for the activation and passivation of SFSB.

Figure 4-3 shows how the application server passivates the EJB.

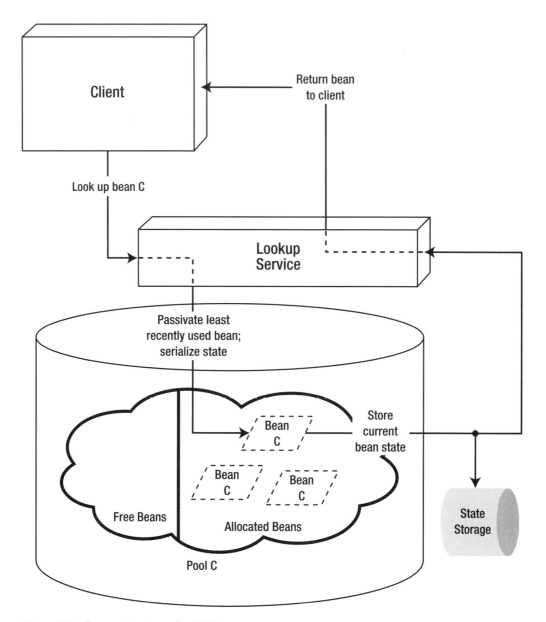

Figure 4-3. *The passivation of a SFSB*

Here the bean is known from the EJB container. We then send the EJB back for its persistable store. Now when we want to retrieve the bean again, we do the opposite, as shown in Figure 4-4.

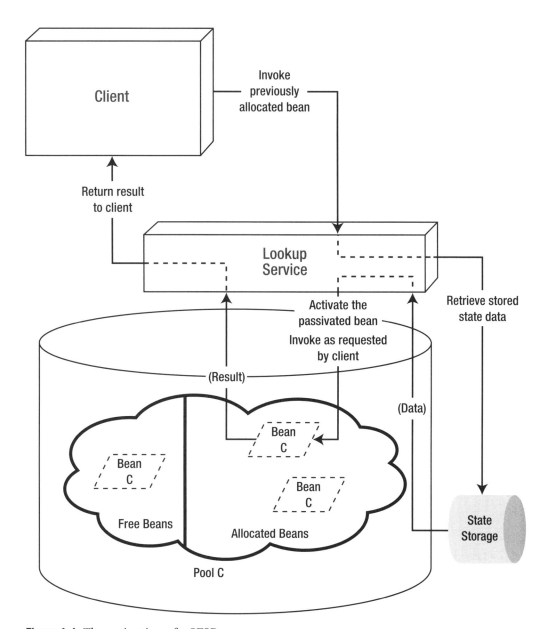

Figure 4-4. *The activation of a SFSB*

Here the bean is being requested for retrieval and is looked up and loaded in storage. After it is loaded, it is sent back to the client for processing. This whole process of activation and passivation of the object does require more processing overhead.

The example often used with a SFSB is the shopping cart. A user uses the SFSB cart to put objects into and out of the cart and then finally to check out, which usually requires a call to persist the data stored in the shopping cart to the server. In previous implementations of SFSBs, these objects became extremely slow and were considerably harder to write than POJOs. The major problem was essentially being able to use SFSBs efficiently. Most developers found it a bit of a pain to do the lookups, and creating the bean itself when using the HttpSession was much easier. Fortunately, creating SFSBs and calling them from the client is considerably easier now, as you will see in Listing 4-7. Also, SFSBs have improved in both performance and resource space, and should no longer be thought of as wasteful. In fact, performance is now quite similar to storing into HttpSession. Another item to remember is that storing in HttpSession is a solution only for users coming over an HttpServlet request and will not be a solution if your users are connecting to the server over a nonservlet connection. SFSB will be defined much like our stateless beans were, except we will use a @Stateful annotation.

Listing 4-7. *Our Stateful Shopping Cart*

```
package com.petradesigns.stateful;

import javax.ejb.Remove;
import javax.ejb.Stateful;

import com.petradesigns.service.ShoppingCart;

@Stateful
public class ShoppingCartBean implements ShoppingCart {

    @Remove
    public void purchase() {
        // persist the items to the database
    }
}
```

As I just mentioned, to make it a stateful bean, we changed the annotation from stateless to stateful. However, there is one other item we had to add. Because this is a stateful bean and the server wants to be able to know when to release the bean for reuse, we had to add a remove method. When this method is executed, it sends a signal to the application server that we can recycle this object. You can have multiple remove methods, but you have to have at a least one designated by the @Remove annotation.

Life Cycle Issues

The life cycle of a SFSB is like the life cycle of the SLSB, except there are two more possible methods that can be defined for it. Remember that because we are storing state and are requiring the client to inform us when to remove the bean, this bean could hang around for a long time. In fact, it could hang around for a long time without even being used.

Think of shopping on a website such as www.amazon.com. You may log on to the site and click to add to your cart the first item you see. Then, you may shop around more, looking at CDs, DVDs, books, leaving reviews, and so forth. None of these options require you to actually add anything to or remove anything from your cart. However, your session is still active and so is this bean. The SFSB itself will then be stored either to memory or if not used for a while will be persisted to the file system until called upon.

Message-Driven Beans

Message-driven beans (MDBs) do not fit entirely into our Seam framework, because they are an asynchronous processing mechanism. They are not used in the direct execution of a web framework; thus their interaction with Seam is quite minimal. In fact, you could use something such as Spring 2 to do asynchronous processing instead. However, because MDBs are part of EJB3, and you may need to perform some asynchronous requests, I will cover it briefly here.

MDBs were not in the initial releases of EJB and were added later for doing asynchronous processing. The purpose of MDBs is to listen to a predefined Java Message Service (JMS) destination (queue or topic) for any new messages. When a message is picked up, it will be processed by that MDB. As in our previous examples, all the traditional items that were defined in the ejb-jar.xml file will now be on the annotation itself. Because there is quite a bit of info for an MDB, Listing 4-8 shows that the class annotation becomes much larger.

Listing 4-8. *An Example of a Message-Driven Bean*

```
@MessageDriven(
    activationConfig =
    {
        @ActivationConfigProperty(
            propertyName="destinationType", propertyValue="javax.jms.Queue"),
        @ActivationConfigProperty(
            propertyName="destination", propertyValue="queue/testQueue")
    })
public class TestQueueBean implements javax.jms.MessageListener {
    public void onMessage(javax.jms.Message message) {
        // Perform operations on the message
    }
```

As I mentioned, the annotation definition is rather large. We are initially defining the activation configuration; the first part of it defines that we are using a queue, and the second defines which queue to use. You will notice that unlike most EJB3 classes, this one is still forced to actually implement a class. So you cannot deal with this as a true POJO, but that was just necessary to work in the Java spec for message listeners. Although this takes away from the traditional POJO development of EJB3, I would not say this takes away from the use of MDBs for asynchronous processing in your application, because in general MDBs serve as a middleman to then pass their payloads onto some SLSBs.

Entity Beans

Entity beans have been around since the beginning of EJB and were supposed to be the heart of the J2EE (now Java EE) persistence tier when they first came out. However, their acceptance was sporadic at best. Mostly they were seen as slow and cumbersome to use. So, for the most part it is a bit rare to see entity beans in the workplace, although some places did use them quite exclusively and effectively.

So people started turning to other solutions to create their data tier. Two of the more common ones were Java Data Objects (JDO) and Hibernate, Hibernate especially in recent years. Hibernate provides a nice separation of tiers and allowed the developers to access the database without using database-specific language. This ease of use was appreciated by many, especially the Java folks. Thus there are many similarities between EBs and Hibernate, so much so that JBoss 4.0.*x* uses Hibernate as its EB implementation. So if you are familiar with Hibernate, your transaction to EBs will be quite painless, especially if you are using the Hibernate annotations.

Basics of an Entity Bean

Like the SLSB, the EB is going to be a POJO, which will help provide us the most flexibility when creating the domain there. The EB for EJB3 should end up looking like a regular JavaBean representing a table in the database. So in the end you will have more of a one-to-one ratio of columns in your table and properties on the bean. Each of the properties will be assumed to be a persistable column on the database. This will then allow us to use `EntityManager` (which we will discuss in a bit) to perform operations on it that will be translated to our table. `EntityManager` can be called from any class, but preferably we would want to call it from a SB. As you can see, this is starting to look a lot like how we use Hibernate.

Take the `House` table we have been using (which we defined in Chapter 2). To start it off as an entity bean, we need the customary annotation at the class level. This time, as you may have guessed, it's `@Entity`. Listing 4-9 defines our `House` EB.

Listing 4-9. *Our House*

```
import javax.persistence.Entity;

@Entity
public class House {

    private long houseId;
    private String address;
    private String city;
    private String state;
    private Date startTime;
    private Date endTime;

    public long getHouseId() {
        return houseId;
    }
    public void setHouseId(long houseId) {
        this.houseId = houseId;
    }

    public String getAddress() {
        return address;
    }
    public void setAddress(String address) {
        this.address = address;
    }
    public String getCity() {
        return city;
    }
    public void setCity(String city) {
        this.city = city;
    }
    public Date getEndTime() {
        return endTime;
    }
    public void setEndTime(Date endTime) {
        this.endTime = endTime;
    }
    public Date getStartTime() {
        return startTime;
    }
}
```

```
    public void setStartTime(Date startTime) {
        this.startTime = startTime;
    }
    public String getState() {
        return state;
    }
    public void setState(String state) {
        this.state = state;
    }

    public String toString() {
        return
          address+","+city+","+state+","+startTime+","+endTime;
    }
}
```

This is pretty much the exact bean code we had before. The only difference is the annotation. However, unfortunately it is not exactly that simple. We do need to define a few more items on the bean, with annotations, in order for it to work fully with the database.

Entity Bean Annotations

There are a variety of annotations that can be used with EBs, much more so than with SBs, and this makes sense when you think of all the options that come with a persistence tier. These annotations are used to define logical mappings and physical mappings of the database on the POJO. Annotations for EBs are defined in the `javax.persistence.*` package. I will go over some of them here. However, it is beyond the scope of this book to go over all of them. So if you feel there is something missing that you want to know more about, I suggest reading *Pro EJB 3: Java Persistence API* by Mike Keith and Merrick Schincariol (Apress, 2006).

@Table

The first question you will probably have is, "How does the container know what table to go off of?" By default, if you do not select anything, the table name will be based on the class name. So for our example this works well, because our table is `House` and our class name is `House`. However, if you need to have a different name, you can use the `@Table` annotation. So if your table were named `houseTable`, your class would look like Listing 4-10.

Listing 4-10. *House Class Based Off of a Table with the Name houseTable*

```
@Entity
@Table(name="houseTable")
public class House {
    // ...
}
```

The table also has a few other parameters, including the `schema` and `catalog` if needed. Another parameter is used to apply unique constraints. Suppose you wanted the address, city, and state to be unique in order to prevent the same location from being added multiple times. You could add
`uniqueConstraints = {@UniqueConstraint(columnNames={"address", "city", "state"})}`.

@Id

Now that we have the table defined, we need to define the primary key for the table. With EJB and Hibernate, it is often better to have an ordinal key, so I would suggest trying to keep to a design like that when using either. That being said, defining which object is the primary key is quite simple. All you have to do is define `@Id` on the getter for the column on the table, as in Listing 4-11.

Listing 4-11. *Getter Defined with the @Id and @GeneratedValue Annotation*

```
@Id @GeneratedValue
    public long getHouseId() {
        return houseId;
    }
```

@GeneratedValue

As I hope you noticed, I snuck another annotation in there—the `@GeneratedValue` annotation. This is used with the `@Id` annotation when you have a value that is generated. This generated value can come from a variety of sources. You can specify the source by defining the strategy as a parameter on the annotation. For example, you could define
`@GeneratedValue(strategy=GenerationType.SEQUENCE, generator="seqGenerator")`, which would define a strategy from a sequence column. The following are the types of strategies allowed (the default is `AUTO`):

AUTO: Indicates that the database should automatically pick the appropriate type

TABLE: Indicates that the database should have an underlying table referencing this unique ID

IDENTITY: Indicates that the database should use this field as an identity column

SEQUENCE: Indicates that the database should use a sequence column to get the column

@Column

We discussed how to identify a table if the table name is not the same as your class name. Well, what if the same problem arises for individual columns? What if your column names are not named with meaningful names? Often DBAs like to have column names to reflect the object type; Java developers do not. That is where @Column comes into play. It allows you to identify the field by simply marking up the column with an annotation. For example, in Listing 4-12, think of our city column as actually cityTuple.

Listing 4-12. *How to Define the city Property to Be the Column cityTuple*

```
@Column(name="cityTuple")
public String getCity() {
        return city;
}
```

@Transient

As I mentioned earlier, the properties on the POJO must correspond to a column on the database. However, there is a chance you could want a column *not* to correspond to a column on the database. Think of a property that combines a few properties together for one getter. If you mark the getter with the @Transient annotation, it will not attempt to persist the property.

@Lob

The @Lob annotation indicates that the property is persisting to a Blob or a Clob field in the database. If the getter returns a type java.sql.Clob, Character[], char[], or java.lang.String, then the container will persist to a Clob field in the database. If the getter returns a type java.sql.Blob, Byte[], or byte[], it will persist to a Blob field in the database.

Collections Annotations

You have taken a look at a House EJB, and each of the columns that it references are for only that table. In other words, none of the columns are foreign keys. However, in many situations a table is linked to other tables. For example, if we had a person table, the house could have a column on it referencing that person. Or if we expand this out to our garage sale, each garage sale will have multiple items.

How do you reference all this? This is done by having foreign key constraints on table A to reference table B. For the House example, we would have each sale item have a houseId property on it to reference the table. Well, you could want your House object to reference a list of sale items, or you may want the SaleItem to reference the House. So the question becomes, "How do we do this without having to add extra plumbing?" The answer is, by using annotations. Two tables can have one of four major relationships: many to one, one to one, one to many, and many to many. I will go over each of them here.

@ManyToOne

The @ManyToOne annotation is used when you have a many-to-one relationship between two tables in the database. A *many-to-one* relationship is when a table A references exactly one record in table B. However, table B can be referenced by many records of table A. The traditional example is an employee and a department. An employee, in theory, can be part of only one department. However, there can be many people in that department.

Consider our Travel Reservations example from Chapter 2 (you can refer to Figure 2-9 in that chapter). We have a CarBooked bean referencing a Car class. The user can book only one particular car. However, this is just an abstract car, so many people can book the same car at different times. There is nothing in the database that prevents this. So for that application, our EB would look like Listing 4-13.

Listing 4-13. *CarBooked Bean Referencing the Car*

```
@Entity
public class CarBooked {
    // ... rest of the class here ...
    Car car = null;

    @ManyToOne
    @JoinColumn(name="carId")
    public Car getCar() {
        return car;
    }
}
```

```
    public void setCar(Car car) {
        this.car = car;
    }
}
```

Hopefully this is fairly straightforward. We have defined our EB to be of the table CarBooked. We did not want to simply reference the integer column carId from our table in the class. Instead, we wanted the entire Car. So we used @ManyToOne to define this as a many-to-one relationship. Then we used the @JoinColumn to define what column we will be joining on the CarBooked table to the primary key on the Car table.

@OneToOne

In practice, a one-to-one relationship works similarly to the many-to-one just discussed. In both situations, the EB will end up with a reference to another EB. A good example of this is at work. You have one cube belonging to just one person. (Well, in theory you do.) There is a one-to-one relationship in the database between a person and a cube. The code will end up looking just like that for @ManyToOne, except you use @OneToOne.

@OneToMany

When you have one entity associated with a collection of other entities, this is considered a one-to-many relationship. In our Garage Sale example, a House would have a number of SaleItems associated with it. Listing 4-14 shows an example.

Listing 4-14. *House with a List of Sale Items*

```
@OneToMany(targetEntity=SaleItem.class, mappedBy="houseId")
public List<SaleItem> getItems() {
    return items;
}
```

Here we use the @OneToMany annotation to define that this list will be derived from another class. The targetEntity property defines the EB; the mappedBy property defines what field on that EB references the primary key (PK) of our class.

@ManyToMany

The last relationship I will discuss is the many-to-many relationship. Many-to-many relationships occur when the relationship can go both ways. Each relationship can reference other relationships on the other side. You could think of students and a class. A student usually takes more than one class, and a class usually has more than one student.

There are references then to both sides. Usually when you have this situation, you will have an intermediary class for storing the relationships. When you have this type of relationship, your code will often look like Listing 4-15.

Listing 4-15. *An Example of a Many-to-Many Relationship of a Course with Students*

```java
@Entity
public class Course {

    private long courseId;
    private String courseName;

    @ManyToMany
    @JoinTable(name="COURSE_TO_STUDENT_TBL",
        joinColumns=@JoinColumn(name="courseId"),
        inverseJoinColumns=@JoinColumn(name="studentId"))
    private Collection<Student> students;

    public long getCourseId() {
        return courseId;
    }

    public void setCourseId(long courseId) {
        this.courseId = courseId;
    }

    public String getCourseName() {
        return courseName;
    }

    public void setCourseName(String courseName) {
        this.courseName = courseName;
    }

    public Collection<Student> getStudents() {
        return students;
    }

    public void setStudents(Collection<Student> students) {
        this.students = students;
    }
}
```

Here we have a table called `Course` and a table called `Student`, and we have joined them via the `COURSE_TO_STUDENT_TBL` table that contains the `studentId` to `courseId` mapping. Here the many-to-many relationship is defined. Then we define which columns are defined toward each other.

Entity Manager

By now you should be able to map the database schemas we defined in Chapter 2 to your entity beans. Now you need to learn how to store and retrieve the database data.

The entity bean by itself is nothing more than a glorified JavaBean with annotations. It does not by itself have the capability to interact with the database. What is required is another object to manage the persisting, retrieving, and deleting from the database. This object is `EntityManager`. You may recall that I briefly talked about it at the beginning of the "Entity Beans" section.

The entity manager will thus be responsible for the entity objects and handling their persistence. The entity manager itself can handle multiple entity instances, the set of which is referred to as a *persistence context*. For each record in the database, there will be only one instance of that entity bean stored inside the persistence context.

`EntityManager` itself comes from factories defined by the `EntityManagerFactory` interface. The factory can then create server persistence units. In fact, different factories can reference the same persistence context. We are able to create an `EntityManager` from the factory via container-managed injection by `@PersistenceContext`.

Persistence Context

The persistence context in Listing 4-16 will be used to inject the entity managers into our session beans.

Listing 4-16. *Injection of EntityManager by the Persistence Context*

```
@PersistenceContext
private EntityManager em;
```

This code is relatively simple and painless. There is a property for the unit name (`unitName`). However, that is not a required field. If no name is specified, then the way that the unit name is determined is vendor specific.

Another option you have for a persistence context is the type. You have two choices: either extended or transactional. By default, when nothing is specified, the persistence context defaults to transactional. This is useful for stateless session beans when you want each call to the initial method to do its own thing. Transactional transactions are considered an eager persistence context; as soon as the method starts, it automatically associates the context to the transaction.

However, what if that is not what you want? What if you are using a SFSB and want to be able to keep this persistence context around until the bean is no longer in use? This is quite useful when you are maintaining a list and want to update it at various times. You will see an example of using the extended persistence context in the next chapter.

Operations on the Entity Manager

So now that we have the entity manager injected into our session bean, we will use this bean to perform a variety of database tasks. In this section, I will go over a few of the basic CRUD commands. Throughout the following chapters that have more-complicated examples, the calls themselves will also get more complicated.

For these examples, we will take excerpts out of the GarageSaleManager SLSB. Also, all these excerpts will reference the EB House.

Add

When you add a record to the database, what you are actually doing is taking an object that is in a transient state and persisting it to the database. Before this record gets persisted, the EB is basically still a JavaBean with no real context. After it gets persisted, it will carry state. Fortunately, persisting is very simple, as shown in Listing 4-17.

Listing 4-17. *Persisting a House to the Database*

```
public void addHouse(House house) {
    em.persist(house);
}
```

As you can see, this code really did not require much, just a call to the entity manager to persist the EB.

Delete

Removing an entity is not as simple as you may think. It is not as simple as saying, "Remove this EB." The EB record you want to remove has to be in the persistence context to be removed, first of all. So there are really two ways to remove an item. Either you have to have a SFSB with an extended persistence context and therefore keep the House EB in the persistence context to remove, or you have to look up the house by ID and remove it that way, as in Listing 4-18.

Listing 4-18. *Removing a House from a Stateless Session Bean*

```
public void deleteHouse(long houseId) {
    House house = em.find(House.class, houseId);
    em.remove(house);
}
```

We simply look up the house and then remove the house. The next chapter includes an example of doing this with a SFSB instead.

I do want to take a minute here to show you how Java 5 has helped the development process (besides by using annotations). Pay close attention to that find call. It may strike you as odd if you are not familiar with Java 5. Two facts should stand out: first, there is no casting of House, and second, we passed a long into an object field. This can be explained by looking at Listing 4-19's find method signature.

Listing 4-19. *The Method Signature for the find Class on EntityManager*

```
<T> T  find(Class<T> entityClass, Object primaryKey)
```

The class returns a generic, allowing the method to define for itself what it returns. In this case, it will return whatever type you have passed in through as entityClass. Also notice that we passed a long into the method that is asking for an Object. This is where autoboxing comes into play, allowing the compiler to automatically convert the long into an Object of type Long.

Update

Updating your EB is going to be quite different from what you are used to. You are not going to be calling anything on the entity manager to update it; you just update the bean itself as in Listing 4-20.

Listing 4-20. *Example of Updating Fields on an Entity Bean*

```
public void updateTime(long houseId, Date startTime, Date endTime) {
        House house = em.find(House.class, houseId);
        house.setStartTime(startTime);
        house.setEndTime(endTime);
    }
```

As you can see, there are no re-persists to the database or anything like that. The key is that you find the object first. After you find the object via EntityManager, it is stored in the persistence context. After it is there, any updates to the object will be persisted automatically to the database. So you are going to want to make sure that the update is permanent unless you decide later in the method to roll it back.

You may also have noticed that we did not have to put any throws declarations for persistent exceptions on the methods. This is because the application server will automatically roll back the call if an exception occurs.

JPQL—EJB3 Query Language

Finally, the last type of manipulation you are going to want to do is to find objects by queries. If you are familiar with the Hibernate way of using Query objects to query the database, this will come fairly easy to you. If not, you will have a bit of a learning curve, but it really is not too hard to understand.

Let's start off with the basics of querying the database. Most of you should be used to using Structured Query Language (SQL) to create your queries. This is the language that almost all databases use to allow interaction with the database. Although similar to SQL, the language we will be using is referred to as *Java Persistence Query Language (JPQL)*, which is similar to Hibernate Query Language. We will be passing JPQL-styled queries to EntityManager to query the database.

JPQL is then implemented as a parameter to EntityManager that will return to you a Query object. Listing 4-21 shows an example of creating a select query.

Listing 4-21. *An Example of a Find All Query in GarageSaleManager*

```
@Stateless
public class GarageSaleManager implements GarageSale {

    @PersistenceContext
    private EntityManager em;

 @SuppressWarnings("unchecked")
    public List<House> findAll() {
        Query query = em.createQuery("Select h from House h");
        return (List<House>)query.getResultList();
    }

}
```

This example is a simple select that has no where clause and that will cause all the House items to be returned. The h is referred to as an *alias* in this context for the entire House object. Then we call for the query to get the result list, which returns a List. You will notice that the code does two things here. First, it casts the object to a list of houses.

Second, it suppresses the warnings for this so that we do not receive an error for trying to cast a List to a List<House>.

Transactions

Now that we have created our EB and you have learned how to have it interact with the persistence layer, there is still one more part: the ability to link these calls together as one single unit. This is necessary because when you make the first call to the database, there is no way to know whether the third call is going to work. In general, if one fails, you want all to fail. And sometimes you want one to work regardless of anything.

Transactions are an intricate part of any application. When writing an application, many developers rush this part. There is no one reason why, but I would say for the most part this occurs because of a combination of a lack of time and a lack of understanding of transactions. In the end, just marking a transaction as required can suffice for most situations, and in the end most developers of an application are more worried about either the look of the presentation tier or their business logic (albeit two very important areas to worry about).

However, do not fret. I will explain how transactions are implemented in EJB3 as well as the various transactions and what they do.

What Is a Transaction?

Before I start explaining how to use transactions, let's go over what a transaction is and what we use them for. In the simplest terms, a *transaction* is a series of operations (generally on a database) that get treated as a single call so that if one fails, they all fail. However, if none fail, they all succeed. As you probably know, this is useful when making multiple calls to a database for a single action. The majority of transactions use what are called ACID properties.

ACID

ACID refers to the four properties that have been established for the majority of transaction processing: atomicity, consistency, isolation, and durability. These properties are defined in further detail in Table 4-1.

Table 4-1. *ACID Properties*

Property	Description
Atomicity	This is the all-or-none property, which represents the idea that either all properties are committed or none are committed.
Consistency	This refers to the data being in a "legal state." In a database system, this could be as simple as making sure you have not violated any integrity constraints in the database. If any violations occur, the transaction is aborted.
Isolation	This is a key feature of transactioning, allowing all the changes you make to not be visible to outside the transaction until it is committed. This is to prevent dirty reads of data.
Durability	This ensures that after the caller has been notified of a successful commit, the transaction is actually committed. Transactions are committed only after they have been written to the log.

As I said before, this covers most transactions. Not all transactions have to be ACIDic. Often people adjust the isolation levels to make reads that are not yet committed; these are referred to of course as *dirty reads*.

Transaction Processing

There are a variety of ways to transact a database with Java, and I will cover a few of them here. The most basic way is on the data source with a rollback and commit. This granular way of doing things is not the most supported way. Of course, this way would also fail if we were transactioning over multiple resources. To transact over multiple resources, you have to use either a Java Transaction API (JTA) transaction or a global transaction. So let's discuss the various ways you can use transactions inside an EJB.

In theory, transactioning can occur at any level you want. You can have transactions in your business or presentation tier, although I'd highly recommend against putting transactioning code inside your servlets (granted, I have it seen done). The most logical place to transact is inside your business logic, which for the purposes of Seam is going to be your EJBs.

When using EJBs, you have two options for transactioning: either container or bean managed. You can define whether you want to use a bean-managed or container-managed transaction at the class level of the EJB. Listing 4-22 shows the class-level annotations.

Listing 4-22. *Example of a Stateless Bean Defined for Bean-Managed Transactions*

```
@Stateless(name="garageSale")
@TransactionManagement(TransactionManagementType.BEAN)
public class GarageSaleManager implements GarageSale {
    // Methods in here
}
```

Listing 4-22 defines the SB to be a bean-managed transaction. Conversely, we could have marked it as a container-managed transaction instead. However, that really is not necessary because the default behavior for the bean is container managed. So if you want to define the bean to be container managed, you do not need to use any annotation at the class level at all.

Container-Managed Transactions

Container-managed transactions (CMTs) are not only the most common way of performing transactions but the preferred way in a Java EE environment. When you use CMTs, the worrying of committing, rolling back, starting the transaction, and so forth is handled entirely by the Java EE container. This is one of the beauties of CMTs: you do not have to code for the transactioning, which allows your SB to exclusively worry about the business logic instead.

It would be quite a waste and annoyance if there were only one possible way of performing transactions. Fortunately, EJB3 allows six types of transactions to choose from. These transaction types in Table 4-2 provide a good variety of ways to transact a business process. If they do not meet your particular needs, you will probably have to use bean-managed transactions instead.

Table 4-2. *Transaction Types*

Name	Description
MANDATORY	This type of transaction must already be started and active before entering the method. If no transaction exists, an exception is thrown.
REQUIRED	This is the simplest transaction. If this type of transaction is active, the method will use that transaction. If the transaction is not active, it will start a new transaction.
REQUIRES_NEW	This is to be used when you want a transaction independent of already-active transactions. The nested transaction in this method is committed or rolled back independently of its caller, if the JDBC driver being used supports nested transactions.
SUPPORTS	Methods marked SUPPORTS do not use anything that requires a transaction. However, they tolerate having a transaction passed through to the method.
NOT_SUPPORTED	This type is used when you do not want a transaction to be a part of the method. The transaction will be suspended as it enters the method (if one exists), and will become reactivated upon leaving the method.
NEVER	A method is marked NEVER if a transaction should never be active when the method is called. If the transaction is active upon calling of the method, the container will cause the method to throw an exception.

The use of the transactioning in CMT is at the bean level. As you may recall in EJB 2.*x*, the transactions for CMT were defined in `ejb-jar.xml` and were defined for an individual or all methods. However, in EJB3 marking methods that are to be transacted is made much simpler by using an annotation at the method level. There are of course positives and negatives to this approach. However, it does provide at a glance a much easier way to see the transaction of the method. The class in Listing 4-23 shows the method with a transaction.

Listing 4-23. *The Stateless Bean with a Transaction on the addHouse Method*

```
import javax.ejb.TransactionAttribute;
import javax.ejb.TransactionAttributeType;

@Stateless(name="garageSale")
public class GarageSaleManager implements GarageSale {

    @TransactionAttribute(TransactionAttributeType.REQUIRES_NEW)
    public void addHouse(House house) {
        em.persist(house);
    }
}
```

In this example, the container will attempt to commit the transaction at the end of the method. If any exception is thrown in this method (albeit in our example of one line, this is harder to do), the container will roll back the transactions. This is the preferred method to roll back a transaction. However, you can also signal the bean to roll back by calling the `setRollbackOnly()` method on `EJBContext`.

■**Note** By default all methods are required transactions. So in the previous session bean examples (in Listings 4-17, 4-18, and 4-20), where we did not define a transaction type or attribute, the transaction type was defaulted to CMT and the methods were defaulted to REQUIRED.

Bean-Managed Transactions

The other side of container-managed transactions is *bean-managed transactions (BMTs)*. These allow a much more fine-grained control of transactions. By using BMTs, you are forced to control the transaction in its entirety. You are responsible for deciding when to start the method to start the transaction—and when the method ends, you have to decide whether to commit or roll back that transaction. So it is of no use to simply throw an exception from the method itself.

Another "problem" with transactions is that they can be propagated only within the bean. If you have one bean that needs to call a transaction on another bean, the second bean will be forced to use a new transaction. As you can begin to imagine, this is going to add a lot of unneeded complexity to your business logic. Therefore, it is best to not use BMTs unless you just cannot achieve the goal you are looking for with the CMT options. However, this will not stop us from taking a look at how you are to implement a BMT here.

So let's try to create some BMTs. We are going to need a few things first. The main thing we are going to need is a transaction object itself. We can use anything that implements the interface `javax.transaction.UserTransaction`, which contains all the necessary methods to manage a transaction. Fortunately, you will not have to create this on your own. Your Java EE application server will have one already implemented for you. This transaction is located in the JNDI at `java:comp/UserTransaction`. With the server-managed user transactions, you can have only one at a time per a thread; thus you can run only one at a time.

As with CMT transactions, there are a few ways to roll back a BMT. The simplest way, of course, is to call the rollback method. However, as with CMT, you can call the `setRollbackOnly()` method, which tells the `UserTransaction` that it may not be committed at all. Let's look at an example in Listing 4-24 to see what is going on.

Listing 4-24. *A Stateless Bean That Uses Bean-Managed Transactions*

```
@Stateless(name="garageSale")
@TransactionManagement(TransactionManagementType.BEAN)
public class GarageSaleManager implements GarageSale {
    @Resource
    UserTransaction tx;

    HouseDAO dao;

    public void deleteHouse(House house) throws IOException {
        try {
            tx.begin();
            try {
                dao.delete(house);
                dao.updateHousingList();
            } catch (DAOException e) {
                tx.setRollbackOnly();
            } finally {
                tx.commit();
            }
```

```
        } catch (Exception e) {
            // Clean up any TX exceptions
        }
    }
}
```

As you can tell, there is a lot going on with this bean. The DAO we have is a made-up DAO that interacts with the database for House. The house will first be deleted, and then a separate table that maintains a list of houses will be updated. If either of these produces errors that trigger the DAOException being thrown, we want to roll back the transaction in its entirety.

The annotation above the class is what you have seen before that defines this bean to be of type BMT. Next we need to get the UserTransaction, which is relatively simple with the annotation injection. The @Resource annotation looks up the UserTransaction at its default JNDI location. Now when the method starts, we manually start the transaction. As it continues, it attempts two calls to the DAO. If either fails, an exception is thrown and we mark the transaction for rollback only. Finally, we commit the transaction, assuming that it has not been marked for rollback. The try–catch surrounding the entire inner try–catch is to handle any unforeseen exceptions generated from the user transaction.

As you can see, BMT is definitely not an easy way of creating a transaction and forces the developer to handle too much of the work. Thus we will not be using BMT for the remainder of this book.

Calling EJBs

Well, obviously, EJBs would be totally useless if we were not able to call them. You will need to be able call EJBs from not only the presentation tier but the business logic tier as well. Back with EJB 2.*x*, this was a rather laborious process, as shown in the following steps:

1. Get the initial context.

2. Look up the bean name in the JNDI by using a predefined name.

3. Get the Home object by using the portable remote interface.

4. Use the Home object to create the remote object that you are able to use.

Yuck—that sure is complicated and a lot of work just to grab an EJB. Fortunately, it is much easier now. As we discussed previously, there no longer is a remote and home interface to worry about. Now all you have to do is call the JNDI by the service name as in Listing 4-25.

Listing 4-25. *Calls to Retrieve the EJB*

```
InitialContext ctx = new InitialContext();
GarageSale garageSale = (GarageSale)ctx.lookup(GarageSale.class);
```

As you can see, this is a lot easier now and much easier to look up. The lookup is either the class name of the service or it can be the string name that you defined on the EJB annotation (`@EJB(name="nameToCallFrom")`).

As easy as this, it can get easier. You can just use the `@EJB` annotation inside your servlet (or whatever front-end framework you are using via the application server). The annotation uses dependency injection to retrieve the EJB from the pool and inject it into your front-end object. Please note, however, that we will not be using this way to inject with Seam, because Seam has its own way of injecting the objects.

Testing

Testing in previous EJB containers was quite tedious. Because the containers were exclusively available for application servers, unit testing was difficult. Now that our EJBs are POJOs, testing is much easier. Also, with the addition of mock objects, we have a framework to mock up `EntityManager` as well. Because testing is such an intricate part of the application, I have dedicated a chapter to that topic later in this book (Chapter 10). However, if need be, you can take the lessons learned from that chapter and apply them strictly to EJBs as well.

Summary

EJB3 represents the heart of the Seam application. EJB is the traditional business and data tier, and even more so with Seam because we get rid of the middleman backing beans (something you will discover in just a few pages).

The chapter started off with a history of EJB and an explanation of the need for it. It went on to discuss the basics of session beans—how we use annotations to make the creation of session beans easier, and the different annotation options in EJB3. We then moved on to message-driven beans (MDBs) and to entity beans (EBs). An EB is the data persistent part of EJB. After I defined the optional annotations for EBs, we went on to actually using them.

This led to a discussion of entity managers and persistent contexts. These were used to convert the EB POJO into a persistable object. This taught us how to add, delete, and create queries. Next, we went over the transactions and how to use them to allow multiple database operations to work together.

Finally, I upgraded our example application from the previous chapter to use EJB, so now we have a full-fledged running app. In the next chapter, you will learn that you no longer need to have backing beans, that you can go straight from the JSF to the session beans.

CHAPTER 5

■■■

Introduction to Seam

The preceding two chapters covered the EJB3 and JSF frameworks, which are the core components of Seam. In those chapters, you learned a simplistic way of designing both presentation and business logic. However, in order to have the JSF pages call the business logic, we had to go through JSF backing beans, the intermediate classes. Doing so often required adding code referencing the backing beans in `faces-config.xml`.

Now it is time to discuss Seam itself. In this chapter, I will show you how to eliminate the backing beans and call the EJB3's SB directly. In addition, I will also start the discussion on using Seam objects to help make common tasks simpler.

In the Figure 5-1 road map, you will see that our main focus is the Seam interception in every tier. To a lesser extent, our focus will be the EJB3 and JSF objects because they will be the target of our interception.

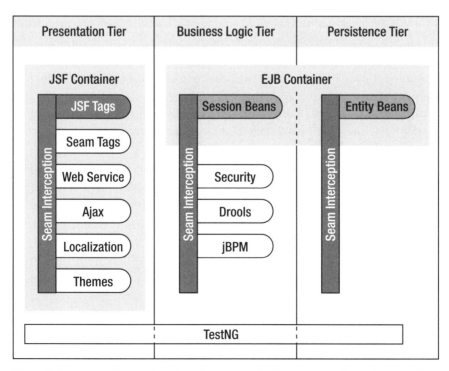

Figure 5-1. *The road map showing that our main focus will be Seam interception across the tiers*

This chapter discusses how we take the EJBs and JSF pages we created before and modify them to leverage Seam. As you will see, the end result will be less code required and an easy separation of barriers. Also, you will be able to see that not only does using Seam save time and space, but it adds functionality that we did not previously have.

The chapter starts off by explaining how to configure and download Seam. It then moves on to Seam's architecture, including an explanation of how it works and various high-level design aspects. You will learn about the injection and conversation mechanisms that Seam is known for. The chapter wraps up with a discussion of the basic components that you can use with Seam. Many of you will want to use these on a day-to-day basis.

■**Note** Although this chapter refers only to the standard EJB3/JSF combination for Seam, there are other frameworks (for example, Hibernate) that can be used with Seam. These are discussed in later chapters.

What Is Seam?

Seam is a new application framework designed by JBoss, a division of Red Hat, to be integrated with many popular next-generation service-oriented architectures. This is achieved not by adding a heavy amount of code surrounding all the common architectures, but by sprinkling interceptors and annotations into already-existing classes. This keeps in line with the idea of using plain old Java objects (POJOs) in Java development by requiring less time for you to worry about the framework piece and leaving more time to spend actually developing the business functionality.

The obvious question you might ask is, "How does adding *more* into a potentially working model help save time?" Seam achieves this by eliminating the need for "plumbing" code. Essentially, we are allowing Seam to handle the plumbing and to have the business logic interact with the JSF pages themselves. One of the nice things about Seam is that even if you already have code you want to use, you will be able to keep your existing EJBs and JSF pages, thus being able to maintain a mixed environment if you choose. Seam does this by integrating with existing layers, as shown in Figure 5-2.

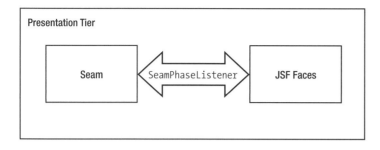

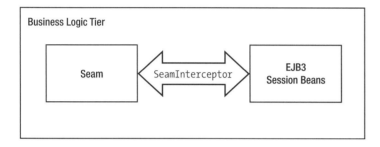

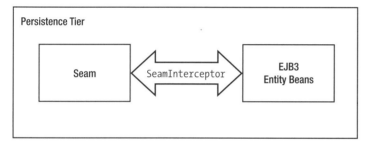

Figure 5-2. *Diagram of Seam intermixing with the various tiers*

Basic Seam Configuration

This section covers the configuration of Seam in an environment that is supporting EJB3, and the deployment of an EAR file.

Downloading Seam

Before configuring Seam, you first have to download the compressed Seam file. Seam is a product of JBoss and can be downloaded as a gun-zipped TAR file or as a ZIP file from `http://labs.jboss.com/portal/jbossseam/download/index.html`. This book uses the Seam 1.1.0 GA release.

The Seam download has many external library files associated with it, because of the large number of configurations possible with Seam. For right now, though, all you have to worry about is the basic configuration, so you will need only the `jboss-seam-ui.jar` and `jboss-seam.jar` files in the root directory of the downloaded file.

However, later in this chapter, you will also need the `jboss-seam-debug.jar` file to use Seam's debug mode.

Configuring Seam

Earlier I mentioned that there are many ways to configure Seam. For our first Seam applications, we are going to use the most basic configuration: the JSF—EJB3 configuration. This is the traditional way that Seam was designed to be set up. This minimalist configuration allows for coupling the presentation tier information to the persistence tier and will enable Seam to work with the examples in this chapter. Later in this chapter, I will discuss further modifications to make life easier in the Seam environment, and in later chapters you can add advanced options depending on the needs of your environment.

Updating XML Files

Let's begin. I will assume that you have an EAR file ready to go from Chapter 4. You will have to modify three of the existing files, one for the business logic and two on the presentation end. We will start with the `faces-config.xml` file in Listing 5-1.

Listing 5-1. *The faces-config.xml File After Adding the Seam Phase Listener*

```
<?xml version="1.0" encoding="UTF-8"?>
<!DOCTYPE faces-config
PUBLIC "-//Sun Microsystems, Inc.//DTD JavaServer Faces Config 1.0//EN"
                      "http://java.sun.com/dtd/web-facesconfig_1_0.dtd">
<faces-config>
    <lifecycle>
        <phase-listener>org.jboss.seam.jsf.SeamPhaseListener</phase-listener>
    </lifecycle>

</faces-config>
```

This first modification integrates Seam with the phase life cycle of the JSF request life cycle. There are actually multiple class files to specify in the phase listener. The one you select depends on how you want to manage the transaction demarcation. I will explain the differences later; for right now, just stick with the basic phase listener.

Next we will move on to the `web.xml` file in Listings 5-2 and 5-3.

Listing 5-2. *In web.xml, Add a Context Parameter for State Saving*

```
<context-param>
            <param-name>javax.faces.STATE_SAVING_METHOD</param-name>
            <param-value>client</param-value>
</context-param>
```

Another item that you need to add to your `faces-config.xml` file, depending on what JSF implementation you are using, is the setting of the state-saving method. If you are using Apache's MyFaces, Seam needs client-side state saving. For our initial examples we will be using MyFaces, so include the previous listing for now.

Listing 5-3. *In web.xml, Add the Listener to the Servlet Request Life Cycle*

```
<listener>
    <listener-class>
        org.jboss.seam.servlet.SeamListener
    </listener-class>
</listener>
```

In every framework that integrates with the web tier, you will have to add either a listener to the life cycle or a front controller servlet to be called by the Web. Seam solves this problem by using a listener to bootstrap the JSF servlet life cycle. The Seam listener is then responsible for moving the data across the tiers as well as for creation and destruction of context objects.

Adding Seam JAR Files

Now that you have your XMLs configured, there are two extra JAR files that you have to add to make the application work: `jboss-seam.jar` and `jboss-seam-ui.jar`. The `jboss-seam-ui.jar` file goes into the `WEB-INF/lib` directory. The `jboss-seam.jar` file belongs at the root level of the EAR file. The server will load up the `jboss-seam-ui.jar` automatically. However, you will have to specify the location of `jboss-seam.jar` in `ejb-jar.xml`, as shown in Listing 5-4.

Listing 5-4. *In ejb-jar, Add the jboss-seam.jar File*

```
<module>
    <java>jboss-seam.jar</java>
</module>
```

Finalizing the Setup

Now that you have your XML and JAR files set up, there is one final thing to do to make Seam work, and although this may seem trivial, if you do not do it you will run into a lot of errors that seem to make no sense at all. So the final step is the addition of the Seam.properties file to the EAR file. This file can be blank but it has to be there. I will explain later in this chapter what you can add to it.

Make these modifications to your files, compile them, and you should be good to go, ready to start using Seam. After the addition of the preceding files, your directory structure should look like the one in Figure 5-3, minus any JSP files.

Figure 5-3. *The file structure of the EAR, EJB3, and WAR directories*

Note Seam has a generation program that provides a shortcut to get Seam up and running. For more information, consult the following websites: http://www.integrallis.com or the Apress website at http://www.apress.com in the Source Code/Download section.

First Example: Stateless Session Bean

Our first example application is the most basic one, a stateless session bean (SLSB). In this page we will be creating a SLSB that will add a House to the database. As I mentioned earlier, Seam does not really add any new code but takes your existing code and modifies it to integrate the business tier and presentation tier for you. So in this section, we will take the HouseManagerAction stateless bean from Chapter 4 and modify it for use with Seam.

For this example, we are going create a relatively simple SLSB that will add a House to the database by starting at a JSF page, setting properties on the House, and inserting the House into the database. In a typical web application, you would have the presentation tier call an action class, which in turn would call a utility class to do a JNDI lookup of the stateless session bean and to do a narrowing on it. At this point, you would have a reference to the home interface, and a method would be called to create the EJB remote. The EJB remote would then be brought to the action class for use, and finally back to the JSP. That is a lot of processing and essentially an extra class in the middle just to convert the request to data to call our session bean. By using Seam, we are going to do the same thing but not have what is essentially a middleman class (the action). We will modify our SLSB so that the JSF page can access it implicitly through Seam. Listing 5-5 shows an example of a SLSB class.

Listing 5-5. *Stateless Session Bean Class-Level Modifications by Seam*

```
@Stateless
@Name("salesManager")
@Interceptors(SeamInterceptor.class)
@JndiName("garage-sale/SaleManagerAction/local")
public class SaleManagerAction implements SaleManager {
    // Put the rest of the method in here
}
```

The first line of this should look familiar; it defines that this is a stateless bean. This is the only part of the class definitions that are not Seam specific.

The @Name attribute defines the Seam component name. This annotation is used by the JSF pages to reference the component or bean. This can of course lead to someone defining the same name in multiple beans. There is really no way to prevent this, or to specify which one will be the overwriting one. Your only indication will be a warning on the console.

The @JndiName annotation specifies the JNDI name that Seam will use to look up the EJB. This of course could get tedious to have in every single EJB, not to mention that the pattern could change per application server. Thankfully, there is a more global way to do this that I will explain later in this chapter.

The @Interceptors annotation is not a Seam-specific annotation, but we are using it for Seam. This annotation is needed for Seam to perform its bijection, validation, and so forth, by intercepting the invocation of the component. However, this is not required for EB because bijection and context demarcations are not defined. As with the @JndiName annotation, there is an easier way to do this that I will explain later in this chapter.

Now that you see how to start creating our Seam-modified session bean, let's go into some of the code itself. Listing 5-6 adds methods.

Listing 5-6. *Stateless Session Bean Method-Level Modifications by Seam*

```
@Stateless
@Name("salesManager")
@Interceptors(SeamInterceptor.class)
@JndiName("garage-sale/SaleManagerAction/local")
public class SaleManagerAction implements SaleManager {

    @PersistenceContext
    private EntityManager em;

    @In @Out
    private House house;

    public String addHouse() {
        em.persist(house);
        return "/homeSuccess.jsp";
    }
}
```

This is the body of our SLSB, with the necessary items in place to perform the house addition. As you can see, it does not take much code—a lot less than Struts would require. EntityManager is a normal component of the SLSB that I discussed in Chapter 4, so I will not explain that any further. The House object is an entity bean, with @In and @Out annotations. I will discuss these annotations further later in the chapter. For now, just realize that these annotations tell the Seam interceptors to populate that object and return it. Listing 5-7 shows our EB House object.

Listing 5-7. *Entity Bean Example*

```
@Entity
@Name("house")
public class House {

    private long houseId;
    private String address;
    private String city;
    private String state;
    private Date startTime;
    private Date endTime;
```

```
@Id @GeneratedValue
public long getHouseId() {
    return houseId;
}
public void setHouseId(long houseId) {
    this.houseId = houseId;
}


@NotNull(message="Address is required")
@Length(min=5, max=15, message="Address should be between 5 and 15")
public String getAddress() {
    return address;
}
public void setAddress(String address) {
    this.address = address;
}
public String getCity() {
    return city;
}
public void setCity(String city) {
    this.city = city;
}
public Date getEndTime() {
    return endTime;
}
public void setEndTime(Date endTime) {
    this.endTime = endTime;
}
public Date getStartTime() {
    return startTime;
}
public void setStartTime(Date startTime) {
    this.startTime = startTime;
}
public String getState() {
    return state;
}
public void setState(String state) {
    this.state = state;
}
```

```
    public String toString() {
        return houseId + ", " +address;
    }
}
```

Well, that is all that's required for the session bean to be ready to be used as a Seam component. As you can see, very little code was added, and what was added were annotations. This helps provide the robustness needed for a web application.

Now onto the changes needed by the JSF page. For reference, Listing 5-8 shows the JSF page from before with the Seam modifications needed.

Listing 5-8. *Seam Modifications to the JSF*

```
<%@ taglib uri="http://java.sun.com/jsf/html" prefix="h" %>
<%@ taglib uri="http://java.sun.com/jsf/core" prefix="f" %>

<f:view>

    <h:form>
        Please enter your address:<br/>
        <h:inputText value="#{house.address}" size="15"/><br/>

         <h:commandButton value="Add House" action="#{salesManager.addHouse}"/>
    </h:form>
</f:view>
```

You may be looking at this very hard, thinking, "I do not see the modifications." Well, you are correct. There are *no* modifications needed to the JSF page to make this work. This is the simplicity that Seam helps bring to a JSF environment. Now that being said, there are Seam-level tag libraries we can use to help make life even easier, but for this example those are not needed.

Well that's it. That's all you have to do to create your first Seam page (see Figure 5-4). In a bit we will get into some additional options for Seam and JSF pages.

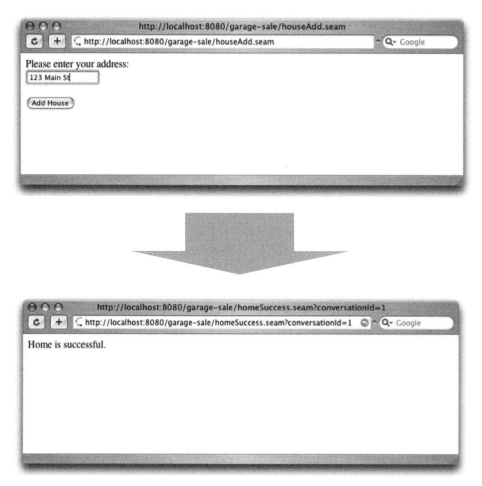

Figure 5-4. *Screen transition of entering a new home*

Architecture

The preceding example showed how easy it is to convert your EJBs and JSF pages to use Seam. As you saw, we added annotated POJOs to allow our objects to use the Seam architecture. You should find this easier than a traditional Java enterprise three-tier architecture.

However, this example raises two questions: what does Seam need with those annotations, and how does it put those together to create seamless application tiers? There are five main topics I will go over to explain how Seam works:

- POJOs and annotations

- Inversion of control and bijection

- Interceptors

- Seam context

- Three-tier architecture with Seam

POJOs and Annotations

Plain old Java objects have become the rage lately in Java development, and there is a good reason for that. They are lightweight service objects that can easily be plugged into any framework. The use of POJOs is one of the core values of many new architectures, and Seam is no different. Seam actually has no base classes to extend or interfaces to implement as do many other frameworks (think Struts and the `Action` interface). Every Seam-related object you create can be a POJO. You could of course use classes that are not POJOs, but there really is no need because POJOs give you straightforward code without the hassle of a lot of plumbing.

However, as is obvious, POJOs are not enough. Seam needs something else to at least help identify that the POJO is a Seam component. In older frameworks, XML files were used to identify these objects. However, that can get messy fast. Now, there are annotations.

As you saw in the first example in this chapter and in our Hello World application in Chapter 1, all Seam needs are POJOs—POJOS with annotations. Annotations provide a flexible way of adding functionality to your existing class structure.

Seam could not easily have been developed without this Java 5 addition. Had Seam's creators not gone this route, they would have had to base all the functionality entirely on XML-based files (which, given the number of things you can do with POJOs, would have gotten messy fast). Imagine in your XML file having to identify not only the class, but then which methods need validating, the type of validation, the time of input/output of objects—yick. So not only do annotations provide a more readable way of understanding the code, they also reduce the number of files needed. In fact, in some situations Seam uses already-existing annotations and then expands on the functionality for them. (The validation framework does this, as you will see this later in this chapter.)

This use of annotations is what sets Seam apart from other frameworks you have used in the past. This is the path that most frameworks in their next versions will be following as well—including Spring, Tapestry, and others.

Inversion of Control and Bijection

Inversion of control (IoC) is not a new concept, but a concept that until recently frameworks did not use. Frameworks such as Spring and Apache's HiveMind have made great use of it, and Seam is no exception in adding it to their repertoire.

Inversion of control, also known by many as *dependency injection*, takes the need to instantiate objects away from the normal user calls. Instead, you allow the container to handle the creation of the component and its subcomponents. Seam is no different in using dependency injection to inject objects. However, Seam takes it to the next step by allowing the injection to go both ways.

IoC is needed because of the nature of Seam. Because we don't use any JSF action classes to translate our presentation tier requests into objects and then set them on the EJB and call the EJB, we have to use IoC to make up for it. This helps us save time and space by letting the container manage the objects.

The usage of IoC in Seam is often referred to as *bijection*, because the injection is two-way (injection and "outjection"). You can specify the direction of the components. However, bijection is so much more in Seam than it is in most typical IoC patterns. Seam takes IoC and expands it by making it dynamic, contextual, and bidirectional, and allowing assembly by the container.

So where can you use bijection? Bijection can be used on any object that is a Seam object. Remember, a Seam object is any object that you have defined with an `@Name` annotation on the class. You can then biject your Seam objects into any SB or JavaBean. However, you cannot biject objects into your EB. This is because the domain model should be independent of business logic and because EBs are instantiated at the application level and Seam could not intercept them anyway.

Seam performs bijection by dividing it into two areas: one going into the system and one going out. As I have said, these are more commonly defined as injection and outjection, and we use `@In` and `@Out` for these, respectively.

You got a brief taste of bijection in the first example. Now let's take a look at what exactly is happening and the options on those annotations. In this example, we have an EB Seam object called `House`:

```
@In @Out
private House house;
```

This code specifies that your EB `House` will be a variable that can be injected in and out of the SLSB and back to the JSF page.

The `@Out` annotation has the following parameters:

`required`: This parameter specifies whether the field coming in/out should be created. By default, this is set to `true` and will automatically be created, or you can specify `required=false` to not have it automatically created.

`scope`: This is used to specify the scope of a non-Seam component. This is not necessary if you are referencing objects that you specified with a Seam name. This is more for objects such as strings, lists, and so forth.

value: This is the context variable name, thus the name you are going to use when referencing this component either in other beans or in your JSF page. This will default to the name of the field or the getter/setter method.

The @In annotation will have all the parameters of @Out as well as the create parameter:

create: This parameter specifies that a component should be created if the context variable is null.

■Note You cannot do bijection directly in an interceptor. You would have to call the objects through other means in the interceptor.

BIJECTION WITH STATELESS SESSION BEANS

One thing that should be noted before we continue is that the bijection in Seam is actually very complex (in a good way). Case in point: how we deal with stateless session beans. If you have worked with them in the past, you are used to a simplistic model in which you send data to the SLSB, it performs some operation, and then you return data. You never have the SLSB access property-specific data on the SLSB. It is not safe to do so with SLSBs, unless the property is a global object such as a database connection or logger reference.

However, with Seam this methodology is thrown out the window a bit. Seam does not use a simplistic creation-time IoC. Instead the bijection happens at invocation. Therefore, the objects you are setting with @In or @Out to be injected or outjected are done at invocation, and when the method is complete, they are disinjected. This is what makes it safe for us in Seam to reference properties of the SLSB inside the methods.

Of course, along with this plus there's a minus. These SLSBs now become somewhat Seam specific, because you would never want to use them in a regular EJB3 container because their behavior would be different. In a non-Seam container, you would not be guaranteed that the properties set on the SLSB would then be the same SLSB that you are calling the method on.

Interceptors

So far, I have discussed the POJO objects that allow you to create both business and domain objects that Seam applies its functionality to. I also discussed using annotations for decorating the POJOs, indicating where we want to apply Seam functionality. So now the question becomes, "How does Seam use these annotations to provide functionality?"

After all, there are no parent interfaces or any classes that get called directly. The answer is, through a combination of interceptors. These interceptors are called directly via the code and the configuration file, or indirectly by classes used by existing interceptors.

There are many ways to wrap calls to the interceptor. In Seam we use Java EE's interceptor classes to wrap the POJOs. The interceptor classes use the `javax.interceptor.` `AroundInvoke` and `javax.interceptor.InvocationContext` annotations for creating the methods that should be called during that interception.

Seam Contexts

Previously I explained how IoC works and its use in the Seam framework. Now part of IoC is the life cycle of the injected object—obviously, it would be bad to have these objects around forever or to have them deleted at each request. This concept is the same with the POJOs themselves; they need to be kept around for sometimes more than one request. The few built-in contexts into the Servlet specification (Request, Session, Servlet context) hardly match everything you could need. Hence Seam has come up with a few more contexts to help you out. I cannot cover them all in detail in this chapter; however, you will see examples of all of them in this or later chapters.

So what exactly are contexts and why do you need them? Any experienced web developer or avid web surfer knows the need to maintain his website as the pages go on. If you are filling out a multipage loan form, you obviously want the information you stored on the first page to go to the second page and so on. You especially do not want to have that information destroyed because you tried to open a new browser window. Or, if you are a system administrator, you might want only certain users to have access to each page. As an even more-advanced example, you may want to have someone interact with the information you are using. You may need to have one person create a request and one person approve it. There are many of these concepts that web developers encounter on a daily or weekly basis.

On most traditional web applications, we handle these contexts by storing information in the request or session objects. Sometimes you have to get tricky and use tokens to prevent the user from using the Back button and refilling in data or using new browser windows. There are many different tricks to the trade. Well, Seam realized this and basically said enough is enough, and instead of forcing developers to add tricks ad hoc by using the request and session objects, just created new conversation states to use.

The following are the contexts available in Seam.

Stateless: The stateless pseudo context.

Event: This is more commonly known as a request scope. This will last the length of a single server request.

Page: This is the culmination of requests for a single Faces request. It will start when you invoke the action to take you to the page, and it lasts until the end of any action invoked from the page.

Conversation: This is for use on a series of requests from the same browser window that all are related to the same topic or conversation. A typical example is a wizard application for a loan.

Business Process: This is used for process management with tools such as jBPM. Applications that require multiple actors to use the same set of items in a process is an example. Chapter 7 covers this topic in greater detail. This context will span multiple conversations with multiple users.

Session: This is a traditional Session context.

Application: This is a traditional Servlet context.

How to Define Context Scope

Before I explain details about each context, you need to know how to set your objects to be those contexts. With Seam they refer to the context of an object as its *scope*; think of it as *the scope of the context*. It is pretty simple. You can define the scope either on your POJO itself, or on the attributes of the POJO by using the scope reference, as in Listing 5-9.

Listing 5-9. *Example of Using Scope*

```
Import org.jboss.seam.ScopeType;

@Scope(ScopeType.Stateless)
public class MyBean {

@Out(scope = ScopeType.Stateless)
String name;

}
```

As you see, we have defined the bean itself as a stateless scope, and we have defined the outjection of name in a stateless scope as well. Under normal circumstances, you can easily define just one, not both.

Now let's delve into more details of each scope type.

Stateless

Stateless contexts are for contexts that are, as you may have guessed, stateless. There really is not much to discuss or show. These are used for a totally stateless object such as a stateless session bean.

Event

For most of your requests that go from one page to another page, this is the context you will be using. This is considered the "narrowest" context. Event contexts are held for one cycle of one request. This can be as simple as going to a list page or just loading the home page.

Page

The Page context is a relatively simple concept; it is when a component is tied to one particular page. Conversely, the page then has access to all the components that referenced it. You will want to use this on pages where you need to persist the components upon multiple subsequent calls to the same page.

Conversation

Have you ever been to a website that requires multiple form submissions and wanted to try multiple scenarios? Suppose you are on a vacation-planning website and you have to go through multiple selections—for example, selecting your airplane travel, hotel, car rental, and maybe even meals. Well, you are not sure what option you want to pick. So you open up your tab-allowed browser such as Mozilla's Firefox and create multiple travel plans. As you may have experienced, there can be one big problem: the site uses session-scoped data and now some of those sessions are overlapping. So you will get a final page with data from different parts. Now there are ways around this, but they have to be programmatically included in the code. That can be a pain.

As a solution, Seam has come up with this idea of a *conversation*, also known as a *workspace*. Conversations are essentially the context every call will initially be in. Most normal conversations will last the duration of one call. However, with Seam we can upgrade these conversations to long-running conversations. Once upgraded, these conversations will last multiple page calls, and in fact will be tied to conversationId. Creating the long-running conversations is basically a way of using the same named context data multiple times. Think in terms of having an HttpSession object with a name, but then if you wanted to start a separate path in the system, you could re-create it again without losing your data from the previous session. Also, another great feature is that the user can access any of these conversations on any of the pages. So let's say that when you were booking your travel, you could still display data from your other selections on that page—for example, showing the total price thus far.

Business Process

The business process mechanism is a way of managing interactions across multiple screens and multiple users all joined together. Because Seam is a JBoss product, it is only natural for it to use the JBoss jBPM (Business Process Manager). Explaining how to use and set up jBPM is too complex for this chapter. However, we will delve into it more in Chapter 7.

Session

This is like a traditional `HttpSession` object. This is necessary when you have SFSBs that need to have their data persisted across multiple session requests. For example, often you will have a request for a list page that you want to make changes to, and you may not want to lose the persistable list data. So you store the data to the Session context, and the data will be persisted until the Seam contexts are destroyed.

Application

This is like the traditional `ServletContext` holding information that is available to all the users. Because this is like the Servlet context, there is no tracking of individual web requests from specific users.

Three-Tier Architecture with Seam

So now that we have all of the major players in place, it is time to put this all together into a functioning Seam application. In this section, I am going to explain how Seam with its interceptors defines the three-tier architecture. This interception for the most part will be transparent to the user. Figure 5-5 presents a diagram of this interception.

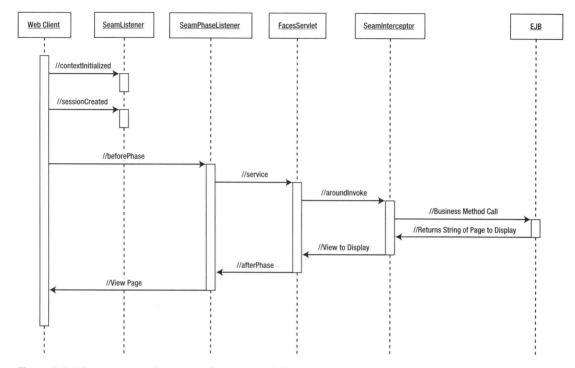

Figure 5-5. *The sequence diagram of an initial full life-cycle call with Seam*

Seam's Integration with the MVC

Most frameworks integrate directly by having you call their framework-specific servlets to integrate with the architecture. Seam is different; it controls items by adding listeners and life cycles into the request. This allows us to maintain the normal life cycle of a JSF request. You saw this already earlier in the chapter when I presented Seam's basic configuration. Here I will explain it in a bit more detail.

Before I start explaining how Seam integrates with the various areas, you need to be aware of a central class: org.jboss.seam.context.Lifecycle. This is the class that will keep our contexts straight. Contexts will handle state in the web tier in a more advanced way than a standard request and session object.

As you may recall, in the web.xml a listener (org.jboss.seam.servlet.SeamListener) was added. You also see this listener being the first thing called in our sequence diagram. This listener is called only at the start of a new session. This will set ServletContext and Session to the Lifecycle object for manipulation later.

Now you see the next object called is SeamPhaseListener. The SeamPhaseListener object is called in connection with FacesServlet. As you saw in faces-config.xml earlier, the SeamPhaseListener is part of the life cycle for FacesServlet. This again is used to control much of the context and to store the request state. This listener is needed to help move the data from the presentation to the business logic tier. In a typical JSF life cycle, you would use backing beans. Now instead of having to worry about your backing beans needing to translate the data and call EJBs, Seam will handle this directly for us.

Seam's Integration with the EJB3

Figure 5-6 represents the integration of Seam with the EJB3 POJO.

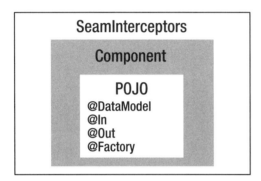

Figure 5-6. *Representation of the layers of the EJB POJO*

So now that you understand the web tier's integration, you're ready to learn about the business logic tier EJB integration. The business logic tier integration uses `SeamInterceptor` to wrap around its call to the EJB. This interceptor wraps around any call to the POJO EJB. This indirectly accesses a `Component` object stored in the Application context, all the while wrapping the call in `Lifecycle`. This `Component` object contains in it the EJB that you are accessing. It is much more than a simple wrapper object. This is the object that holds all the field-level objects—from the injected fields, to the data model objects, to the validators—basically, anything associated with the POJO's attribute-level Seam annotations. Also, another big extra is the inclusion of additional default interceptors. These interceptors handle everything from bijection to validation to transaction management. Additionally, you are able to add your own interceptors into the POJOs or even additional default interceptors. The interceptors are defined in the `org.jboss.seam.interceptors` package.

Put It All Together

Putting it all together, you have the ability to initiate calls from the JSP page to the EJB without having to worry about the middle-management bean. At the same time, you are also not losing any functionality.

JSF PAGES

I have discussed the changes to the business logic tiers. Now I want to briefly mention the presentation tier. All the JSF tags you are currently using can be kept without any modifications. There are some custom tag libraries from Seam; in general, these are tied to components used on the business logic tier (for example, `DataModel`). Throughout this chapter and the rest of the book, we will be using a mixture of JSF tags and Seam tags for our pages.

Components

Hopefully by now you have a very basic understanding of using Seam with the code you have created in Chapters 3 and 4. This section covers additional tools to help you create your Seam pages, including logging and debugging. In addition, I am going to introduce Seam-level components that will help make your pages more robust—for example, data models and validation components. By the end of this section, you will know enough to start writing even more-complex Seam pages.

Seam Configuration Options

As you may have noticed, these JSF pages tend to get a lot of annotations at the class level, and this can get quite messy. What is worse is that some of those annotations are quite repetitive. The interceptor is required on every single page that you want to become a Seam page. In addition, the JNDI name has to be defined on each page, and worse yet, the JNDI name is application server–specific. So take a look at the following code in Listing 5-10.

Listing 5-10. *The Standard Code We Have Been Using for Our Classes*

```
@Stateless
@Name("houseManager")
@JndiName("garage-sale/HouseManagerAction/local")
@Interceptors(SeamInterceptor.class)
public class HouseManagerAction implements HouseManager {
    // Add the rest of the code here
}
```

By modifying two configuration files, we can eliminate having to use `@JndiName` and `@Interceptors`.

JNDI Name

You can define the JNDI name in `components.xml`, which is placed in the `WEB-INF` directory. You are going to use a wildcard expression for the pattern of the EJB name. Listing 5-11 contains an example of defining a `jndiPattern` to be used for JBoss. Consult your documentation if you plan to use a different application server.

Listing 5-11. *Our components.xml file with the JNDI Name Pattern*

```
<components>
    <component name="org.jboss.seam.core.init">
        <property name="debug">true</property>
        <property name="myFacesLifecycleBug">true</property>
        <property name="jndiPattern">garage-sale/#{ejbName}/local</property>
    </component>
</components>
```

Seam Interceptor

There is a rather easy way to define the Seam interceptor, and unfortunately it uses a file that you may have thought you had gotten rid of: `ejb-jar.xml`. Because we define most EJB configurations now in annotations (optionally still definable in `ejb-jar`), we use a new attribute for EJB3: `interceptor-binding`. Here we just define `SeamInterceptor` for all the EJBs. Of course, if you wanted Seam to work only on a specific subset, you could specify that in Listing 5-12 as well.

Listing 5-12. *The ejb-jar.xml File with the Seam Interception*

```
<?xml version="1.0" encoding="UTF-8"?>
<ejb-jar xmlns="http://java.sun.com/xml/ns/javaee"
        xmlns:xsi="http://www.w3.org/2001/XMLSchema-instance"
        xsi:schemaLocation="http://java.sun.com/xml/ns/javaee
          http://java.sun.com/xml/ns/javaee/ejb-jar_3_0.xsd"
        version="3.0">
    <interceptors>
      <interceptor>
        <interceptor-class>org.jboss.seam.ejb.SeamInterceptor</interceptor-class>
      </interceptor>
    </interceptors>
```

```
    <assembly-descriptor>
        <interceptor-binding>
            <ejb-name>*</ejb-name>
            <interceptor-class>
                org.jboss.seam.ejb.SeamInterceptor
            </interceptor-class>
        </interceptor-binding>
    </assembly-descriptor>
</ejb-jar>
```

So from now on in the examples, assume that we are using these two optional configurations.

Logging

One good habit that many, from beginners to experts, forget is proper logging. Logging is such a core fundamental to good programming that I wanted to include it sooner rather than later. One of the issues some people have is which logger to use. The main two are Log4J and Apache commons-logging. Another issue with logging is how to properly do it. Listing 5-13 shows an example of logging.

Listing 5-13. *Logging by Using LogFactory*

```
private static final Log log = LogFactory.getLog(SaleManagerAction.class);

public String addHouse() {
    if (log.isDebugEnabled()) {
        log.debug("House address to add is "+ house.getAddress());
    }
    em.persist(house);
    return "/homeSuccess.jsp";
}
```

That is the proper way to write a debug or info log message. Not only does creating the debug statement add many lines, but many developers (even experienced ones) screw up the instantiation of it. Often they will forget to declare the Log static or have to change the class name and forget to change it on the logger as well. This can cause all sorts of problems. Also, when debugging, you use isDebugEnabled mainly because creating the string that is accessing the object requires processing time, so often people forgo using isDebugEnabled and just use the debug statement.

So as you can see, there is a lot of extra effort here and room for mistakes. Fortunately, Seam realized this in advanced and used annotations and scriptlets, which has made logging much simpler. Listing 5-14 shows the previous code written with Seam logging.

Listing 5-14. *Logging with Seam*

```
@Logger
private Log log;

 public String addHouse() {
    log.debug("House address to add is #{house.address}");
    em.persist(house);
    return "/homeSuccess.jsp";
}
```

Well, look at that—not only did we cut down on code, but we made it simpler. Now the obvious question is, "Did we lose any of the functionality?" The answer is no. Seam uses Apache commons-logging for its logging behind the scenes. The annotation itself then defines the static log element to be used in the page. Also, you notice that isDebugEnabled is no longer there either. This happens because, as you can see, the debug method is not retriev- ing the address via string concatenation of the object. So this way, the object is not being forced to resolve until well within the debug method; hence the isDebugEnabled method is no longer needed. All in all, this is a smooth way to perform debugging. Try adding some debug statements to your code now and check the server.log file for the output.

Debug Mode

Another nice feature of Seam is its *debug mode*. This idea of having easily debuggable abilities via the container is something that is catching on. Tapestry has an error page that details the error and stack trace and all the variables associated with the request. This is a bit different. Both are displayed on a web page built into the debugging software. With Seam, you merely go to an independent web page that shows you all the informa- tion. This is more for debugging complex problems that arrive with an application of this nature. As I said before, there are many Conversation contexts to use, so consequently knowing all of them and keeping track of them can be tricky. So what does the debug mode tell you? It tells you the following:

- Conversations

- Component

- Conversation context

- Business Process context

- Session context

- Application context

These are all associated with the current session you are in—which makes sense, because you would not necessarily want to see all the sessions. Figure 5-7 shows the debug screen.

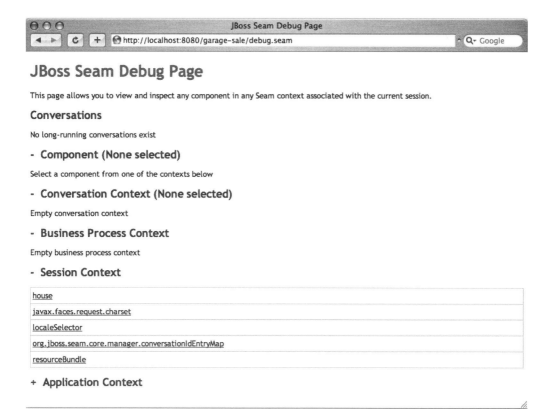

Figure 5-7. *Screen shot of Seam in debug mode*

How to Make This Work

Well hopefully you are thinking, "Wow, this is neat! How do I do it?" Well, it is quite simple. It requires one change to your web.xml file and the addition of four other JARs. The debug addition to web.xml is shown in listing 5-15.

Listing 5-15. *Add This to web.xml to Turn On Seam Debugging*

```
<context-param>
    <param-name>org.jboss.seam.core.init.debug</param-name>
    <param-value>true</param-value>
</context-param>
```

The JAR files are located in two areas. First, from the base of the download, you will find `jboss-seam-debug.jar`. You will take all the JAR files from the `facelets/lib` directory as well. Figure 5-8 shows the directory structure.

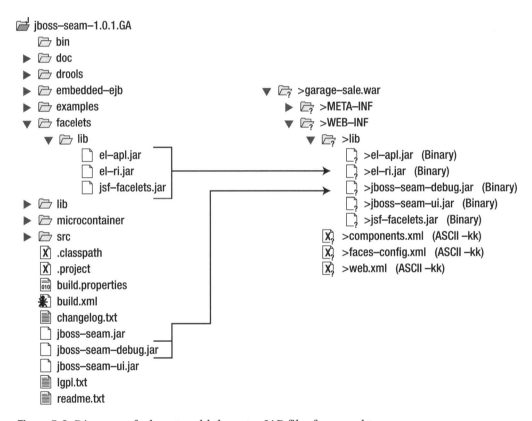

Figure 5-8. *Diagram of where to add the extra JAR files from and to*

Now all you have to do is open a separate web browser in the same session and call `http://localhost:8080/garage-sale/debug.seam`. The `localhost:8080` represents where you configured the server to run, `garage-sale` is the context root, `debug` is specified by default, and `.seam` is what you specified in the URL pattern for your Faces servlet mapping in the `web.xml` file. Listing 5-16 defines the additional entry for the URI.

Listing 5-16. *Web Configuration for the application.xml File*

```
<web>
    <web-uri>garage-sale.war</web-uri>
    <context-root>/garage-sale</context-root>
</web>
```

Listing 5-17 provides the definition for the web suffix.

Listing 5-17. *Configuration for web.xml*

```
<servlet-mapping>
    <servlet-name>Faces Servlet</servlet-name>
    <url-pattern>*.seam</url-pattern>
</servlet-mapping>
```

Data Model

The *data model* is a useful set of Seam annotations and JSP tag libraries for processing lists on the presentation tier. Quite often you will have a list of items for a page and you will need to either edit parts of the list or delete parts of the list. This is actually quite simple. You get a list of items from the database. Then you display the list on the presentation tier with a link and an ID. When you click the link, you are taken back to the action page, where you can use that ID to either look up the item from the list or from the database. This is a basic operation that happens throughout many web applications the world over. This tends to become a routine, cumbersome process. Fortunately, Seam has some components to help you with it.

For our example, we will display a list of addresses and a Delete button for each to remove them from the database.

Seam has made this much simpler by adding framework pieces into an SFSB that makes life easier for the developer. All you have to do is specify three items in the SB. Specify the item that is the list, the individual item you want selected to be injected, and the factory method to instantiate the list.

In this example, we want to get a list of houses back and be able to edit them one at a time. The page will display with a list of text boxes that each have a Delete button. The user can hit the Delete button and delete any address desired. This code is built onto the same Garage Sale application we used earlier. Let's start off with the SFSB, which is a new item we have not discussed before.

POJO Service

Listing 5-18 shows our stateful session bean.

Listing 5-18. *The SFSB for Our Edit Action*

```
@Stateful
@Name("houseManagerEdit")
@Scope(ScopeType.SESSION)
public class HouseManagerEditAction implements HouseManagerEdit {
    //...
}
```

This style should look fairly familiar by now for defining our Seam Session objects. The new part this time is the @Stateful annotation, which of course denotes that we are using an SFSB.

The @Scope annotation is a Seam-specific annotation that sets the context for binding the instance of the POJO. In this case, we are binding to the Session context. The combination of making it stateful and setting the scope to Session is necessary to allow us to persist the list objects, so when we go back to the server we know which object of the list that the user selected. If we did not persist this in Session, the list would be lost and we could not persist it.

Now that we have our code to create the bean, let's add the guts of it, which gives the real functionality. We are going to define two objects to use: DataModel and DataModelSelection. The DataModel object will represent the list of items, and the DataModelSelection object will represent the selected item. Listing 5-19 displays the DataModel selection.

Listing 5-19. *The DataModel Selection Example*

```
@Stateful
@Name("houseManagerEdit")
public class HouseManagerEditAction implements HouseManagerEdit {

@PersistenceContext
private EntityManager em;

@DataModelSelection
@Out(required=false)
private House house;

@DataModel
private List<House> houses;
```

```
@Factory("houses")
public void findHomes() {
    List list = em.createQuery("From House hs order by hs.houseId").getResultList();
    houses = list;
}
}
```

@DataModel is a Seam annotation that allows us to use java.util.Collections from the EJB in the JSF <h:dataTable> tag on the front side. This is achieved by having Seam convert the list into an instance of javax.faces.model.DataModel. This can be a powerful component for use in an SFSB by allowing us to select and bring back objects into the bean for processing. However, the question remains, "How does the page know to populate that object?"

The @Factory annotation comes into play in telling the page how to initialize the houses bean. Seam uses this to tell it to instantiate the houses object and run this method when the presentation tier requests the houses object. As you can see, this method then sets our houses object by using a simple query from our entity bean. Note that this method will be called upon each request to it, regardless of whether you have a stateless or stateful bean.

The @DataModelSelection annotation tells Seam that this is the object to be injected from the list that is selected on the presentation tier. This object then can be used in your method that wants to use it and that is called from the JSF page. Listing 5-20 shows the method for performing the deletion.

Listing 5-20. *SFSB Delete*

```
public String remove() {
    em.remove(house);
    return null;
}
```

Here is our method we will call from the JSF page that will call for the deletion of the house from the database.

Listing 5-21 shows our change to make the persistence context extended.

Listing 5-21. *The Change of Our Persisentece Context*

```
import static javax.persistence.PersistenceContextType.EXTENDED;

@PersistenceContext(type=EXTENDED)
private EntityManager em;
```

We change `EntityManager` to `type=EXTENDED` in order to give it an extended persistence context. This keeps our house list in a managed state, and therefore subsequent calls to the page will not need to requery the list to get the full data.

JSF Presentation Tier

Now that we have covered the business logic object, let's go over the JSP that is going to display the list of houses in Listing 5-22.

Listing 5-22. *The JSP to Display the List of Addresses*

```
<%@ taglib uri="http://java.sun.com/jsf/html" prefix="h" %>
<%@ taglib uri="http://java.sun.com/jsf/core" prefix="f" %>
<%@ taglib uri="http://jboss.com/products/seam/taglib" prefix="s" %>

<f:view>

    <h:dataTable var="house" value="#{houses}" rendered="#{houses.rowCount>0}">

        <h:column>
            <f:facet name="header">
                <h:outputText value="Address"/>
            </f:facet>
            <h:outputText value="#{house.address}"/>
        </h:column>
        <h:column>
            <f:facet name="header">
                <h:outputText value="Action"/>
            </f:facet>
            <s:link value="Delete" action="#{houseManagerEdit.update}"
                        linkStyle="button"/>
        </h:column>
    </h:dataTable>
</f:view>
```

This JSF is doing quite a bit here. As you can see, we use the `dataTable` discussed in Chapter 3. However, we introduce our first use of one of the Seam tag libraries. This creates a button link that will reference the specific list item. When the user clicks on this tag library, the page will call the SFSB, setting the `house` property with the item from that row selected. The action defines the name of the SFSB and the method on it to call. The method is a simple delete, as you would have had in any standard SFSB. This JSF page rendered with example data will produce the output in Figure 5-9.

Figure 5-9. *The display of our JSF page*

Bringing this all together, you should be able to see how easy it is to use Seam to create a presentation tier that display lists and allow us to perform operations on each individual item in that list.

Validation

Validation is an intricate part of any application, especially a web application. Unfortunately, the EJB3 specification alone does not contain any validation specs. However, the Hibernate framework does. The Hibernate validation framework is already part of JBoss, so we are able to easily use it. Figure 5-10 steps through our validation process for the garage sale house addition.

This is the validation for Seam, making use of the Hibernate validator. It is a relatively simple concept. You apply the Hibernate @Valid annotation to any attribute that needs to be validated on the POJO. If the action method you call from the JSF page has the @IfInvalid annotation on the method, Seam will attempt to validate all those Hibernate validations. If any of the validations error out, a message for the JSF page will be displayed. Now let's dive into the code changes.

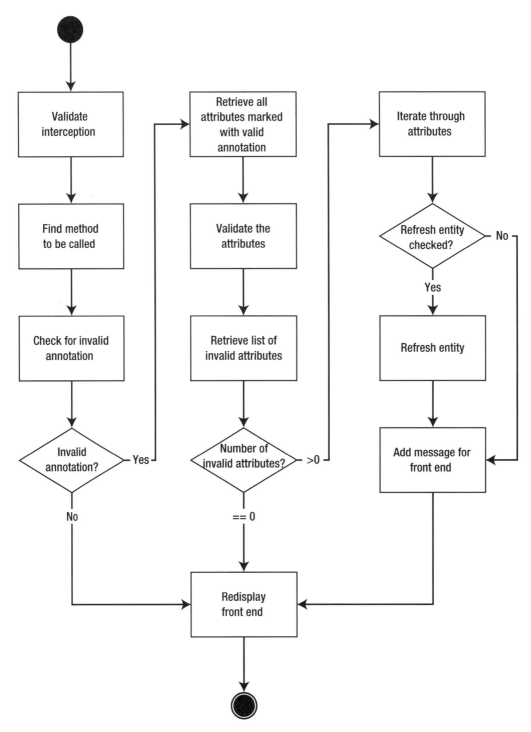

Figure 5-10. *Activity diagram of the validation mechanism in Seam*

Validation on the Domain Model

The validation specification works by allowing validation annotations on the domain-level objects. Because we are using a full EJB cadre for our framework, the EBs would be the domain-level objects. Thus, in order to implement the validation, all you would have to do is annotate the EB as in Listing 5-23.

Listing 5-23. *An Example of an Entity Bean with NotNull Validations*

```java
import org.hibernate.validator.NotNull;

@Entity
public class House implements Serializable {

    private static final long serialVersionUID = -3823531857349759805L;

    private long houseId;
    private String address;

    @Id @GeneratedValue
    public long getHouseId() {
        return houseId;
    }
    public void setHouseId(long houseId) {
        this.houseId = houseId;
    }

    @NotNull(message="Address required")
    public String getAddress() {
        return address;
    }
    public void setAddress(String address) {
        this.address = address;
    }
}
```

As you can see, it is a fairly simple process. Just attach the validation on the getter of the value that you wish to validate. This then allows the framework to be able to determine whether this is a valid object. Table 5-1 shows the possible Hibernate validations.

Table 5-1. *Validation Annotations in Hibernate*

Annotation	Description
@Length(min=, max=)	Checks whether the string length matches the range
@Max(value=)	Checks that the value is less than or equal to the max
@Min(value=)	Checks that the value is greater than or equal to the min
@NotNull	Checks that the value is not null
@Past	For a date object, checks that the date is in the past
@Future	For a date object, checks that the date is in the future
@Pattern(regex="regexp", flag=)	For a string, checks that the string matches this pattern
@Range(min=, max=)	Checks whether the value is between the min and the max
@Size(min=, max=)	For collections, checks that the size is between the two
@AssertFalse	Asserts that the evaluation of the method is false
@AssertTrue	Asserts that the evaluation of the method is true
@Valid	For a collection or a map, checks that all the objects they contain are valid
@Email	Checks whether the string conforms to the email address specification

You will notice that in Listing 5-23 we also added a `message=` parameter to our `@NotNull` annotation. This allows us to pass a message back to the presentation tier specifying the error message.

Calling the Validator from the Business Tier

We have gone over how to define the validation on the domain objects, but have not yet gone over how to tell Seam when to validate the domain objects. The Hibernate validator can be called from different layers, thus making it so we can perform checks on the domain bean from layers not near the validator. This will work well for our needs.

The validation on the business logic tier is accomplished in two steps. First, you define what properties should be validated, and then you define which methods will trigger validation to be performed. Listing 5-24 defines the validation.

Listing 5-24. *A SLSB That Will Validate the House Before Adding It*

```
import org.hibernate.validator.Valid;
import org.jboss.seam.annotations.Outcome;

@Stateless
@Name("salesManager")
@Interceptors(SeamInterceptor.class)
@JndiName("garage-sale/SaleManagerAction/local")
public class SaleManagerAction implements Serializable, SaleManager {

    private static final long serialVersionUID = -5814583678795046052L;

    @PersistenceContext
    private EntityManager em;

    @Valid
    @In @Out
    private House house;

    public String addHouse() {
        em.persist(house);
        return "/homeSuccess.jsp";
    }
}
```

The @Valid annotation tells Seam which object needs to be validated. This annotation is not Seam specific; this is another Hibernate validator that Seam uses to determine that this object needs to be validated.

■**Note** Earlier versions of Seam used the @IfInvalid annotation. This has been semi-deprecated in favor of using <s:validateAll/> in the JSF page.

Validation on the JSF Pages

So now you know how to set the domain objects to validate and how to trigger the validation on the business tier. Now let's go over how to add the code to our JSP to display the validation error. Listing 5-25 shows our modified code with validation.

Listing 5-25. *The JSP for Our houseAdd.jsp*

```
<%@ taglib uri="http://java.sun.com/jsf/html" prefix="h" %>
<%@ taglib uri="http://java.sun.com/jsf/core" prefix="f" %>


<f:view>
   <h:messages/></div>

   <h:form>
       <s:validateAll>
       Please enter your address:<br/>
       <h:inputText value="#{house.address}" size="15"/><br/>
       <h:commandButton value="Add House" action="#{salesManager.addHouse}"/>
       </s:validateAll>
   </h:form>
</f:view>
```

The only major addition you can see is the `<h:messages/>` tag, which will allow the display of any errors that occur. The Seam `<s:validateAll>` tag has also been added, to signify that these elements need validating.

Figure 5-11 shows the display that occurs when a user tries to add a house that doesn't meet the minimal validation rules.

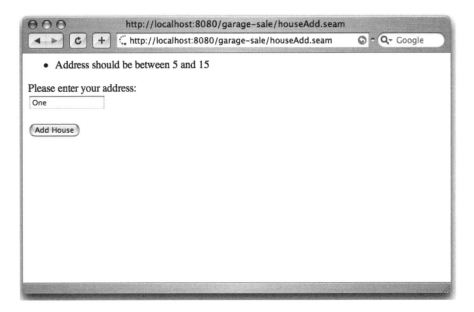

Figure 5-11. *House Add Page with an error*

Schema Generation

One final positive side about the validator mechanisms is in its use for schema generation. If you are having your schema automatically generated, the validation framework will add the appropriate not-nulls, lengths, and so forth to it. Obviously, not all the validations will be there, because constraints such as `@EmailChecks` are not normal database checks.

Summary

At this point, we have gone over the basics of MVC, JSF, EJB3, and now Seam. So you should have a basic understanding of how Seam works and how to write a basic Seam-enabled Java EE application. You have also learned about the different contexts that Seam uses to manage state. Although some of that information may be confusing right now, as you read the next two chapters, you will understand the usefulness of these contexts.

This chapter also covered a few additional components such as logging, data models, and debugging. These are all tools specific to Seam to help with web application development. There are of course many more, and some are tied to more-complex processes that you will read about later in this book. Most of these components are tied to higher-end processing.

In the next few chapters, you will learn about some progressively more-complex Seam processing.

CHAPTER 6

■ ■ ■

Seam Contexts

As you may recall, in Chapter 5 I talked about contexts. There are seven of them, and I gave a brief description of what they are and how they are used. To review, the contexts are as follows:

- Stateless context

- Session context

- Application context

- Event context

- Page context

- Conversation context

- Business Process context

Now, in my opinion, Seam would have been a great framework even without the use of multiple contexts. Without the use of extra contexts beyond the standard Request, Session, and Servlet contexts, you would still have the ability to skip the necessity of backing beans and go straight to the business logic tier. The use of multiple contexts adds an additional level of functionality beyond the traditional web contexts and can ease much of your development, which sometimes can be hampered by overuse of the Session object especially.

I briefly described the Seam contexts in the preceding chapter. Now I will provide more details and examples. Some of the contexts do not require an entire application to explain or to examine their use and are rather simple. Most of these contexts are quite easy to understand and correspond to regular servlet requests—for example, the HttpSession object has a corresponding Session context. Others, such as the Conversation context, are much different and will require more explanation.

I will start by going over, in detail, each of the contexts except for the Business Process context. (The Business Process context adds a great deal of complexity, so I have devoted Chapter 7 to that topic.) I will then provide a more detailed explanation of how to make your beans have multiple context states based on name. I will explain how to access these contexts outside of the normal injection process. I will then wrap up this chapter with an explanation of our business objects and their uses in a Seam application.

The major focus for us in this chapter from a technology point of view will be squarely on the business logic tier. All of our settings on the process will be done there. Although the JSF tier does play a role, for the most part the context that the objects are in will not affect how the JSF pages interact with the objects.

Figure 6-1 diagrams the road map once again.

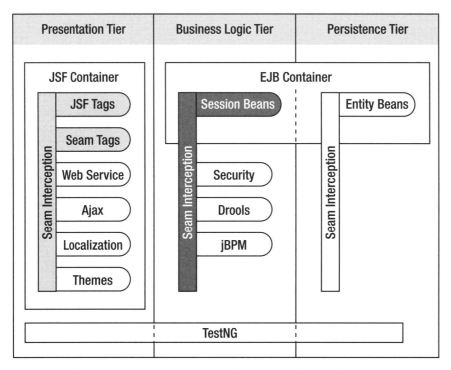

Figure 6-1. *The road map for this chapter focuses mostly on the Seam aspects of development.*

I am going to start these discussions with a few familiar faces, ones that are part of our normal Servlet objects.

Stateless Context

Let's begin with the Stateless context. We already have stateless session beans, which are stateless, so why do we need a Stateless context? Well the answer is, we do not. However, the Stateless context does have limited usefulness. As you may remember, earlier I explained that Seam business objects do not necessarily *have* to be session beans; JavaBeans can be used as business objects within the Seam container as well.

The use of the Stateless context allows us to have a JavaBean in a stateless manner—as shown in Listing 6-1.

Listing 6-1. *A Stateless Hello World JavaBean*

```
@Name("statelessHelloWorld")
@Scope(ScopeType.STATELESS)
public class StatelessHelloWorld {

    @RequestParameter("name")
    String userName;

    public String getText() {
        return "Hello World! - " + userName;
    }
}
```

This simple Hello World example takes in the name of a user and outputs "Hello World! -" + the user name to that user. As you may have noticed, I introduced a new annotation, @RequestParameter. This annotation, as you may have guessed, is for a request parameter. It takes an optional parameter that specifies the name of the parameter. So in this example, if you did not define the name, your parameter on the JSF page would have been userName. However, in our example the parameter on the JSF page would be name. This is useful because if you need to change the parameter name on the JSF page, you have to change it in only one location in the class file as opposed to changing it in multiple areas.

I would use this context sparingly on the class level. Although this context is useful, it is not necessary to annotate our stateless session beans with it. Just remember that when using the Stateless context, you should not persist the state across multiple calls.

Session Context

Our next context is the Session context. If you have ever worked with a web application or Hibernate, you should be familiar with the concept of a session. A *session*, in the simplest terms, refers to an object that is used across multiple calls. For a web request, this refers to multiple calls to the server. For Hibernate, it can refer to multiple calls to the database.

Our Session context is most like the web request. It is used for those global pieces of information that all our conversations need to have access to. You are going to want to annotate the classes or properties that need to be persistable. These in general are objects that you would have stored onto the HttpSession object when using servlet-based classes.

Although a session example may not be the most interesting to see, I want to give you an example anyway. My goal is to show you not only how simple using the session is, but also how transparent it will be to other objects thanks to injection.

In this example, you are simply logging in and setting a Session context of userName, which will forward you to a page that displays the variable. Finally, that page will call a different listener that will also have that variable to display, and forward again to our final page for display. I will not show all the pages here, but I will show most of them and the code for you to get an idea of the process. Listing 6-2 shows our stateless page with the Session context variable being set.

Listing 6-2. *A Stateless Class with a Session Context Object on It*

```
@Stateless
@Name("sessionExample")
public class SessionExampleAction implements SessionExample {

    @Out(scope = ScopeType.SESSION, required = true)
    private String userName;

    @Logger
    Log log;

    public String login() {
        log.info("login");
        userName = "Joseph";
        return "/pageOne.jsp";
    }
}
```

Although this is an SLSB, it is still allowed to contain a reference to a Seam Session context object. This may go against your perceived notions of what an SLSB has in it, and I partially agree with you. If you wanted to, you could just as easily make this an SFSB if it makes you feel any better. However, you have to remember that one goal of Seam is to eliminate the need for a backing bean. And if your backing bean was simply going to log you in and add this variable to the session, that would be a bit of a waste. This way, you are simply cutting out the middleman. The code that displays this page is in Listing 6-3, with its corresponding display in Figure 6-2.

Listing 6-3. *The Code for Our Display Page of Our Session Context Object*

```
<%@ taglib uri="http://java.sun.com/jsf/html" prefix="h" %>
<%@ taglib uri="http://java.sun.com/jsf/core" prefix="f" %>
<%@ taglib uri="http://jboss.com/products/seam/taglib" prefix="s" %>

<f:view>
    User Name - <h:outputText value="#{userName}"/> <br/>
    <s:link action="#{nextPage.continueToNextPage}" value="Continue"/><br/>
</f:view>
```

Figure 6-2. *The display of the user session on the page*

As you can see from the code, you are simply accessing the variable by using the variable name that we set in the SessionExampleAction class. This is because that variable name was bound to a Seam Session context with the name username, which in turn bound it to the HttpSession context. Recall that we could have added a name parameter to the @Out annotation if we wanted to customize the name of the property.

The final class I want to show you is the class that is accessed when clicking the Continue link. This class is interesting because it shows that we can inject that session variable back into the class without even specifying the scope. This is done because Seam searched for that variable via the specific contexts whose order is defined at the end of this chapter. Listing 6-4 shows the simple code for injecting the property and displaying the name.

Listing 6-4. *Code for Getting the Session Context Username and Outputting It to the Log*

```
@Name("nextPage")
public class NextPageAction {

    @In
    private String userName;
```

```
    @Logger
    Log log;

    public String continueToNextPage() {
        log.info("User name - #{userName}");
        return "/pageTwo.jsp";
    }
}
```

Now that you have seen the Session context examples, you should appreciate how easy and unobtrusive it is to set the Session context. It is also worthy to note that in the portal environment, the POJOs that you annotate as a Session context will represent the portlet session as defined in JSR 168.

A best practice to remember when using the Session context is that you should use this context only with something that is truly session specific. Although this may seem an obvious comment, you will often find with normal web applications that people fall into the pattern of using the session too often. This is mainly due to needing an object to persist longer than a single request but shorter than an entire session. With Seam, however, because we have many other contexts that give us much more fine-grained control, such as the Conversation context, you will probably not need to use this "cheat." So think carefully when using a Session context when creating your Seam-based application.

Application Context

As I mentioned in Chapter 5, the Application context is like the Servlet context used by the Servlet specification. The Servlet context is where you store static type data that is not differentiable for multiple users. Listing 6-5 creates a class that will be used to retrieve static content.

Listing 6-5. *Simple Example of a Class Creating an Appliation*

```
@Name("configurationData")
@Scope(ScopeType.APPLICATION)
public class ConfigurationData implements Serializable {
    // ... content goes here ...
}
```

One thing to watch out for is that if you decide to put an SFSB in the Application context, you could have a problem because an SFSB does not allow concurrent calls to it. To get around this, you will have to mark the class as @Synchronized if you choose to use an SFSB.

Event Context

We are going to move on to the Event context, which ironically has the smallest section in this chapter even though it's probably one of the most used contexts. I describe it in this small section because it is an extremely simple context. It is short-lived and can be well used for quick calls. The Event context is alive only from the restore view to render response scope. It is destroyed at the end of a request cycle. The Event context is used for items that you want to have around for a short time. By default, Event context objects are used by the system for the Seam Remote Method Invocation (RMI) and remoting calls. The context for this call is used only for the invocation of the request. You will learn about the specifics of RMI and remoting in Chapter 8.

Page Context

One of the issues I always had with Struts was the way in which you had to retrieve dynamic lists back to the page. Most of the time, the lists I am referring to had to populate select boxes on the pages. The easy way of doing it was to retrieve the list in the Action, set the lists on the request, and send it back—which would work perfectly the first time the request was sent back to the page. However, after you submitted the page back to the server, that's when problems could arise. You could have either a validation error or a business exception that would send you back to the page. Well, you would want to return to that page, but now that request object would be gone, so you would have to re-create the request object, which usually required calling the database. *Yuck!* I always found this to be a wasteful way of setting lists.

So instead you would usually have to find a more advanced way of saving the objects. You could re-create the objects each time, which usually was a waste of resources and time. Or you could save the objects to the session the first time around, thus having that list object always available. Of course, you would have to find a way to manage that session information so you were not keeping it indefinitely. Or you could store the list of objects as a hidden variable as well. None of those ideas ever appealed to me, because they required unnecessary extra calls, polluting your HTML code, or abusing the session. I always thought, wow, wouldn't it be nice to have a mechanism that allows us to keep state for the length of a page? And in actuality I ended up for a few projects upgrading the Request context to do just that. Well, fortunately, there is no longer a need to hack the code.

The Page context is another one of those contexts that you do not usually find in standard web frameworks, but in all fairness I think you should. As its name indicates, the Page context allows you to keep state for the length of the page request—so while you are on the page, you have access to the object. Whenever you make a Faces request to the server, you will access and set an object that is scoped on the Page context. After the variable is stored and the listener returns from the method, the page will get rendered and retrieve the data stored on the object. So as of right now we are basically working just as we would with a regular *Event* context. Now here is where it starts to behave differently, when you post back to the page from the originating page. During the invoke application phase, the Page context variables are manipulated in order to allow the object to be persisted onto the page, whereas with the Event context you would no longer have these objects.

Using the Page context allows you to keep objects scoped while you are on the page. This is perfect for any page requiring dynamic data, so you can post back to that same page many times either because of validation failures or to add information to the page. This would also be great for a list that you want to iterate through. In fact, the `DataModel` discussed in the previous chapter will use the page or the unspecified scope only to perform its processing for this reason.

You may also wonder what happens in a multiwindow environment, where you could have multiple windows, but each window is on the same URL. Well, because the data is serialized to the client, the Page context works easily in the case of multiwindow or Back button environments.

Conversation Context

The ability to sustain multiple conversations in Seam is a great feature that (if thought out well in design) can add useful functionality to a website. The Conversation context allows a user to mimic multiple sessions without actually having to have multiple sessions. So think of a web application: You log in to a website or arrive at a website. That website creates a session object for you. If you are using a shopping cart or a sequence of steps for a final operation, you will hold those objects' state in the session. So for our travel example, you log in, select your airline, hotel, and car, and can see the price as you go along. This is a normal feature of any travel site.

So what happens if you want to price out another flight? Well, you could create a complex session management tool to keep a map of the session value tied to some ID for each of the new sessions. However, most sites do not work that way, because, wow, that's complex. Instead, they usually rely on the user to open a new browser window (which in turn triggers a new session to be created) and price out that flight. At that point, you can price out your flights. However, it is impossible for those two session objects to know anything about each other. Well, there are ways to be aware of the other sessions, but the methods that allowed that have been deprecated for quite some time. There are advanced tricks you could do, but nothing you want to try in reality. At any rate, what if you wanted those two "sessions" to be aware of each other? What if there was shared data between them that you did not want to repeat? Well, you could not do it. However, this is the problem that Conversation contexts attempt to overcome.

Figure 6-3 shows what the first page of the Travel Reservations application will look like when entering for the first time and the starting conversation.

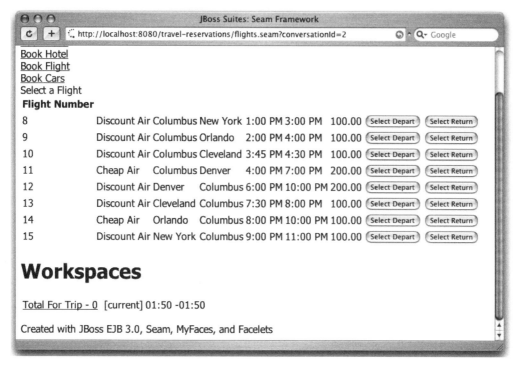

Figure 6-3. *The flights page when entering for the first time to book a flight*

What the Conversation Context Brings You

A conversation gives you the ability to make a class span multiple instances within the same session, while keeping its state through multiple calls. This provides a first-class object to the web application world. As I have already pointed out, this quite brilliantly gives you features that you have never had before. Of course, you could do the same even with normal session management by writing some custom session management wrappers. However, what if you want complex session management to be accomplished under only a few circumstances? Then it would get harder. Okay, so let's take a look at exactly how we are going to accomplish this.

How It Works

So how does this work? Well, first you have to decide what object you are going to want to keep in the conversation. Personally, I believe this is the hardest part (it's nice to know that the hardest part is not too hard and just requires some thinking and planning).

First things first: you have to pick the type of class you can use. Your class has to be a class that can keep its state for multiple calls, so your only choices are SFSB, EB, or JavaBeans. It makes sense based on this need that you will not be able to use SLSBs, because they are stateless. For our examples we will use the SFSB. (Personally I find this to be the easiest to use of all our choices). The reason is that you are going to want an object that can hold state and can perform operations. This makes sense if you think about our travel example and what you want to keep persisted. You are going to want to be able to not only make multiple travel reservations, but also to perform multiple operations on that object. Now you may think, "Well, I could have other beans performing operations on the object" if that was your goal. Although this is possible, when it comes to redirecting the lack of a conversation, coding the work-around gets trickier.

Understanding the Conversation

Before we begin to go in depth about how to make the conversations span multiple screens, let's go over again what a conversation is. In its basic form, a *conversation* is a single unit of work. Think of it as what you are doing at a given point on a given page. You could be "creating a garage sale," "creating a ticket," or "making a travel reservation." A conversation is that single life cycle of a request. If you have three windows open and are making three separate requests, you will have three separate conversations.

As you will learn later, many of the Seam components you create are by default conversations. These components and requests use what are called *temporary conversations*. Why temporary? Because they last only the span of the request. After the render response occurs, the conversation is destroyed.

So the question that you may have is, "How then do these temporary conversations allow us all the complex functionality just described?" Well, it's quite simple: we can make these temporary conversations *long-running* conversations. A long-running conversation can then span multiple screens and multiple calls. This becomes very interesting because we can make it so this long-running conversation can "worry" about itself. Now those three separate windows can perform independently of each other and yet at the same time be aware of each other if they want to. Long-term conversational states will be stored in an object like the `HttpSession` object between calls, and like `HttpSessions`, you can set a time-out for your conversations so that they do not grow unbounded.

Long-running conversations—unlike their short-term brethren that get destroyed after each page—will be propagated from page to page. When using a Faces request, this propagation will be performed automatically by a `conversationId` variable. When using standard HTTP `GET` requests, you do not have this luxury and thus your conversations in those cases will be temporary.

So not only can we have long-running and temporary conversations, but we can also take those long-running conversations and nest conversations underneath them (these are then called *nested conversations*). In addition, we will use conversations implicitly when we use the business processes.

So hopefully you now understand the purpose of a conversation; it is to have a single talking point or to span multiple talking points. Now let's get into how to make this temporary conversation a long-running conversation.

Creating a Long-Running Conversation

We have to mark the class as conversational to signify that we want the class to be part of a long-running conversation. We are going to use the `BookingCartBean` from our travel reservations that will have a member variable `Booking`, which is an entity bean. You can see the start of the class in Listing 6-6.

Listing 6-6. *The Start of Our Booking Cart Stateful Conversation Object*

```
@Stateful
@Name("bookingCart")
@Conversational()
public class BookingCartBean implements BookingCart {
// ... more ...
}
```

We start by creating an SFSB and mark it as a Seam component named `bookingCart`. The third line is what defines that this bean is going to be a part of a long-running conversation. This means that every single method on this class is going to be part of a long-running conversation. The `@Conversational` annotation will cause the class itsclf to be intercepted by `ConversationInterceptor`, which will check every method to make sure that it is part of a conversation or that it is a trigger for a conversation to begin.

Now because every method and property in this class is tied to a conversation, there are only three options for the methods that have been defined for this long-running conversation class as follows:

- The method is part of the long-running conversation.

- The method is beginning the long-running conversation for the bean.

- The method is ending the long-running conversation for the bean.

Beginning a Long-Running Conversation

For everything there is a beginning, so first things first: we have to start the long-running conversation, and this does not happen automatically. A normal conversation has a beginning, middle, and an end. This is the same with a Seam long-running conversation as well. So let's discuss how we start the conversation. It is fairly straightforward, as Listing 6-7 shows. We just use the `@Begin` annotation on the method that we want to begin the conversation.

Listing 6-7. *The Start of Our Long-Running Conversation in the BookingCartBean*

```
@Begin
public String starTravelPlans() {
    return "flights";
}
```

The code is straightforward, as I said it was. When you click on the first page to start the process, this will start a new set of travel plans by taking you to the flight page and starting a long-running conversation. Now if you tried to go to this method again while still on a page in a long-running conversation, Seam would return to you an error like the one in Listing 6-8, stating that you cannot create a new conversation while in an existing conversation.

Listing 6-8. *Error Displayed When Trying to Run Long-Running Conversations*

```
[[Faces Servlet]] Servlet.service() for servlet Faces Servlet threw exception
javax.faces.el.EvaluationException:
    Exception while invoking expression #{bookingCart.starTravelPlans}
    at org.apache.myfaces.el.MethodBindingImpl.invoke(MethodBindingImpl.java:153)
    at org.jboss.seam.core.Pages.callAction(Pages.java:212)
    at org.jboss.seam.jsf.AbstractSeamPhaseListener.callPageActions(
        AbstractSeamPhaseListener.java:127)
...
Caused by: javax.ejb.EJBException:
java.lang.IllegalStateException:
 begin method invoked from a long running conversation, try using @Begin(join=true)
    at org.jboss.ejb3.tx.Ejb3TxPolicy.handleExceptionInOurTx(Ejb3TxPolicy.java:69)
    at org.jboss.aspects.tx.TxPolicy.invokeInOurTx(TxPolicy.java:83)
```

Middle of a Long-Running Conversation

After you start a conversation, you are in the middle of the conversation, which is where we are now in this example. The methods without any annotations to signify the beginning or end of a conversation are the ones that have to run while a long-running conversation is in progress. Listing 6-9 shows the `selectHotel()` method in our class. As you notice, no annotations are necessary for it. The method has already been annotated with `@Conversational` at the class level to indicate that this has to be in a conversation.

Listing 6-9. *The selectHotel() Method in our BookingCartBean.java Class*

```
public String selectHotel() {
        Hotel hotel = hotelReservations.getSelectedHotel();
        log.info("Book Hotel");
        if (booking.getHotelBooked() == null) {
            booking.setHotelBooked(hotelBooked);
        }
        booking.getHotelBooked().setHotel(hotel);

        return "hotels";
    }
```

This method will be used later when we select a hotel we want to add to our stateful booking object. If you try to call this method before you have begun a conversation, ConversationInterceptor will intercept the call and detect that you are calling a non-begin method, and will direct you to a starting page. The starting page you are directed to is defined in the pages.xml which we will discuss in a few sections.

Ending a Long-Running Conversation

Finally, as in real life, you will finish talking and want to end the conversation. In our example, we no longer need to keep the long-running conversation after the reservation is made. Ending is as simple as beginning the conversation. Listing 6-10 shows how we use the @End annotation to end the conversation.

Listing 6-10. *The Method to Mark the End of a Long-Running Conversation on the Booking-CartBean*

```
@Remove
@End
public void makeReservation() {
    em.persist(booking);
}
```

This method is also marked with the @Remove annotation. This is because the bean on this is a SFSB and when we end its context, we are also signaling to the application server that we no longer need this bean either, which is an obvious decision.

■**Note** You can have multiple @Begin and @End methods for a conversation but all will still react within that same conversation.

So we just went over how to mark up our SFSB to signal that it will be part of a long-running conversation. So by now you should understand the difference between a temporary and a long-running conversation. The temporary conversation would be the default for our SFSB; however, we have marked it to be long-running so that we can propagate the conversation over multiple calls.

Now we will move on to the options on our JSF pages to affect the conversation. These options include reading the conversations as well as using the links to be part of the conversations.

Additional Configuration

For the most part, there are no extra configurations to mark that your conversations should be run as long-running conversations. However, there is one addition you may need depending on your JSF calls. When you want Seam to maintain the long-running conversation and you are using post-then-redirect in JSF, you will have to add an extra filter in your `web.xml`, as in Listing 6-11.

Listing 6-11. *Addition to web.xml Needed for Seam*

```
<filter>
    <filter-name>Seam Redirect Filter</filter-name>
    <filter-class>org.jboss.seam.servlet.SeamRedirectFilter</filter-class>
</filter>
```

This will basically just add `conversationId` to the URL of the requests made.

JSF Integration with Conversations

Now let's head over to the presentation tier and see what it gives us for long-running conversations. If you are using just temporary conversations, you have nothing to worry about. However, let's be fair—a temporary conversation is not the more interesting part, and that is not what we want to see in this section. So let's see what we can do with the long-running conversations in the JSF pages. There are essentially a few things we can do. We can create links to new conversations, the same conversations, nested conversations, and so forth. We also can take all those long-running conversations we have and display them on each of our workspaces. (*Workspaces* is a fancy name for the different pages holding their own unique conversation IDs.) Not only can we display the conversations, but we can jump to different conversations as well. Well, let's get started so you can understand how long-running conversations can affect the link tags on our pages.

Creating Links with Long-Running Conversations

When you are in or are starting a long-running conversation, you have many options for the link tags. The choice you have to make depends on what you want the next page to do. You have to decide whether you want that link to be part of the long-running conversation, be part of a nested conversation, or not be part of the conversation at all.

Normal Propagation of the Conversation

Under most circumstances, as you move along you merely want to keep the page in the same conversation. For this you can use either the JSF `commandLink` or you can use the Seam `link` component as shown here:

```
<s:link action="hotels" value="Book Hotel"/>
```

This is a fairly straightforward, regular Seam link. The HTML that gets outputted will automatically have the conversation ID with it. And if you are building your Seam application from scratch, I would suggest going ahead and using the `<s:link>` tag. However, as I explained earlier, Seam can be used with normal JSF tags as well. This is most often the case if you are changing an existing JSF application, or do not want to add Seam-specific components to your JSF page. We can add the `conversationId` parameter to a regular JSF page, but we will have to do it the old-fashioned way, by passing it along as a regular variable. The preceding code marked as a command link looks like the following:

```
<h:outputLink action="hotels">
    <f:param name="conversationId" value="#{conversation.id}"/>
    <h:outputText value="Book Hotel"/>
</h:outputLink>
```

This code was created with regular JSF tags. However, the `conversationId` insertion is a bit sloppy, and being that it is inputted as a parameter and thus not checked until runtime, is prone to typing mistakes. There is an additional Seam tag you can add to the `<h:outputLink>` tag if you want to preserve the JSF structure but sprinkle Seam into the JSF page. So we will take the preceding regular JSF component, sprinkle Seam into it, and the result is as follows:

```
<h:outputLink value="hotels">
    <s:conversationId/>
    <h:outputText value="Book Hotel"/>
</h:outputLink>
```

The code looks just as it did before except we got rid of the sloppy way of adding the conversation ID by using a Seam component instead.

The final way to perform the ID propagation is with a normal `href` output:

```
<a href="hotels.seam?conversationId=#{conversation.id}">Book Hotels</a>
```

The only extra warning I would give is against using the `commandLink` tag without any markups for the `conversationId` if the page is supposed to be part of a long-running conversation. If you do, you will more likely get an error when trying to render the page, as shown here:

```
java.lang.IllegalStateException: Client-id : _id0 is duplicated in the faces tree.
```

So to avoid getting these exceptions, try using one of the previous methods for your links.

Other Propagations of the Conversation

If all we could do is propagate the conversation with our tags, that would not be much fun. Surely we should be able to do more with the tags. And we can. JSF tags can give us about as much leverage as some of the class-level annotations. By using a combination of the JSF `commandLink` and the Seam `conversationPropagation` tag, we can do some interesting things with the conversation—for example, beginning it, ending it, or nesting it. The `conversationPropagation` tag gives us the option of controlling the conversations from within the JSF itself. So let's see how we will perform these operations.

The general look of a `commandLink` using the conversation propagation is as follows:

```
<h:commandLink action="hotels" value="Select Hotel">
    <s:conversationPropagation type=""/>
</h:commandLink>
```

This is pretty simple. Depending on what we want to do, we just change the type. You will notice in the preceding code that I have left the type blank. Table 6-1 lists the names of the parameters for the `type` property.

Table 6-1. *Parameter Options for the conversationPropagation Types Property*

Parameter	Description
begin	The link will trigger the beginning of a conversation.
end	The link will trigger the end of a conversation.
join	The link will join with an already-existing long-running conversation.
nested	The link will create a child conversation.
none	The link will not be part of a conversation.

It is useful to note here that the `join` and `nested` properties can also be used on the `@Begin` annotation as Boolean parameters (that is, `@Begin(join=true)`).

The `join` property tells the container to join an existing long-running conversation that has already begun. However, if there is no long-running conversation running at the time, an exception will be thrown.

Nesting is used when you want to have a new conversation while there is already a long-running conversation present. The current conversation is suspended until this new nested conversation reaches a method marked with the `@End` annotation. After the nested conversation ends, the previous conversation resumes.

So now we have the ability to manipulate the calling of our conversations, and the ability to determine when the conversations are propagated and how to propagate them. In the next section, we will move on to something I find more interesting: messing with the conversations themselves.

Performing Workspace Management

When using Conversation contexts, one of the more interesting capabilities is managing your workspaces. This ability allows you to switch back and forth between your conversations, basically to manage multiple workspaces without having to have multiple browser windows open. In this section, I am going to explain how to set your pages to view the extra workspaces and in fact how to switch the workspaces around.

Viewing Lists of Conversations

Viewing multiple lists of conversations requires doing a few things first. First, you have to add an entry to an XML file to describe how you want the workspace description to display. Second, you have to insert that formatted information into the Extensible Hypertext Markup Language (XHTML) code.

Let's get started with the `pages.xml` file, which is used to display the page descriptions. For this first example, we are going to display at the bottom of the page a list of workspaces. Each workspace will show a summation of the trip's expenses, as described in Figure 6-4.

This page displays the total cost for the trip under the Workspaces section. The first part of the line reads Total For Trip, and we define this in the `pages.xml` file in Listing 6-12.

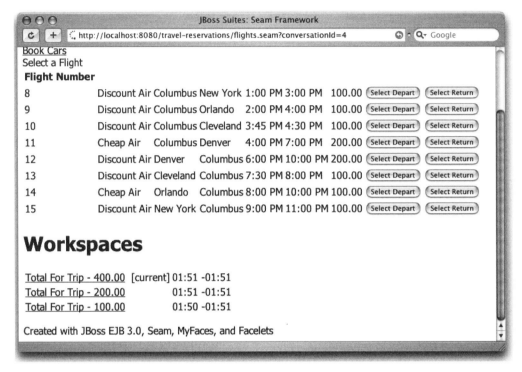

Figure 6-4. *Screen shot of our flights page with a list of the conversations*

Listing 6-12. *The pages.xml File Example*

```
<pages>
    <page view-id="/flights.xhtml">Total For Trip - #{booking.totalCost}</page>
</pages>
```

Here you can define the text based on the page you are on. In this example, we have defined the text for the flights.xhtml page. And as you see, we are displaying the total cost of the trip thus far.

Now of course we have to display the cost on the page, and to do this we are going to use a template and include the conversationList.xhtml file as part of that template. Listing 6-13 displays conversationList.xhtml.

Listing 6-13. *A Portion of the conversationList.xhtml File*

```
<div xmlns="http://www.w3.org/1999/xhtml"
     xmlns:c="http://java.sun.com/jstl/core"
     xmlns:ui="http://java.sun.com/jsf/facelets"
     xmlns:f="http://java.sun.com/jsf/core"
     xmlns:h="http://java.sun.com/jsf/html">
<div class="section">
    <h1>
      <h:outputText rendered="#{not empty conversationList}" value="Workspaces"/>
    </h1>
</div>
<div class="section">
    <h:form>
        <h:dataTable value="#{conversationList}" var="entry">
            <h:column>
                <h:commandLink action="#{entry.select}"
                    value="#{entry.description}"/>
                 
                <h:outputText value="[current]" rendered="#{entry.current}"/>
            </h:column>
            <h:column>
                <h:outputText value="#{entry.startDatetime}">
                    <f:convertDateTime type="time" pattern="hh:mm"/>
                </h:outputText>
                -
                <h:outputText value="#{entry.lastDatetime}">
                    <f:convertDateTime type="time" pattern="hh:mm"/>
                </h:outputText>
            </h:column>
        </h:dataTable>
    </h:form>
</div>

</div>
```

So take a quick look at the listing. Focus on the second section and you will see the
`<h:dataTable/>` component. In that section of code, we are going to display the list of
conversation workspaces. We retrieve the list of conversations by using the built-in
Seam component `conversationList`, which will reference the object
`org.jboss.seam.core.ConversationList`. If you look up this object in the APIs, you will
notice that it contains a list of `org.jboss.seam.core.ConversationEntry` objects. Table 6-2
lists the properties available to you for this object.

Table 6-2. *Properties of ConversationEntry*

Property	Description
description	Displays the description of the workspace
startDatetime	Gets the start date and time of the conversation
lastDatetime	Gets the last date and time you accessed the conversation
current	Boolean value displaying true if this is the workspace you are on, false if not
displayable select	Returns a string that has information to link to access this workspace

Most of these properties should be easily understandable. The only one that you may not understand is the description property. This is where pages.xml comes into play. The description we defined in pages.xml is what gets propagated when calling the description on the ConversationEntry object.

Switching Workspaces

So now you should have the knowledge to modify the workspace to display it the way you want and set it up in any way. And even though we have the ability to display the list of workspaces and select each one, there is an alternative way to do it. We can also display a list of workspaces in a select box and then use a drop-down to switch to the workspace we want. The code is fairly straightforward, as shown in Listing 6-14.

Listing 6-14. *Select Box Switcher to Switch Workspaces*

```
<h:selectOneMenu value="#{switcher.conversationIdOrOutcome}">
    <f:selectItems value="#{switcher.selectItems}"/>
</h:selectOneMenu>
<h:commandButton action="#{switcher.select}" value="Switch"/>
```

This code will retrieve the org.jboss.seam.core.Switcher object to be used to display the list of items in the workspace in order to give you the opportunity to switch. This drop-down will look like that in Figure 6-5.

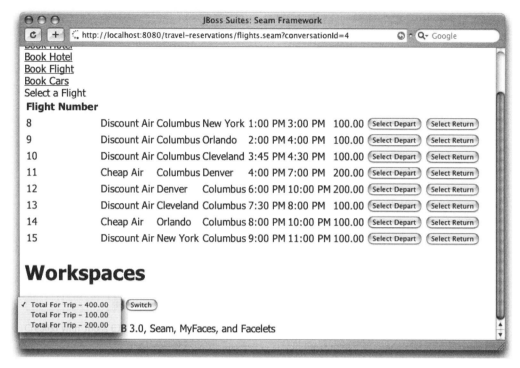

Figure 6-5. *Screen shot of a drop-down for switching workspaces*

Redirecting a Long-Running Conversation Not Started

Previously I discussed the starting, middle, and end points of a long-running conversation. I also discussed how Seam would intercept any long-running conversation marked by the @Conversational annotation. If you are trying to call a method other than one marked with @Begin while a long-running conversation is started, Seam will reject that call and redirect you. The question becomes, redirect you to where? This is based on something I discussed previously, the pages.xml configuration. We can take our listing and modify it by adding a no-conversation-id property to it, as in Listing 6-15.

Listing 6-15. *The Additional Parameter to Tell Where to Redirect a Long-Running Conversation*

```
<pages>
    <page view-id="/flights.xhtml" no-conversation-view-id="/index.xhtml">
        Total For Trip - #{booking.totalCost}
    </page>
</pages>
```

This code indicates that if there is no long-running conversation, the request should be redirected to the `index.xhtml` page. If you are familiar with Seam 1, please note that this is a change to the framework. Previously, the `ifNotBegunOutcome` property on `@Conversational` was used, but this has since been deprecated.

Seam Debugging

I mentioned in Chapter 5 the ability to debug applications by calling the `/debug.seam` URI. I want to bring up this topic again, to point out the usefulness of the debugger when debugging a conversation. Figure 6-6 shows the debug page after starting three conversations on one particular session.

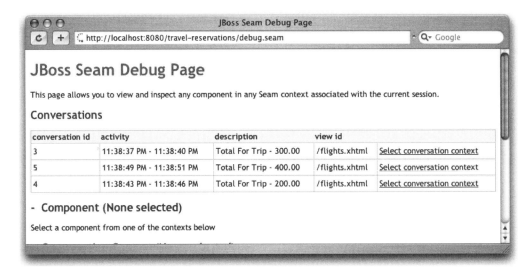

Figure 6-6. *Screen shot of the debug page after starting multiple conversations*

Hopefully this section helped enlighten you on how to use a Conversation context to its maximum benefit. By using this context, we can use workspaces to manage multiple conversations without having to create complex session management frameworks. In our example, we have used the Conversation context to make a simple travel reservation system have more-complex functionality, enabling the user to plan multiple trips and then select only one to book based on pricing.

More on How to Access Contexts

So except for the Business Process context, we have gone over all the possible contexts that you can use with Seam. The examples provided here and in later chapters should illuminate the usefulness that having more than three contexts gives the user. Before we move on, however, there are some extra items and information about the contexts in general to go over. Mainly, you need to know that classes can have multiple contexts and you need to learn where the contexts live.

Using Roles

You can now go ahead and use the various contexts for your POJOs or the properties on the POJOs. You can define what the scope is by using the annotation @Scope on the bean class itself. However, what happens if this POJO can be used in two different ways at different times? Basically, sometimes you want to be able to call this bean as a session-scoped object, and at other times an event-scoped object.

When you think about it, this situation is rather a predicament. After all, it's a bit of a waste to copy the class just to redefine it. Well, by using the @Role annotation, having one object support multiple scopes is not that hard, as you can see in Listing 6-16.

Listing 6-16. *A POJO Defined to Be Either Session or Event Scoped*

```
@Name("temp")
@Entity
@Scope(SESSION)
@Role(name="tempEvent", scope=EVENT)
public class Temp {
    // ...
}
```

We use the @Role annotation to define two things: the name and the scope. As with all Seam components, the name must be unique, which is why we have to define a different name for the role. So what if we decide we want to add an additional role to this as well? Because a modifier cannot have multiple annotations of the same type, we use another modifier—@Roles, as in Listing 6-17.

Listing 6-17. *A POJO Defined to be Either Session or Event Scoped*

```
@Name("temp")
@Entity
@Scope(SESSION)
@Roles({@Role(name="tempEvent", scope=EVENT)
@Role(name="tempPage", scope=PAGE)})
public class Temp {
    // ...
}
```

Using the `@Roles` annotation allows the user to embed an array of `@Role` annotations into the `@Roles` annotation. This allows the class to have multiple roles assigned to it. Do take note, though, that unlike most Java lists, there are no commas separating the contents of the `Roles` array.

■Note Even though `@Role` allows you to create multiple roles, you still need to mark the POJO with the `@Name` annotation to initially create it as a Seam component.

Where Do Contexts Live?

While reading about the preceding contexts, I think it is easy to see that a lot of thought was put into adding these as a major functional piece of Seam. These contexts provide functionality that is not usually found in most web architectures but has been deemed useful. Most of the reasoning for adding these items came about simply through the authors of Seam having issues at various assignments with being able to use only three specific Servlet contexts and having to create solutions to overcome this limitation. Their pain is our gain.

However, if you are the curious sort, you may be interested in where all of these live. Although the handling and maintaining of these contexts can become complex, the simple storage of them is not so bad. Seam uses a `Contexts` class, which contains numerous static member variables of `Context`. The `Contexts` are all stored as `ThreadLocals` so that multiple sessions won't have access to each other's instances. Each specific context (such as the Event, Page, and Session contexts) has a concrete corresponding class that implements `Context`. If you want to examine these further, they are stored in the package `org.jboss.seam.contexts`.

Accessing the Contexts

So if these contexts are stored in these readily accessible objects, what stops us from accessing them manually? The answer is, nothing. In fact, accessing them is actually easy and built in. We have access not only to the preceding contexts, but also to the Faces context.

Accessing the contexts is fairly straightforward. You use the `@In` annotation as follows:

```
@In private Context sessionContext
```

Table 6-3 lists other contexts that you can use.

Table 6-3. *Contexts That Are Injectable into Your POJO*

Name	Context
sessionContext	The Session context object
eventContext	The Event context object
pageContext	The Page context object
conversationContext	The Conversation context object
applicationContext	The Application context object
businessProcessContext	The Business Process context object
statelessContext	The Stateless context object
facesContext	The Faces context object

Order of Lookup

As in any framework (including Struts), when looking up an object by name, the application will default to looking it up in a certain order. The main reason is simple: you have to look up items in some order. Now remember that nothing prevents you from giving multiple contexts the same name (although this is not recommended). Doing so will prevent you from accessing some of them, however. The following is the order in which contexts are looked up:

1. Event context

2. Page context

3. Conversation context

4. Session context

5. Business Process context

6. Application context

This is the priority order for the contexts, so you can either directly specify the context you want to look for or—if the context does not matter— you can let Seam look up the object progressively through the contexts.

Default Bindings

As you are reading about the various components nested within Seam, one question you should be asking yourself is when to use which business object with these contexts. In the previous chapter, we started with some examples of how to annotate our EJB3 and JavaBean objects with Seam. However, you could not really fully appreciate or understand how these objects work without some entry-level knowledge of Seam as well as a better understanding of Seam contexts. Well now you have that knowledge, so in this section I will explain how the various business logic tier objects interact with Seam. I'll also tell you a bit about how to use them when building your system.

Stateless Session Beans

Stateless beans by default are in the Stateless context, and are going to be used in various interactions between your client and business tier. They are good at allowing their methods to be used as action listeners by the JSF pages. Therefore, they are good at doing some of the simpler types of lookups such as looking up an address from the database or logging in a user.

Entity Beans

Entity beans will primarily be used for our persistent information. As you have seen thus far, they are great in persisting data, and because they are POJOs, they are still easy to transport between layers. Because they are persistent objects, they are also perfect for use as backing beans to represent objects on the page. By default they are bound to the Conversation context as well.

Of course because these are persistent objects, there are certain limitations when using entity beans. You cannot use EBs for bijection or context demarcation, nor can you bind them to the Stateless context either. Also, invocation of an entity bean will not cause validation to occur. Validation must be triggered within the calling listeners as described previously.

Message-Driven Beans

I seriously debated whether to include MDBs in this section, because in reality they do not fit neatly into the flow of web applications. Do not get me wrong; they are extremely useful for asynchronous processing. And I have used them before quite effectively for long-running web calls as well. Because of all this, their Seam functionality is quite limited and is not bound to any context. They do support bijection and a few other items. If you are going to use a message-driven bean, it is best to just use it in the traditional manner.

Stateful Session Beans

Last but not least of the EJB3 components is the SFSB. I have included this one last because even though it is different from the SLSB and EB, it can be used in both backing beans and action listeners. If you are used to creating J2EE or Java EE applications, you are probably used to two things: not using SFSBs, and storing data in `HttpSession`. Well, you are going to have to get used to changing both of these when using Seam.

First, as mentioned in Chapter 5, SFSBs are inherently faster and less cumbersome than they were before. Second, because we are skipping the web layer, you really do not have easy access to `HttpSession` directly. This allows us to have Seam manage our state, and without this we would not be able to use things such as the Conversation context.

If you have your SFSB become a Seam component, it will bind by default to the Conversation context. You will then be able to store persistent data in it and will be able to use it as both a place to store backing beans and as a JSF action listener. However, because SFSBs are objects that tend to stay in state until they are triggered to be destroyed, they are not able to be set of context type Page.

JavaBeans

The last type of object that can be used with Seam is your plain old JavaBean. I think because of the focus on Seam's ability to skip the use of backing beans, JavaBeans are sometimes left out of the discussion. However, I feel they do serve a good purpose. And they can serve two big purposes.

First, with Seam we are able to get away from using backing beans, which are more often than not just being used to pass through data to the business logic tier. Most of the time, traditional JSF backing beans or Struts `Action` classes just serve the purpose of receiving data from the JSF/JSP pages and using that data to create objects that can be sent to the EJBs. Doing this task requires you to create more classes and more configurations, and the end result is just more points of failure. All of this is obviously a waste of code that Seam helps you avoid.

However, in some situations you actually do need a backing bean. Often in complex web applications, there is functionality a backing bean must perform before passing the parameters on to the business logic tier. This functionality is not business specific, but purely presentation tier. If you feel you have to do some intermediary processing that is more part of presentation tier than the business logic tier, you can use a normal JavaBean and yet still call your EJB3 business tier.

Another reason you may want to use JavaBeans is simply that using an EJB can be overkill. For the most part, there are two reasons to use a SLSB: either to use pooling or to run transactions. If you have no need for either, then why add the extra overhead?

Unlike the other EJBs, JavaBeans are stored by default in the Event context.

Summary

The point of this chapter was to give you a clear understanding of six of the contexts in Seam: Stateless, Session, Application, Event, Page, and Conversation. Each of these contexts is useful for persisting data from page to page and even within individual pages. I think you will agree that the Conversation context can definitely provide functionality that was cumbersome to code in previous web frameworks. The chapter ended with some more-advanced techniques of handling contexts in general.

The only topic that was left out of this chapter was the Business Process context. That is our final context to discuss and is the topic of Chapter 7.

CHAPTER 7

■■■

Business Process in Seam

Business process management tools are used by businesses to increase their speed and efficiency in the workplace. The basic purpose of business process tools is to create a way to document business processes outside of the code. A business process itself generally references a sequence of steps that are followed to complete a process—anything from creating a trouble ticket at work to ordering from an online merchant. The processes generally have alternate paths to follow and generally involve some level of multiple-user interaction. The business process tool we use for Seam is *JBoss Business Process Management (jBPM)*.

The Business Process context is different from the other Seam contexts because it provides mechanisms to interact with the jBPM. In addition, there is a page flow mechanism associated with jBPM, which can be used with or without it to manage the flow of pages. This mechanism allows for the use of dynamic page flows in our application. This means you can configure the flow in an XML file based on dynamic data of the application. For example, if you are performing calculations based on buying an item, you could configure the application so that if the total cost of the purchase is more than $100, the user is brought to page A, and if under, to page B.

Because jBPM is an entirely separate application, I wanted to segregate it into its own chapter. The entire jBPM is quite complex and does not have to be run with Seam or even EJB3. In fact, running jBPM with Seam or EJB3 requires many custom calls within the application to the jBPM framework. However, one of the advantages with Seam is that we are able to create these calls with annotations instead.

This chapter covers the jBPM business process and its page flow and how it relates directly to Seam. I will show you why and how to use the jBPM process, and after I cover the basics, I will show you how to inject it directly into Seam-annotated business components. As is shown in the Figure 7-1 road map, this chapter also focuses on the Seam interception, JSF tags, and Seam tags that will interact with the jBPM.

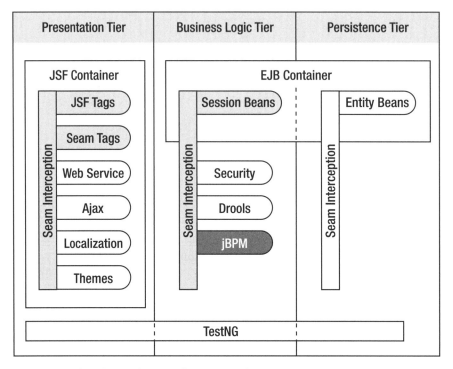

Figure 7-1. *This chapter's main focus is on the jBPM component.*

What Is JBoss jBPM?

The jBPM is a JBoss open source product designed to create business processes that can interact with people, applications, and services. This can be accomplished through workflow diagrams and by allowing for dynamic switching of processes. Using jBPM will allow you to have maximum flexibility in designing your workflow.

The brilliance of this is that developers can focus on implementing the business services and not have to constantly worry about flow and change. Conversely, business analysts can be left to worry about creating the process flow, and if they make changes later, switching to a different process is relatively painless.

There are two components of the jBPM system that I will present in this chapter: the process definitions and the page flow.

The process definitions are used to create tokens, which can then be managed by the system. These tokens are passed along from task to task until complete, and they can even be sent back to the same task. You can also swap out different tokens.

The other component in jBPM is the page flow, which can be used to create a sequence of pages that have specific steps. You can specify the action listener and page the jBPM call. This is similar to the process definition flow and can be used with it but can also work independently of it. The page flow controls the sequence of steps from page to page, including alternate paths and what actions are taken for each part of the flow.

Process Definitions

Your first step in understanding the jBPM component is to focus on the process definitions that jBPM provides. According to the JBoss documentation, jBPM is an "extensible workflow management system" that allows you to create a graphical or textual model of a workflow. The textual model is a defined XML file, and the graphical model is interpreted from this XML description through an Eclipse plug-in. I will show you how to use this and other tools to make the work easier in Chapter 10; for now we'll do it the hard way.

When I first read about process definitions and workflows and page flows, I kept thinking, "This is very interesting; I can't wait to use jBPM." Then my next thought was, "When do I use it?" JBoss provides some examples, but I found it hard to pinpoint the exact criteria for using jBPM. And I am very against using frameworks just for the sake of frameworks. I believe using frameworks just for the sake of frameworks has been abused by the Java community. So let's first examine when you are going to want to use jBPM. There are about three major items that you should have in place when using jBPM.

First (and this may seem like an obvious one), there needs to be a *workflow* that exists no matter how small—so that you need to complete step A, step B, and so forth, and each step can have a few moving parts to it as well. I will go over the workflow specifics later in this chapter; however, you can see a graphical representation of it in Figure 7-2.

Now although this workflow may encompass many actions (for example, a credit card application that asks you for information striped on many pages), this of course should not be your sole reason for using a process definition.

So the second point is that the framework should incorporate the concept of actors. An *actor* is a predefined application user, either a person or another system, that you set at login. An actor has a user ID defined for them and can belong to a set of groups. Because we are going to define actors and groups (such as a user group, manager group, admin group, and so forth), it would be useful for your application to have a hierarchy of groups. However, it is not necessary if the application is dealing with a collaborative website, just as long as you have the concept of assigning user(s) to a task.

The third and final item that your application should have is *tasks*. Now these tasks do not have to be specifically defined for the site but will be implicitly used. Consider a task as an instance of the workflow. If you have three steps in your workflow, your task starts at the beginning of the step and is finished at the end of it. Therefore, your website could have not only multiple tasks, but multiple simultaneous tasks in the system. Each of these tasks would then have certain actors assigned to them.

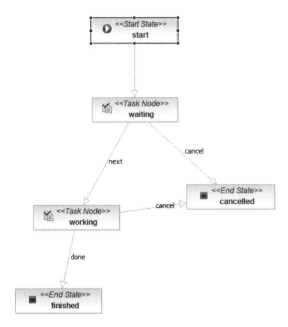

Figure 7-2. *An example of a workflow*

So the key here is to make sure your system makes use of the preceding three points. Now that being said, you do not have to meet all these requirements. You are going to have to judge for yourself whether the overhead is worth it. Because design and database interaction requires quite a bit of overhead, this overhead is worth it if you are using jBPM for the right purpose. A good example of this is the ticketing system outlined in this book.

How jBPM Works

Although I do not want to get into a lot of detail on how jBPM works behind the scenes, there are a few things you should know. The first step of using jBPM is to create an XML file that defines your workflow. In this workflow, you define a start and a middle and an end. All of the items of the XML including all the tasks, the sequence of tasks, and the actions associated with the tasks, are objects that are stored in a database. There are quite a bit of database interactions.

An Example for Using jBPM: Ticketing System

Before I dive into explaining the workflow, I am going to discuss the example we will be modeling, to give you a solid idea on why you want to use jBPM. Why is the ticketing system a good example? Well, let's start with what a ticketing system does. Our ticketing system allows a user to go to the site and create a ticket. The ticket then moves through a process, where people can update its current state, cancel the ticket, send it for work, and so forth. This allows an admin actor to maintain various tickets in various states. Because this scenario has a workflow, a set of tasks, and actors, it provides a good mechanism for using jBPM.

There are two basic steps to creating a jBPM project: creating the XML schema of the workflow and creating the code that will call it.

Creating a Workflow

Now that we have established this wonderful concept of using jBPM, it is time to learn how to design your workflow. There are two ways to do this, with the end result being an XML file. For now we are going to create the XML by hand. In Chapter 10 I will go over using tools to make our lives easier.

Let's start this with a basic example of the workflow we are going to use. We are going to be adding to this example, and I will be explaining it as we go along. The standard XML file is in Listing 7-1.

Listing 7-1. *Our Workflow XML File*

```xml
<?xml version="1.0" encoding="UTF-8"?>

<!DOCTYPE process-definition PUBLIC
                    "-//jBpm/jBpm Mapping DTD 2.0//EN"
                    "http://jbpm.org/dtd/processdefinition-2.0.dtd">

<process-definition name="TicketingSystem">

    <start-state name="start">
        <transition to="waiting"/>
    </start-state>

    <task-node name="waiting" end-tasks="true">
        <task name="taskAssignment" description="Tasks waiting for assignment">
            <assignment pooled-actors="ticket-user"/>
        </task>

        <transition name="next" to="working"/>
        <transition name="cancel" to="cancelled"/>
    </task-node>
```

```
    <task-node name="working" end-tasks="true">
        <task name="taskWorking" description="Tasks are reassigned to be workable">
            <assignment pooled-actors="ticket-user"/>
        </task>

        <transition name="done" to="finished"/>
        <transition name="cancel" to="cancelled"/>
    </task-node>

    <end-state name="finished"/>
    <end-state name="cancelled"/>
</process-definition>
```

This is our standard XML file. It starts by defining the name for the process. Then it defines the start state of the process. After that it defines multiple task nodes. You can have one or multiple task nodes, which in turn contain multiple tasks. At the very end you have an end state.

Along with tasks, there are also other items you can include, such as forks, decisions, or basically anything that you can use to help guide you through decision-making possibilities.

When a workflow starts, it creates a token, which contains the elements that the system will be providing work on. The token will live until it reaches the end state. Later in this chapter, you will see more-concrete examples on how this component works.

Components Involved in Creating a Process Definition

So the XML file in Listing 7-1 may look fancy, but you probably could not make out too much of it besides the superficial—where there is a start and an end, and the tasks in between. However, you have quite a few choices based on your needs when creating your workflows.

Although I will not go over everything in this chapter's example, my hope is that it will give you a firm basis for creating whatever workflow you need.

Start State

The *start state* is your entryway into the workflow. This component will start you on the workflow and can be defined with a view ID as well. The start state's main attribute holds the transition component. Listing 7-2 provides an example of a start state.

Listing 7-2. *An Example of Using the Start State Component*

```
<start-state name="start">
    <transition name="wait "to="waiting"/>
 </start-state>
```

As you can see, the name is defined as `start`, and because there is no task, the start state is defined to move to a task labeled `waiting`.

Transition

The preceding example—and quite a few examples you are going to see—will have *transitions*. These define what task or state the user should be forwarded to next. The name defined there will always point to a `name` on another component. In Listing 7-2, we defined a `name` and a `to`. The `name` is not necessarily needed because there is only one transition, and by default the application would have to go to that transition labeled in `to`. If there had been multiple transitions, a `name` would be required to differentiate them.

Task Node

If we were to follow along chronologically in our workflow, the *task node* would be next. The task node is quite a complex and important node. This is where all the work will be taking place within the token. Any operations that the token needs to run will be here. A typical task node looks like Listing 7-3 and has a task and a transition. In fact, there can even be multiple tasks and multiple transitions.

Listing 7-3. *An Example of a Task Node with a Task and an Assignment*

```
<task-node name="task-step1" end-tasks="true">
      <task name="task-step1" description="#{task-step1.description}">
          <assignment actor-id="user"/>
      </task>
      <transition name="cancel" to="cancelled"/>
</task-node>
```

Task

Tasks are used to perform the work of the token. Here is where most of your actual work on the token will occur. Because nodes have multiple tasks, you can control the flow between each task. I will show you how to implement it later in this chapter. One other item of importance to note is the `actor` assignment. This is a required field for the task and tells the system what actor is allowed to have access to the task on the token.

Actor Assignment

One of the benefits of using jBPM is that you can specify an *actor* for each task. This defines who has control of the token to process for that task. There are two types of assignment definitions you can use; you can define the item either per actor or per group. Listing 7-4 provides two examples of defining per actor.

Listing 7-4. *Defining Actors for a Task by Using the Actor ID*

```
<task name="step1" description="Generic Step">
    <assignment actor-id="#{actor.id}"/>
</task>

<task name="step1" description="Generic Step">
    <assignment actor-id="user1"/>
</task>
```

The first example uses a regular expression to reference the actor ID. This will allow anyone who is logged in to access that task. The second example, however, references one particular user by using a hard-coded value. In reality, when you use the actor assignment, you might instead want to reference a value totally different from one saved to a database.

Instead of referencing a particular user, another option is to reference a particular group such as an admin or managers group. Listing 7-5 provides an example of this declaration.

Listing 7-5. *Defining Actors for a Task by Using Pooled Actors*

```
<task name="step1" description="Generic Step">
    <assignment pooled-actors="ticket-admin"/>
</task>
```

This example allows access to the task based on whether the user has been assigned to the `ticket-admin` group. You can use a comma-delimited string here if you want multiple actors to have access to this ticket as well. In addition, you can use JSF regular expressions to reference either a string or a string array for multiple actor groups.

Another option you have for assignment is to use Drools for the assignment piece. I will show you how to do this in the last part of Chapter 8, because Drools requires a few customizations to use.

State

The *state* component is used to signal a wait within the application—when the system needs to wait for a process to come back from an external system. After the response is received, the application will send a signal to the token that it is available.

Decision

Another key item for process definitions is the *decision*, which allows jBPM to decide which task nodes to go to. This can be accomplished by using regular expressions to check back with an object. Listing 7-6 provides an example of a decision.

Listing 7-6. *A Decision on Where to Go Based on Whether an Item Is Positive or Negative*

```
<decision name="decide" expression="#{numberCheck.isPositive}">
    <transition name="positive" to="pos-task-node"/>
    <transition name="negative" to="neg-task-node"/>
</decision>
```

This example is determining whether some number is positive. If it is, the user can go to the pos-task-node; if the number is negative, the user goes to the neg-task-node. The method isPositive will be the one returning the string values positive or negative.

Fork

In a decision, the application is using criteria to decide which path to choose, either path A or path B. However, a *fork* differs in that it allows the application to run both paths simultaneously. Listing 7-7 shows an example of a fork.

Listing 7-7. *A Fork That Has You Run create-task1 and create-task2*

```
<fork name="run-processes">
    <transition name="create-task1" to="task1"></transition>
    <transition name="create-task2" to="task2"></transition>
</fork>
```

When this fork is transitioned to, it will call both nodes task1 and task2 to be run concurrently.

Join

After using the preceding fork to fork off to separate concurrent branches, you may need to bring those nodes back together after they are done processing. This is what a *join* does. It uses tokens from the same parent, and if one or more of the joined nodes is still running, the ones that are already complete go into a wait state to wait for all the joined nodes to be complete. Listing 7-8 shows an example of a join building up from our fork.

Listing 7-8. *A Join Node That Joins Two States Together*

```
<state name="task1">
    <transition to="joinPoint" />
</state>

<state name="task2">
    <transition to="joinPoint" />
</state>

<join name=" joinPoint ">
    <transition to="end" />
</join>
```

Here the two tasks we sent to the fork come back together. In reality, you would probably have a few tasks in between, but the end result is that they join back. The state nodes allow you to wait for the processing to complete.

End State

Well, all along between these items, we were passing the token between the different components. To finally end the token, the application will reach an *end state*. You can have multiple end states in your workflow. Listing 7-9 shows an example of two.

Listing 7-9. *A finished and cancelled End State*

```
<end-state name="finished"/>
<end-state name="cancelled"/>
```

Process Definition Creation in Seam

So by now you should have an understanding of how to create your process definition file and what you need to write to create each step. The only thing left now is to tie the process definition workflow to our code. Under normal processes, this requires a decent amount of Java code. However, with Seam the process is relatively painless and we can do it all with annotations. We will start by configuring Seam to use jBPM workflows. Then we will start the process, and finally define the tasks needed for each of the tasks.

Configuring jBPM with Seam

Configuring the application to use jBPM is simple. The configuration requires adding a JAR file and updating two XML files.

The JAR file `jbpm-3.1.2.jar` is required for jBPM and it is located under the `lib` directory of the Seam distribution. We need to place this JAR file at the root of the EAR and then add a reference to the JAR in the `application.xml` file. The newly modified `application.xml` with the jBPM JAR file is displayed in Listing 7-10.

Listing 7-10. *The Modified application.xml with the jBPM JAR File*

```
<application>
    <display-name>Ticketing System</display-name>

    <module>
        <ejb>chapter7_ts-business.ejb3</ejb>
    </module>
    <module>
        <web>
            <web-uri>chapter7_ts.war</web-uri>
            <context-root>/ticketing-system</context-root>
        </web>
    </module>
    <module>
        <java>jboss-seam.jar</java>
    </module>
    <module>
        <java>jbpm-3.1.2.jar</java>
    </module>
</application>
```

Now that we have configured the application to have the jBPM files in its class path, we have to configure it to read the XML process definitions. The process definition files can be defined in `components.xml`. Listing 7-11 shows the component definition.

Listing 7-11. *The jBPM Process Definition XML Defined in components.xml*

```
<component class="org.jboss.seam.core.Jbpm">
    <property name="processDefinitions">ticketing-system.jpdl.xml</property>
</component>
```

That is almost all you have to do to configure jBPM to work with Seam. The last thing, of course, is to make sure you include the jBPM JAR file in the build, in the root of the EAR.

jBPM-Specific Configuration Files

In addition to the updates to the existing configuration files and the addition of a JAR, you also need to add a couple of custom configuration files to the root of the EAR. The first one to add is a Hibernate configuration file. As I said earlier, jBPM works by interacting with a database, and it uses Hibernate as its persistence mechanism for the database. You can use the `hibernate.cfg.xml` file that comes with the jBPM release. Listing 7-12 displays this file.

Listing 7-12. *The hibernate.cfg.xml File for jBPM That Needs to be Put into the Root of the EAR*

```
<?xml version='1.0' encoding='utf-8'?>

<!DOCTYPE hibernate-configuration PUBLIC
        "-//Hibernate/Hibernate Configuration DTD 3.0//EN"
        "http://hibernate.sourceforge.net/hibernate-configuration-3.0.dtd">

<hibernate-configuration>
  <session-factory>

    <property name="show_sql">true</property>
    <property name="connection.datasource">java:/DefaultDS</property>
    <property name="transaction.factory_class">
        org.hibernate.transaction.JTATransactionFactory
    </property>
    <property name="transaction.manager_lookup_class">
        org.hibernate.transaction.JBossTransactionManagerLookup
    </property>
```

```xml
<property name="cache.provider_class">
    org.hibernate.cache.HashtableCacheProvider
</property>
<property name="hbm2ddl.auto">create-drop</property>
<!-- property name="transaction.flush_before_completion">true</property-->

<!-- hql queries and type defs -->
<mapping resource="org/jbpm/db/hibernate.queries.hbm.xml" />

<!-- graph.def mapping files -->
<mapping resource="org/jbpm/graph/def/ProcessDefinition.hbm.xml"/>
<mapping resource="org/jbpm/graph/def/Node.hbm.xml"/>
<mapping resource="org/jbpm/graph/def/Transition.hbm.xml"/>
<mapping resource="org/jbpm/graph/def/Event.hbm.xml"/>
<mapping resource="org/jbpm/graph/def/Action.hbm.xml"/>
<mapping resource="org/jbpm/graph/def/SuperState.hbm.xml"/>
<mapping resource="org/jbpm/graph/def/ExceptionHandler.hbm.xml"/>
<mapping resource="org/jbpm/instantiation/Delegation.hbm.xml"/>

<!-- graph.node mapping files -->
<mapping resource="org/jbpm/graph/node/StartState.hbm.xml"/>
<mapping resource="org/jbpm/graph/node/EndState.hbm.xml"/>
<mapping resource="org/jbpm/graph/node/ProcessState.hbm.xml"/>
<mapping resource="org/jbpm/graph/node/Decision.hbm.xml"/>
<mapping resource="org/jbpm/graph/node/Fork.hbm.xml"/>
<mapping resource="org/jbpm/graph/node/Join.hbm.xml"/>
<mapping resource="org/jbpm/graph/node/State.hbm.xml"/>
<mapping resource="org/jbpm/graph/node/TaskNode.hbm.xml"/>

<!-- context.def mapping files -->
<mapping resource="org/jbpm/context/def/ContextDefinition.hbm.xml"/>
<mapping resource="org/jbpm/context/def/VariableAccess.hbm.xml"/>

<!-- taskmgmt.def mapping files -->
<mapping resource="org/jbpm/taskmgmt/def/TaskMgmtDefinition.hbm.xml"/>
<mapping resource="org/jbpm/taskmgmt/def/Swimlane.hbm.xml"/>
<mapping resource="org/jbpm/taskmgmt/def/Task.hbm.xml"/>
<mapping resource="org/jbpm/taskmgmt/def/TaskController.hbm.xml"/>

<!-- module.def mapping files -->
<mapping resource="org/jbpm/module/def/ModuleDefinition.hbm.xml"/>
```

```
<!-- bytes mapping files -->
<mapping resource="org/jbpm/bytes/ByteArray.hbm.xml"/>

<!-- file.def mapping files -->
<mapping resource="org/jbpm/file/def/FileDefinition.hbm.xml"/>

<!-- scheduler.def mapping files -->
<mapping resource="org/jbpm/scheduler/def/CreateTimerAction.hbm.xml"/>
<mapping resource="org/jbpm/scheduler/def/CancelTimerAction.hbm.xml"/>

<!-- graph.exe mapping files -->
<mapping resource="org/jbpm/graph/exe/Comment.hbm.xml"/>
<mapping resource="org/jbpm/graph/exe/ProcessInstance.hbm.xml"/>
<mapping resource="org/jbpm/graph/exe/Token.hbm.xml"/>
<mapping resource="org/jbpm/graph/exe/RuntimeAction.hbm.xml"/>

<!-- module.exe mapping files -->
<mapping resource="org/jbpm/module/exe/ModuleInstance.hbm.xml"/>

<!-- context.exe mapping files -->
<mapping resource="org/jbpm/context/exe/ContextInstance.hbm.xml"/>
<mapping resource="org/jbpm/context/exe/TokenVariableMap.hbm.xml"/>
<mapping resource="org/jbpm/context/exe/VariableInstance.hbm.xml"/>
<mapping
  resource="org/jbpm/context/exe/variableinstance/ByteArrayInstance.hbm.xml"/>
<mapping resource="org/jbpm/context/exe/variableinstance/DateInstance.hbm.xml"/>
<mapping
    resource="org/jbpm/context/exe/variableinstance/DoubleInstance.hbm.xml"/>
<mapping
resource="org/jbpm/context/exe/variableinstance/HibernateLongInstance.hbm.xml"/>
<mapping
resource="org/jbpm/context/exe/variableinstance/HibernateStringInstance.hbm.xml"/>
<mapping resource="org/jbpm/context/exe/variableinstance/LongInstance.hbm.xml"/>
<mapping resource="org/jbpm/context/exe/variableinstance/NullInstance.hbm.xml"/>
<mapping
  resource="org/jbpm/context/exe/variableinstance/StringInstance.hbm.xml"/>

<!-- msg.db mapping files -->
<mapping resource="org/jbpm/msg/Message.hbm.xml"/>
<mapping resource="org/jbpm/msg/db/TextMessage.hbm.xml"/>
<mapping resource="org/jbpm/command/ExecuteActionCommand.hbm.xml"/>
<mapping resource="org/jbpm/command/ExecuteNodeCommand.hbm.xml"/>
```

```
<mapping resource="org/jbpm/command/SignalCommand.hbm.xml"/>
<mapping resource="org/jbpm/command/TaskInstanceEndCommand.hbm.xml"/>

<!-- taskmgmt.exe mapping files -->
<mapping resource="org/jbpm/taskmgmt/exe/TaskMgmtInstance.hbm.xml"/>
<mapping resource="org/jbpm/taskmgmt/exe/TaskInstance.hbm.xml"/>
<mapping resource="org/jbpm/taskmgmt/exe/PooledActor.hbm.xml"/>
<mapping resource="org/jbpm/taskmgmt/exe/SwimlaneInstance.hbm.xml"/>

<!-- scheduler.exe mapping files -->
<mapping resource="org/jbpm/scheduler/exe/Timer.hbm.xml"/>

<!-- logging mapping files -->
<mapping resource="org/jbpm/logging/log/ProcessLog.hbm.xml"/>
<mapping resource="org/jbpm/logging/log/MessageLog.hbm.xml"/>
<mapping resource="org/jbpm/logging/log/CompositeLog.hbm.xml"/>
<mapping resource="org/jbpm/graph/log/ActionLog.hbm.xml"/>
<mapping resource="org/jbpm/graph/log/NodeLog.hbm.xml"/>
<mapping resource="org/jbpm/graph/log/ProcessInstanceCreateLog.hbm.xml"/>
<mapping resource="org/jbpm/graph/log/ProcessInstanceEndLog.hbm.xml"/>
<mapping resource="org/jbpm/graph/log/SignalLog.hbm.xml"/>
<mapping resource="org/jbpm/graph/log/TokenCreateLog.hbm.xml"/>
<mapping resource="org/jbpm/graph/log/TokenEndLog.hbm.xml"/>
<mapping resource="org/jbpm/graph/log/TransitionLog.hbm.xml"/>
<mapping resource="org/jbpm/context/log/VariableLog.hbm.xml"/>
<mapping resource="org/jbpm/context/log/VariableCreateLog.hbm.xml"/>
<mapping resource="org/jbpm/context/log/VariableDeleteLog.hbm.xml"/>
<mapping resource="org/jbpm/context/log/VariableUpdateLog.hbm.xml"/>
<mapping
  resource="org/jbpm/context/log/variableinstance/ByteArrayUpdateLog.hbm.xml"/>
<mapping
  resource="org/jbpm/context/log/variableinstance/DateUpdateLog.hbm.xml"/>
<mapping
  resource="org/jbpm/context/log/variableinstance/DoubleUpdateLog.hbm.xml"/>
<mapping
  resource="org/jbpm/context/log/variableinstance/HibernateLongUpdateLog.hbm.xml"/>
<mapping
  resource="org/jbpm/context/log/variableinstance/HibernateStringUpdateLog.hbm.xml"/>
<mapping
  resource="org/jbpm/context/log/variableinstance/LongUpdateLog.hbm.xml"/>
<mapping
  resource="org/jbpm/context/log/variableinstance/StringUpdateLog.hbm.xml"/>
```

```
    <mapping resource="org/jbpm/taskmgmt/log/TaskLog.hbm.xml"/>
    <mapping resource="org/jbpm/taskmgmt/log/TaskCreateLog.hbm.xml"/>
    <mapping resource="org/jbpm/taskmgmt/log/TaskAssignLog.hbm.xml"/>
    <mapping resource="org/jbpm/taskmgmt/log/TaskEndLog.hbm.xml"/>
    <mapping resource="org/jbpm/taskmgmt/log/SwimlaneLog.hbm.xml"/>
    <mapping resource="org/jbpm/taskmgmt/log/SwimlaneCreateLog.hbm.xml"/>
    <mapping resource="org/jbpm/taskmgmt/log/SwimlaneAssignLog.hbm.xml"/>

  </session-factory>
</hibernate-configuration>
```

In this example, the application is configured to use `java:/DefaultDS` in JBoss as its database persistence. The other file we are going to have to include is a jBPM-specific configuration file. This is another cut-and-paste example you can use from a jBPM distribution. Listing 7-13 shows the XML file.

Listing 7-13. *The XML jbpm.cfg.xml File for jBPM That Needs to Be Put into the Root of the EAR*

```
<jbpm-configuration>

  <jbpm-context>
    <service name="persistence">
      <factory>
        <bean class="org.jbpm.persistence.db.DbPersistenceServiceFactory">
          <field name="isTransactionEnabled"><false/></field>
        </bean>
      </factory>
    </service>
    <service name="message" factory="org.jbpm.msg.db.DbMessageServiceFactory" />
    <service name="scheduler"
      factory="org.jbpm.scheduler.db.DbSchedulerServiceFactory" />
    <service name="logging" factory="org.jbpm.logging.db.DbLoggingServiceFactory" />
    <service name="authentication"
   factory="org.jbpm.security.authentication.DefaultAuthenticationServiceFactory"/>
  </jbpm-context>

</jbpm-configuration>
```

Creating the Process Definition

The first step to start the process of using a jBPM process definition is to create the process and the associated token. The purpose of creating the process is to tell the system that a new token is out there and that we are going to have to manage it. Also in this step we will be identifying what fields are needed for tracking the ticket. These fields will be tied to the token, in this case a ticket.

Now although the token itself is persisted to the jBPM database, you also have the option to persist parts of it to your own database. This will undoubtedly be necessary because you probably want outside systems to be able to track back to the object. The thing to make sure of is that you save to the ticket the ID to track the ticket with.

So the create task starts when we are submitting a ticket. This method has been marked with the @CreateProcess annotation, and the items we want to save to the token are marked with ScopeType.BUSINESS_PROCESS. Listing 7-14 defines the code.

Listing 7-14. *The Create Process Definition*

```
@Stateful
@Name("ticketCreation")
public class TicketCreationAction implements TicketCreation {

    @PersistenceContext(type=PersistenceContextType.EXTENDED)
    EntityManager em;

    @Logger
    Log log;

    @In(create = true)
    @Out
    private Ticket ticket;

    @Out(scope=ScopeType.BUSINESS_PROCESS, required=false)
    long ticketId;
    @Out(scope=ScopeType.BUSINESS_PROCESS, required=false)
    String ticketName;
    @Out(scope=ScopeType.BUSINESS_PROCESS, required=false)
    String owner;

    @CreateProcess(definition="TicketingSystem")
    public String createTicket() {
        ticket.setTicketComplete(false);
```

```
        em.persist(ticket);

        // save fields of the ticket.
        ticketId = ticket.getTicketId();
        owner = ticket.getOwner();
        ticketName = ticket.getName();

        return "/ticket_list.xhtml";
    }

    @Destroy
    @Remove
    public void destroy() {
        log.info("destroy");
    }

}
```

Here we have a SFSB with the method `createTicket()` annotated to create the process `TicketingSystem`. The method will first save the ticket to the database. Then we save the `BUSINESS_PROCESS`-scoped fields based on what is in the ticket. This will be used later to display the ticket on the ticket list page. We are saving the ID, the name, and the owner of the ticket, and then forwarding this data to the list page.

Resuming a Process

If you have a process that is already started and want to resume it, this is performed with the `@ResumeProcess` annotation. This method will take the parameter `processIdParameter`, which defaults to `processed`.

Viewing Tasks

The next page of the system in Listing 7-14 sent you to the ticket list page. Now for a normal user, you may not have anything displayed. However, if you are an administrator, you are able to view the page, find any tickets, and assign them to users. Suppose we add one ticket. The page in Figure 7-3 then displays, showing the list of tickets out there.

As you can see, the task is currently in the assignment stage, waiting to be used. However, there are also four other areas on the screen. This code uses table data to display the list with the `<h:dataTable>` tag. Listing 7-15 shows an example of our code for the first ticket listing.

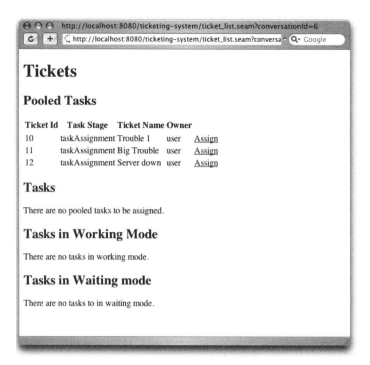

Figure 7-3. *The list page displaying the list of the tickets viewable to the user*

Listing 7-15. *The Display of the Pooled Tasks*

```
<h2>Pooled Tasks</h2>
    <c:choose>
        <c:when test="#{empty pooledTaskInstanceList}">
            <p>There are no pooled tasks to be assigned.</p>
        </c:when>
        <c:otherwise>
            <h:dataTable value="#{pooledTaskInstanceList}"
                        var="task"
                        styleClass="dvdtable"
                        headerClass="dvdtablehead"
                        rowClasses="dvdtableodd,dvdtableeven"
                        columnClasses="dvdtablecol">
                <h:column>
                    <f:facet name="header">Ticket Id</f:facet>
                    #{task.variables['ticketId']}
                </h:column>
```

```
        <h:column>
            <f:facet name="header">Task Stage</f:facet>
            <h:outputText value="#{task.name}" />
        </h:column>
        <h:column>
            <f:facet name="header">Ticket Name</f:facet>
            #{task.variables['ticketName']}
        </h:column>
        <h:column>
            <f:facet name="header">Owner</f:facet>
            #{task.variables['owner']}
        </h:column>
        <h:column>
            <s:link action="#{pooledTask.assignToCurrentActor}"
                    taskInstance="#{task}"
                    value="Assign" linkStyle="button"/>
        </h:column>
    </h:dataTable>
  </c:otherwise>
</c:choose>
```

Most of the preceding code should look like a fairly standard display of a table. The only unfamiliar part may be pooledTaskInstanceList. This is a core Seam component that you have access to. There are quite a few options you can put in the code; I have listed them in Table 7-1.

Table 7-1. *Optional List of jBPM Tokens to Display*

Type	Description
pooledTaskInstanceList	Stores a list of pooled tasks available to be assigned to yourself.
taskInstanceList	Contains a list of tasks that are currently assigned to the logged-in user.
taskInstanceListForType['task_name']	Displays a list of tasks currently assigned for that particular task type. The task_name correlates to the task name in our XML.

So the rest of the lists are similar to the preceding code except we switch out the types for each. Now in the other area of the code, we print out two items: items that are properties on task, and items that are parameters on task.variables[]. The ones that are properties, such as #{task.name}, are properties directly on the object. In this case, the task name refers to the name of the task. Now #{task.variables['owner']} is the more interesting reference. Remember back in Listing 7-14 that we defined the page-level business process variables, `ticketId`, `ticketName`, and `owner`. Well, here is where you can reference those objects. This example displays only `ticketName`.

Finally, the last item on the row is a link to assign the task to the current user. The link `#{pooledTask.assignToCurrentActor}` calls the core Seam component `poolTask`, which will assign the task to whomever is logged in. After the task is assigned, it will show up in the Tasks section of the page as well as in the Tasks in Waiting Mode section, as in Figure 7-4.

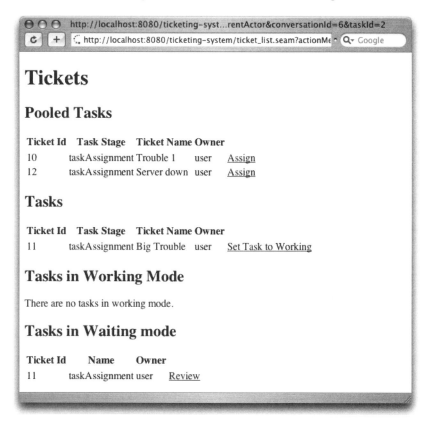

Figure 7-4. *The page after assigning a task to yourself*

Creating a Task

The next step is to create a task. In the XML file we defined the tasks under `<task-node>`. The tasks are defined individually per Seam component. Each Seam component can have only one task, and annotations define where methods start and end a task. Listing 7-16 defines the task. After a task starts, the task will be in start mode and you can perform any operation you want on it.

When you are ready to complete the task, you can call one of the ending methods. You can have multiple end tasks and begin tasks in your code. Check out the example in Listing 7-16.

Listing 7-16. *The Task Defined*

```
@Stateful
@Name("taskAssignment")
public class TicketAssignmentAction implements TicketAssignment {

    @Logger
    Log log;

    @PersistenceContext(type=PersistenceContextType.EXTENDED)
    EntityManager em;

    @Out(required=false, scope=ScopeType.CONVERSATION)
    Ticket ticket;

    @In(required=false)
    Long ticketId;

    @In(required = false)
    String name;

    @BeginTask
    public String viewTask() {
        ticket = (Ticket) em.find(Ticket.class, ticketId);
        return "/ticket_list.xhtml";
    }

    @EndTask(transition="next")
    public String assign() {
        if (name == null || name.length()==0) {
            return null;
        }

        ticket.setName(name);

        return "/ticket_list.xhtml";
    }
```

```
    @EndTask(transition="cancel")
    public String cancel() {
        return "/ticket_list.xhtml";
    }

    @Destroy
    @Remove
    public void destroy() {

    }
}
```

When starting a task, we will also start a long-running conversation. This is necessary because the task needs to keep track of its conversation. This long-running conversation is the same type of conversation we used when discussing Page contexts in Chapter 6. This time the conversation will run from the start of @StartTask to the end of @EndTask.

The @StartTask-defined method processes items for the task. Assuming there is a successful completion of the method, it will create a long-running conversation. A successful completion is defined as no exceptions thrown and a return of a non-null response. The following are the parameters allowed for @StartTask:

taskIdParameter: This will correspond to the name of a request parameter that holds the ID of the task. If this property is not filled in, Seam will default to taskId.

flushMode: If you are running this application by using the Seam-managed Hibernate transactions, this will specify the flush mode.

The @EndTask method ends the long-running conversation upon successful completion of the method. After the method is completed successfully, it triggers a transition to be called. The method has a transition property that will transition to the name defined if there is one. If not, the task will just transition to the default transition. There are two other properties that you can define as well:

ifOutcome: This will specify the JSF outcome(s) triggered at the end of a successful task.

beforeRedirect: This will specify when the long-running conversation is destroyed. If it is true, it will be destroyed before the redirect. If it is false, it will be destroyed after the redirect. This is false by default.

The Actor

Actor assignment is an important part of your process and in fact if you do not have your actor created, you will not even be able to create a token in the first place. The *actor* is a Seam component that is stored in the session. In general, you should create your actor component when you are logging in to the website. The following code shows the LoginAction, which would be the same code that is called by a login screen.

```
@Name("loginAction")
public class LoginAction implements Login {

    @Logger
    Log log;

    @In(create=true)
    private Actor actor;

    private String user;

    public String loginTicketingSystem() {
        actor.setId(user);

        if (user.equals("admin")) {
            actor.getGroupActorIds().add("ticket-admin");
        }
        else {
            actor.getGroupActorIds().add("ticket-user");
        }
        log.info("Log in with #{actor} - ticket system");
        return "/ticket_create.xhtml";
    }

    public String getUser() {
        return user;
    }

    public void setUser(String user) {
        this.user = user;
    }
}
```

You can inject the actor component. The name of the component is `actor`, and so as long as you name your variable the same, you will be fine. Otherwise, you will have to set the value parameter on the `@In` annotation to `value="actor"`. So the first step is to set the ID, and the second step is to set the group IDs. Here we set the actor group ID as `ticket-admin` for anyone logging in as admin, and `ticket-user` for any other user.

Resuming a Task

If you have a task that is not complete and want to resume the task, you would use `@BeginTask`. The task works the same as `@StartTask` and has the same properties.

Switching Process Definitions

Sometimes it can become necessary to switch to a different process flow. Think about our ticketing system. You may have one workflow for normal tickets and another for a fast-track workflow needed in an emergency. Switching workflows could be totally at the discretion of a user or administrator. You could put each process into one gigantic work-flow, but then manageability becomes in issue. Fortunately, by using Seam and jBPM, we can switch process definitions dynamically.

The one thing to realize about process definitions is that they are just that—definitions. There is nothing that makes them 100 percent strict. After all, if they were, then there would not be much difference between using them and hard-coding the flow and logic in your code. You can even switch them on the fly, and in fact it is a pretty easy process. All it takes is one component and some JSF code.

Let's first go over the Java code in Listing 7-17.

Listing 7-17. *The Seam Component That Will Allow You to Switch Process Definitions*

```
@Name("processDefinitionAction")
@Scope(ScopeType.APPLICATION)
public class ProcessDefinitionAction {

    static final String[] PROCESS_DEFINITIONS = {
            "process1.jpdl.xml",
            "process2.jpdl.xml",
            "process3.jpdl.xml",
            "process4.jpdl.xml"
        };

    @In(value="org.jboss.seam.core.jbpm")
    private Jbpm jbpm;
```

```java
@In
private JbpmContext jbpmContext;

public List<SelectItem> getProcessDefinitions()
{
    List<SelectItem> definitionList = new ArrayList<SelectItem>();
    for (String definition: PROCESS_DEFINITIONS)
    {
        definitionList.add(new SelectItem(definition));
    }
    return definitionList;
}

private String currentProcessDefinition;

public String getCurrentProcessDefinition()
{
    return currentProcessDefinition;
}

public void setCurrentProcessDefinition(String def)
{
    currentProcessDefinition = def;
}

public String changeProcessDefinition()
{
    jbpmContext.deployProcessDefinition(
            jbpm.getProcessDefinitionFromResource(currentProcessDefinition) );
    // returns you back to your original page.
    return null;
}
}
```

This listing defines a few things we are going to need in order to change the process definitions:

- The XML process definition files that we are able to switch between

- The injected Seam jBPM component

- The jBPM context component

The getProcessDefinitions() method will be called by our JSF page in order to get a list of the definitions. Of course, we could have just hard-coded the definitions in the JSF page. The last method, changeProcessDefinition(), is used to do the actual switching of process definitions and will return you back to the page after it is complete. The JSF page that displays this is in Listing 7-18.

Listing 7-18. *The JSF Page to Display Our Process Switching*

```
<f:subview rendered="#{login.admin}"
          xmlns="http://www.w3.org/1999/xhtml"
          xmlns:ui="http://java.sun.com/jsf/facelets"
          xmlns:f="http://java.sun.com/jsf/core"
          xmlns:h="http://java.sun.com/jsf/html">

    <h:form>
        <h:selectOneMenu
          value="#{processDefinitionAction.currentProcessDefinition}">
            <f:selectItems value="#{processDefinitionAction.processDefinitions}"/>
        </h:selectOneMenu><br/>

        <h:commandButton action="#{processDefinitionAction.changeProcessDefinition}"
            value="Change"/>
    </h:form>
</f:subview>
```

The preceding listing defines a simple select drop-down that retrieves the process definition list from our component and then will call the changeProcessDefinition method when wanting to switch between components.

Page Flow Definitions

The other item associated with jBPM and mentioned at the beginning of this chapter is the page flow definition. We are treating it as a separate concept and technology, because although it is packaged with jBPM, it can be used independently of a business process definition. The purpose of the page flow is to give some independence to the way an application flows and what actions and decisions can happen in each place. This also allows you to easily switch what flow to use based on events or outside conditions. As with the business process definitions, this ability allows your flows to become independent of the application code.

Of course, as with all frameworks you learn about, one of the biggest things to do is learn when to use it and when not. So carefully picking your battles is the key. For the right application, jBPM page flows can provide quite a bit of flexibility. Let's start with when *not* to use page flow definitions.

Page flow definitions do not work well on web pages that are flow independent—in other words, when you can switch from page to page to page independently of a process. For example, look at the website use case diagram with independent flow shown in Figure 7-5.

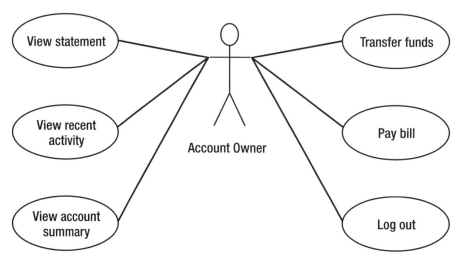

Figure 7-5. *An example of a website with independent flow*

This is an example of a credit card/banking website with multiple pages to define screen flow. There are usually a variety of screens for such processes as viewing your transactions, making a payment, changing your address, and so forth. The main menu bar links at the top will not use a page flow. The actor here represents the person using the website, and that user can access any page independently. The user can go from transactions, back to banking, and so forth.

Now consider a page that links to multiple pages in a row. For example, when you pay a bill, you are not filling out only one page but multiple pages with different flows based on input. Figure 7-6 shows an example of a user paying an account.

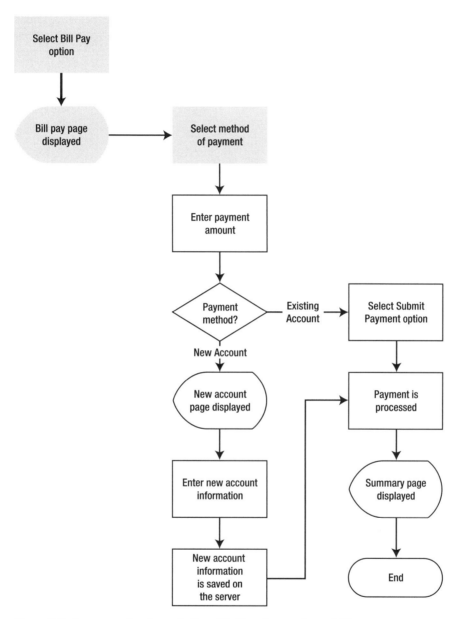

Figure 7-6. *An example of a website with flow for paying a bill*

As you can see on this page, paying a bill requires multiple steps to complete. You have to select the amount you want to pay and the payment method, and then pay the bill. The page also has alternate paths of flow throughout it. Depending on whether you select a previous account or need to create a new account, the flow changes. Listing 7-19 shows the XML page flow definition for our application.

Listing 7-19. *An Example of a Page Flow XML*

```xml
<?xml version="1.0"?>

<pageflow-definition name="pay-bill">

    <start-state name="start">
        <transition to="payment-amount"/>
    </start-state>

    <page name="payment-amount" view-id="/payment.jsp">
        <transition name="next" to="payment-type"/>
    </page>

    <page name="payment-type" view-id="/payment_type.jsp"
          no-conversation-view-id="/payment.jsp">
        <redirect/>
        <transition name="next" to="payment-type-decision"/>
    </page>

    <decision name="payment-type-decision"
      expression="#{paymentManager.isNewAccountType}">
        <transition name="false" to="complete">
            <action expression="#{paymentManager.createPayment}"/>
        </transition>
        <transition name="true" to="create-account"/>
    </decision>

    <page name="create-acount" view-id="/create_account.jsp"
          no-conversation-view-id="/payment.jsp">
        <redirect/>
        <transition name="next" to="complete">
            <action expression="#{paymentManager.createPayment}"/>
        </transition>
    </page>

    <page name="complete" view-id="/complete.jsp"
          no-conversation-view-id="/payment.jsp">
        <redirect/>
        <end-conversation/>
    </page>
</pageflow-definition>
```

As you can see, there are different sections with starts, pages, and decisions. Each of these has various options and outcomes. We will be using this as a basis to discuss what components are available and what these components provide us. Figure 7-7 shows a graphical representation of the preceding listing.

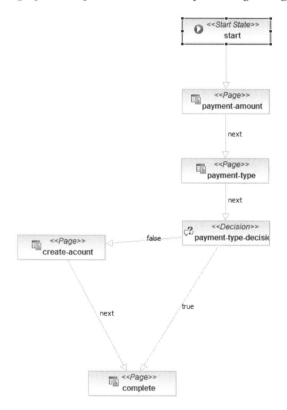

Figure 7-7. *A graphical representation of the XML listing*

Components Involved in Creating a Page Flow

As I did earlier with the process definition components, here I will define the components that can be used to make a process flow.

Start State

The *start state* is like the start state in the process definition. It starts the process and transitions to what is defined in the transition definition. In actuality, for page flows we can define start states with multiple transitions. In that case, an action listener would forward to the string of the name passed back. Look at the example in Listing 7-20.

Listing 7-20. *The Start State for a Process Definition*

```
<start-state name="start">
    <transition name="first" to="firstPage"/>
    <transition name="second" to="secondPage"/>
</start-state>
```

In this example with two transitions, if first was the string returned, jBPM would forward to the page firstPage. Conversely, if second was returned, jBPM would forward to the tag named secondPage.

Start Page

Although the start state is triggered to start by an action listener, you can also define the start by the page that the code is on. Listing 7-21 provides an example.

Listing 7-21. *An Example of a Start Page*

```
<start-page name="hello" view-id="/hello.jsp">
    <transition to="hello">
        <action expression="#{helloWorld.hello}"/>
    </transition>
</start-page>
```

Page

The *page* is used to define the information for the page you are going to and the actions of that page after you are on it. Listing 7-22 shows the page content used previously.

Listing 7-22. *An Example of a Page Definition*

```
<page name="create-account" view-id="/create_account.jsp"
        no-conversation-view-id="/payment.jsp">
    <redirect/>
    <transition name="next" to="complete">
        <action expression="#{paymentManager.createPayment}"/>
    </transition>
</page>
```

This listing uses the standard name that is used by other tags to know where to forward to. The view-id will be used to set the page to display. In addition, `no-conversation-view-id` indicates that if there is no long-running conversation, forward to that entry page. After you are on the page, you can define multiple transitions. These transitions will forward to another page flow tag, unless the redirect tag is used. In addition, if an action needs to be executed before the next page flow, it can be set inside the transition.

Redirect

The redirect we used previously, when inserted into a page tag, will cause a browser redirect as opposed to a forward.

Action

As I said, the action will allow you to run a server-side execution. This action will use a regular expression to identify the class and the method that should be executed.

Decision

Decisions are used here much like they are in task definitions to control the page flow. They will use a regular expression to decide which page to go to next. Listing 7-23 shows an example of a decision.

Listing 7-23. *A Decision Deciding Whether an Account Is New*

```
<decision name="payment-type-decision"
    expression="#{paymentManager.isNewAccountType}">
        <transition name="false" to="complete">
            <action expression="#{paymentManager.createPayment}"/>
        </transition>
        <transition name="true" to="create-account"/>
</decision>
```

Here you have a regular expression that references a Java component and method. Depending on the result, Seam can either perform an action and then forward to a page, or simply forward to a new page. Here we are deciding whether this is a new account. If it is, the user goes to a page to create a new account. If this account is existing, the user can just go ahead and create the payment and then forward to the `complete` page.

Additionally you can embed Drools into the decision to make it a rules-based decision. I will explain this further in Chapter 8.

End Conversation

Another option to put into the page tag is `<end-conversation/>`. This will signify that the conversation has ended and to shut down the long-running conversation.

Page Flow Creation in Seam

Page flow creation in Seam is fairly trivial. In fact, there is not much coding at all required. The main items are to configure the application to use page flows and then to tell it when to start the page flow.

Configuring Page Flow with Seam

We already defined jBPM in the previous section, so most of the jBPM configurations are already done. However, if you skipped ahead or were implementing only page flow, you are going to have to reference the jBPM configuration we did previously. There is only one additional change. All you have to do is add a line to `components.xml`, as in Listing 7-24.

Listing 7-24. *The Addition of the jPDL Reference*

```
<component class="org.jboss.seam.core.Jbpm">
    <property name="processDefinitions">ticketing-system.jpdl.xml</property>
    <property name="pageflowDefinitions">new-ticket.jpdl.xml</property>
</component>
```

As you can see, there is only the addition of one line. Note that if you decided to implement only the page flow without the process definitions, you could have eliminated the process definition line. However, you would still need the JAR file reference.

Starting the Page Flow

As you should have been able to see from the page flow definitions, the code was not overly complex, requiring us to identify tasks and definitions. Most of the items were simply transferring from page to page and calling Seam components. The regular expressions we defined previously will work like the Seam components we defined previously for action listeners.

In reality, the only thing to do is to start the conversation. Because these are long-running conversations, we are going to use the `@Begin` annotation that we used in Chapter 6, except now we are going to set the parameter `pageflow` to the page flow definition name. You can see this in Listing 7-25.

Listing 7-25. *Method That Is Beginning a Page Flow*

```
@Begin(nested=true, pageflow="newuser")
public void start() {
    // ... do work here ...
}
```

Here the start method will start a long-running conversation and start the page flow labeled newuser.

Summary

This chapter went over our last Seam context object, the Business Process component, as well as the incorporated page flow component. They both provide good flexibility in your application. And with Seam implementing jBPM, creating jBPM components for Seam is an extremely painless process and can add some much needed flexibility to your architecture. This is of course in keeping with the agile methodology that Seam is designed for. This chapter also marks the end of discussing all the major Seam components. In the next chapter, you will learn about some optional items that can enhance your website.

CHAPTER 8

■ ■ ■

Advanced Topics

Although I have called this chapter *Advanced*, do not be scared. This does not mean that this chapter is exponentially harder—in fact, I would argue that the preceding two chapters were probably the hardest to understand conceptually, because they presented ideas that most people do not work with on a daily basis. This chapter covers topics that are nice goodies to have in any web application: internationalization, Ajax, and security. It also covers web services, with a focus on RESTful web services. In addition, it covers Drools support and a new idea called themes. Ideas outlined here should help you make the most of Seam and to expand your web applications to be as dynamic as possible.

Internationalization

The world is becoming a smaller and smaller place, and websites are becoming more international. No longer are people restricted from purchasing things only from a store. (In fact, for some reason I can get certain CDs only from Amazon.co.uk that Amazon.com does not seem to have. I digress, though.) Most people, and especially larger companies, want to be able to sell their products around the world. And even in the United States it is becoming much more common for all kinds of services to be presented in English and Spanish—been to an ATM lately? The same can be said for websites.

As you may recall, we have hard-coded all the text in our pages so far. All of the instructions, titles, and database information have been hard-coded in the JSP/XHTML pages. Wouldn't it be nice to externalize this data so that if we changed languages, we would not be creating multiple JSP files? Well if any of you have experience with internationalization, you know that it is not only possible, but also quite common.

There are few ways to do this. The most common is to have a properties file that is in your class path. Another way is to externalize the data to an outside file or source. Externalizing the data outside of the class path is out of the scope of this book, but there are many good content management tools to do that with if that's what you want.

As in most frameworks out there, the internationalization is accomplished through the use of *language bundles* (also known as *resource bundles* when not being used for multiple language support but rather for externalization of content). These files contain a name/value pair that you can reference in your JSF pages. You then have multiple versions of these files based on the languages that your website supports.

In this section, I will show you the two ways to do this within Seam. The first one is JSF specific and can be used in Seam. The second is totally Seam specific. Later in this section, I will tell you how to customize some of the internationalization options.

DIFFERENCES IN PROPERTY FILES

Often you will see resource bundles, language bundles, and property files used interchangeably. Although all of these files are property files, there is a hierarchical separation of the three. The property file is the lowest; it represents name/value pairs. These name/value pairs can be used for anything, including configurations (for example, our Seam.properties file). A resource bundle is used to externalize resource data. Usually you use a resource bundle if you have content you do not want to hard-code in your pages. A resource bundle that is used specifically for internationalization is then called a language bundle. In theory, a language bundle could be a resource bundle or a property file—it just depends on the depth of the explanation you want.

Understanding Language Bundles

The way Java systems define and use language bundles is virtually the same from framework to framework. Usually the only difference lies in the specific implementations of the language bundles. In Java the `java.util.Locale` object is used to represent a "geographical, political, or cultural region,"[1] and is what we will be using to indicate our pages' language and geographical needs.

The `Locale` object keeps track of three items: the language, the country, and a variant. Out of the three, we will worry about only the first two. The variant is a vendor- and browser-specific item. The other two codes are the more interesting ones, especially the first one.

The language code is a two-digit code that represents the language you want your page to display. The code you use is listed in ISO 639. You can find a list of these codes at `http://ftp.ics.uci.edu/pub/ietf/http/related/iso639.txt`.

The second variable is your country code, which is a two-digit representation of the country. These codes are also based on an ISO standard; the codes are from ISO 3166. You can find the list of country codes at `http://userpage.chemie.fu-berlin.de/diverse/doc/ISO_3166.html`.

It's obvious why you need the language code. Why you need the country code may not be as obvious. The country portion is used when you want to display country-specific information on the screen—for example, the name of the country, or more obviously, the

---

1. `http://java.sun.com/j2se/1.5.0/docs/api/java/util/Locale.html`

monetary designation for the country. The language plus the country code combined are used for countries where multiple languages are spoken (such as Canada), to identify both the country and the language.

Language Bundle

Setting up a language bundle file for multiple languages is pretty straightforward. You set the bundle's filename by using the following format:

```
<bundle_name>_<language code>_<country code>.properties
```

The language code and country code are optional when creating language bundles. So if you want to, you can leave out either the language code or country code when creating the bundle's filename. It is fairly common to leave out the country code, because most applications are not country specific. In fact, one of the only reasons you would need the country is if your application had anything country specific such as monetary display (for example, if you wanted to display a dollar sign ($) for the United States and pound sign (£) for the United Kingdom).

The following are three language bundles we will be using. They are all used for our displays to greet people; therefore, I named them `greeting`:

- `greeting.properties` is the format for indicating a default language.

- `greeting_en.properties` is the format for indicating the English language.

- `greeting_en_US.properties` is the format for indicating the English language and the United States.

Notice how the language code in this example is lowercase, and the country code is uppercase. This will always be the case for each language and country code. For our examples, we will be using only language property files (as opposed to language/country files), and the languages will be English, Spanish, and French. If you decided to use a language that does not use English-type characters (for example, Japanese or Arabic), the values for your property files will have to be stored in Unicode.

Our examples will use derivations of the `greeting_en.properties` file. Listing 8-1 shows our language file in English. This will be a good reference for you, so that the next sets of examples will make more sense.

Listing 8-1. *The Contents of the greeting_en.properties File*

```
hello=Hello
helloPerson=Hello Bobby
howAreYou=How are you?
thankYou=Thanks
```

Location of Language Files

Your language files should be located in the `WEB-INF/classes` directory. The examples in this chapter reference files as if they are stored in that directory. If you are working on a large-scale application, however, it may not be wise or even allowed to locate your files at the base root directory. In that case, you can store them in a package structure such as a regular Java file. If you do, though, you will have to reference the package name first, before the property filename. So instead of referencing `greeting`, you would reference `com.company.greeting` if `com.company` were the package in which your language files were located.

Using Language Bundles with Seam

As I have said all along, Seam provides a way of attaching JSF and EJB3 technologies with a few extra goodies. The language output is one of those areas as well, where we use basic JSF processing, but we can sprinkle some Seam in there for some added functionality.

Internationalization with JSF Alone

Internationalization in JSF is straightforward. First you have to load up the language bundle and then you can display the property from the language file. There are two ways to load up the language file: either in the individual JSP or at a global level.

First, let's consider loading it up at the page level. This is not really the preferred method of loading up the language bundles because it requires you to add a tag library to every JSP page to recognize the language bundles. However, this can be useful if you have one particular page that needs to load up the properties file from a different source, and for some reason the names in that properties file and the one you are using for the site have the same names in them.

Okay, now that I justified its existence, I'll show it to you. Listing 8-2 shows the internationalization for the page level.

Listing 8-2. *Our Example for Page-Level Lookup of Internationalization Files*

```
<%@ taglib uri="http://java.sun.com/jsf/html" prefix="h" %>
<%@ taglib uri="http://java.sun.com/jsf/core" prefix="f" %>

<f:view>
    <f:loadBundle basename="greeting" var="msg"/>
    <h:outputText value="#{msg.hello}"/>, <h:outputText value="#{msg.howAreYou}"/>
    <br/>
</f:view>
```

This is a fairly straightforward way of doing simple internationalization. The first part loads up the language bundle. The particular language bundle it loads up will be based on the language that is set on the global `Locale` object. The `basename` is the name of the language bundle, and `var` sets the variable. You can then load up the particular entry from the page by using `<var>.<name in properties file>`. As I said, this is not the preferred way of internationalization, because you have to add `<f:loadBundle/>` into every JSP page. Figure 8-1 shows the output generated by the code in Listing 8-2.

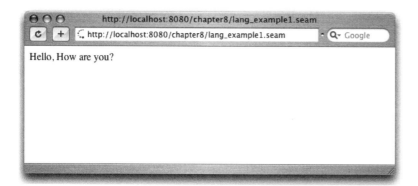

Figure 8-1. *Our JSP display with the language displayed in English*

In addition, you will want to set the bundles in the `faces-config.xml`. Here you will define the languages that the application will provide support for. This will become more useful later on when we want to auto populate a display showing the languages available (see Listing 8-3).

Listing 8-3. *Our faces-config.xml File with an Entry for the Supported Language and Message Bundle*

```
<application>
    <locale-config>
        <default-locale>en</default-locale>
        <supported-locale>es</supported-locale>
        <supported-locale>fr</supported-locale>
    </locale-config>
    <message-bundle>greeting</message-bundle>
</application>
```

There are two main parts of this code. The first part defines the languages we will support and the bundles available. Our example supports three languages, and the default one is English. There is also only one bundle here, the greeting file.

For this example, we will have three property files for changing the data: `greeting_en.properties`, `greeting_es.properties`, and `greeting_fr.properties`.

Internationalization with JSF and Seam

Loading the properties in the page is just as easy as it was previously, except now you reference the bundle name instead of a `var` property. Listing 8-4 shows the code for our JSF page when referencing the language bundle from a global resource.

Listing 8-4. *The Display of our Page When Referencing a Global Property*

```
<%@ taglib uri="http://java.sun.com/jsf/html" prefix="h" %>
<%@ taglib uri="http://java.sun.com/jsf/core" prefix="f" %>

<f:view>
    <h:outputText value="#{messages.helloPerson}"/>,
    <h:outputText value="#{messages['howAreYou']}"/><br/>
</f:view>
```

One item that may be initially confusing is that our tag references `messages`, even though we set the message bundle to `greeting` in Listing 8-3. There is a good reason for this. The message `greeting` references a lookup on the message bundle. The `messages` calls a Seam component, `org.jboss.seam.core.Messages`, and it is this component that performs lookups into our message bundles.

As you can tell, Listing 8-2 is virtually identical to Listing 8-4, except we do not need to load up the language bundle this time. Also you will notice that we loaded the `howAreYou` message by using `[ ]` notation instead of using dot notation (`.`). This is an alternative way of referencing the name on the properties. Personally I prefer dot notation because it's more the Java-esque of way doing things. But you are free to do it whichever way you prefer; the end result is the same. Note that in order to do this we will have to add a resource bundle configuration in the `components.xml`, which I will explain shortly.

So now that we can load up the locale file, the question is, what can we do with it? Seam's contribution to internationalization adds the ability to switch locales on the fly with already-created Seam components and the ability to use JSF EL in the properties files, and allow the bundles to be looked up in the page without the need for `<f:loadBundle/>`.

One of the problems developers can have when creating internationalizations is that in general they are not displaying *just* text. Usually it is text intermixed with code lookups. So to accomplish this, you have to break up sentences and intermix calls to components—yuck. I have had to do this quite a few times, and it is annoying every time.

So what Seam brings you is the ability to reference components inside our properties file. Take our preceding example that displays, "Hello, How are you?" What if we wanted to insert a user's name for that personal touch? Well, we can reference it inside the properties file in a JSF-EL-like way. So, to our `greeting` properties file we add `helloPerson=Hello #{user.name}`. This references the Seam component `user`, which is defined in Listing 8-5.

Listing 8-5. *Our user Seam Component*

```
@Name("user")
public class User {

    private String name = "Bob";

    public void setName(String s) {
        name = s;
    }

    public String getName() {
        return name;
    }
}
```

And to our JSP all we have to do is switch out our reference from `hello` to `helloPerson`, giving us the result in Figure 8-2.

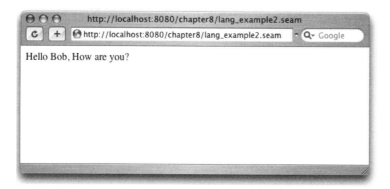

Figure 8-2. *The display of our Hello page when adding the Seam user component to it*

Now if you updated your code and ran it right now, you probably would not get the proper display. Instead, your display would read, "Hello #{user.name} … ". This is because we have to tell Seam that we are going to use the language bundles and where they are referenced. To do this, you can add a reference to the multiple bundles, as shown in Listing 8-6.

XML NAMESPACES

XML namespaces are used to qualify element and attribute values in XML. This can help define more-customized names in XML documents and hopefully prevent conflict if two documents have the same element names.

You set the namespace by defining a lookup to the namespace. This is defined by using the `xmlns` tag in a start tag of an element. This is usually done with the following format:

```
xmlns:namespace-prefix="namespaceURI"
```

We will use namespaces in Listing 8.6 for our output of components.

Listing 8-6. *Our Reference to the Resource Bundle in components.xml*

```xml
<?xml version="1.0" encoding="UTF-8"?>

<components xmlns="http://jboss.com/products/seam/components"
            xmlns:core="http://jboss.com/products/seam/core">

    <core:init jndi-pattern="chapter8/#{ejbName}/local"/>

    <core:resource-bundle>
        <core:bundle-names>
            <value>greeting</value>
        </core:bundle-names>
    </core:resource-bundle>

</components>
```

Another item to note about the XML in Listing 8-6 is that the core objects are referencing the `xmlns:core` namespace. However, the `<value>greeting</value>` is using the default namespace referenced as `http://jboss.com/products/seam/components`.

You can define multiple bundle names under `<core:bundle-names>`, because the `bundleNames` variable is an array. One thing of interest to note about Seam is that by default you do not have to define anything in `components.xml` if—and this is a big if—you named your bundle `messages`. This is because Seam defaults the `bundleNames` to be `messages`. With Seam you can inject the messages in the class level as well. If, for example, you wanted to inject `greeting.hello` into a property called `customGreeting`, you would write the following:

```
@In("#{greeting.hello}") private String customGreeting;
```

This can be useful if you have to send the localized message to a server or to be replaced in an email. In addition, if you want the locale to be remembered when the user exits the browser and comes back, you can store the locale in a cookie. Simply add the line shown in Listing 8-7 to the `components.xml` file.

Listing 8-7. *Setting Seam to Remember the Locale via a Cookie*

```
<component name="localeSelector">
    <property name="cookieEnabled">true</property>
</component>
```

Selecting a Language

Obviously, if you are going to go through the hassle of creating multiple files for multiple languages, you want to give the user a chance to display those languages. By default, the language will be selected based on browser settings. So if a user's browser or OS is configured to be in French, that's the language the server will pick up and then display to the user.

For the most part, that is how internationalization worked exclusively for years— until people noticed one minor problem. And that is, many people do not have their browsers and OS configured properly. Many bi-, tri-, and quadrilingual people have their systems set up for English but prefer to read in other languages, for instance. So, nowadays sites will perform the autodetection but will give you the option to switch your languages as well.

This ability to switch manually is what we will discuss here, and fortunately there really is not much you have to do because this capability is built into Seam with `LocaleSelector`. You have only two options for manually selecting the language: you display the languages either from a predefined set or automatically.

Manually Selecting the Language

The actual switching of languages is fairly easy. In fact, the only code you have to add is in the JSP page for the display. Listing 8-8 shows the code for adding a drop-down list for language selection on our pages. The listener it calls has already been created for us by the Seam core code.

Listing 8-8. *Our Example Page with a Drop-Down Language Selector*

```
<%@ taglib uri="http://java.sun.com/jsf/html" prefix="h" %>
<%@ taglib uri="http://java.sun.com/jsf/core" prefix="f" %>
```

```
<f:view>
    <h:form>
        <h:selectOneMenu value="#{localeSelector.language}">
            <f:selectItem itemLabel="English" itemValue="en"/>
            <f:selectItem itemLabel="Espagna" itemValue="es"/>
            <f:selectItem itemLabel="Francais" itemValue="fr"/>
        </h:selectOneMenu>
<h:commandButton action="#{localeSelector.select}"
        value="#{messages['ChangeLanguage']}"/><br/>
    </h:form>

<h:outputText value="#{messages.helloPerson}"/>,
<h:outputText value="#{messages['howAreYou']}"/><br/>
</f:view>
```

This code will display a page with the selection of English, Spanish, or French. Figure 8-3 shows the output of the page in French with the drop-down.

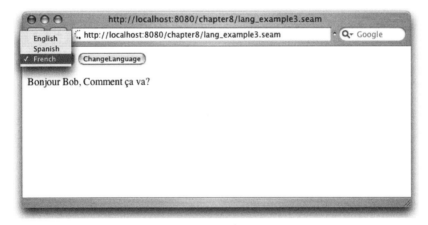

Figure 8-3. *The display of the examples page in French, with a language selection drop-down*

Alternative Language Selection

As I mentioned, there are two ways to display the language selection. The second way looks a lot like the first, except that you don't have to manually write out all the supported languages. As you can imagine, the first method could be tedious, especially if the drop-down list appears on a variety of pages and areas. If you add more languages, you would have to add them to the configurations *and* the pages.

As you may recall, earlier we defined in the faces-config.xml file the supported locales. So assuming you keep this file up-to-date, you can simply tell Seam to reference that file to get all the language names. Listing 8-9 does just that, which of course simplifies the JSP code—and code simplification is almost always a plus.

Listing 8-9. *Our Code to Use Our Locale Definitions from faces-config.xml to Generate the Drop-Down*

```
<h:selectOneMenu value="#{localeSelector.language}">
    <f:selectItems value="#{localeSelector.supportedLocales}"/>
</h:selectOneMenu>
<h:commandButton action="#{localeSelector.select}"
        value="#{messages['ChangeLanguage']}"/><br/>
```

Another added bonus is that the drop-down display presents the language name in the native language, as you can see in Figure 8-4. This definitely makes better sense than having to have the person know what the name of their language looks like in a different language. (Of course, you could have done this earlier as well; this process is just easier.)

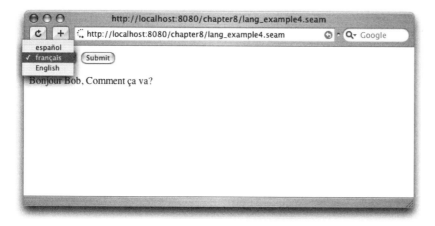

Figure 8-4. *The display of the drop-down when having the system reference the language names*

As you can see, this provides a slick and easy way to embed the code to switch the languages in your pages without having to add any extra POJOs.

■**Note** Although you do not have to use the Seam components for internationalization if you do not want to, I think you can agree that they do provide some added functionality. If your JSF pages have already been created, there is not much need to use the Seam components (although the integration between the two is fairly straightforward). From here you should be able to internationalize your pages with ease. I will not be using internationalization in the rest of the book, simply because of the overhead required to create the files.

Themes

One of the problems these days with designing websites is that you want to attract people to your site and at the same time you have to make the site useful. This often leads to complex page layouts that sometimes include options to reduce the complexity.

You are probably familiar with sites that have an option to make the page printable, for instance. This option usually takes the border away and may apply some additional formatting changes. Seam has a built-in way to change page formatting automatically. This works like internationalization, and the options are referred to as *themes*.

The themes work by defining certain attributes for the pages. Because the idea is to change the look and feel of the page, the two most common parts to change are the template and the cascading style sheet (CSS).

Creating Themes

Creating a theme works on the same principle as creating language bundles, except this time you will create property files that include your theme-specific information. Our example will include two items: the CSS and a template file. In reality, you could customize the theme as much as you want.

Listing 8-10 shows an example of our default theme.

Listing 8-10. *Our Default Theme, Saved as default.properties*

```
css css/default.css
template defaultTemplate.xhtml
```

In our default theme, we define two properties: the location of the style sheet and the location of the default template, which in this case is in the root web directory. As with internationalization, these bundles need to be stored in the WEB-INF/classes directory and can be stored at different package levels. Of course, for our examples, we will assume that they are stored at the root level.

Also as with internationalization, we will set the properties for these in the components.xml file. They will be stored in the Seam session-scoped object ThemeSelector.

Listing 8-11 shows three themes we have defined: default, printable, and text-only. This way, you or the user can define how the site is displayed. If you want to print out the page, you select printable. If you are using a dial-up modem, you can select text-only. Of course, for each item you do have to configure certain options, which can get more and more complicated.

Listing 8-11. *Our components.xml Class with Three Available Themes Defined for It*

```
<component name="org.jboss.seam.theme.themeSelector">
    <property name="availableThemes">
        <value>default</value>
        <value>printable</value>
        <value>text-only</value>
    </property>
    <property name="cookieEnabled">true</property>
</component>
```

In addition, notice that there is a cookieEnabled property on the ThemeSelector component. This works the same way as the cookie does on the internationalization data; this will allow you to store the theme of the site you were just on via the cookie. This is useful when you have a varying sets of themes. If you are using themes simply to go back and forth between printable and nonprintable displays, this option would be less useful.

DEFINING THEMES WITH NAMESPACES

You can also define your themes with XML namespaces. If you want to define Listing 8-11 with XML namespaces, use the following as a template:

```
<?xml version="1.0" encoding="UTF-8"?>

<components xmlns="http://jboss.com/products/seam/components"
    xmlns:theme="http://jboss.com/products/seam/theme">

    <theme:theme-selector cookie-enabled="true">
        <theme:available-themes>
            <value>default</value>
            <value>printable</value>
            <value>text-only</value>
        </theme:available-themes>
    </theme:theme-selector>

</components>
```

Using Themes

Our Travel Reservations application in Chapter 6 used Facelets for the presentation tier. The Facelets had a tag at the very beginning: a `composition` UI tag defines the namespaces to load up and also defines the location of the template for the page. The template will be used as the outline of the page, with the insertions being dictated by definitions in the page itself. Our example from the Travel Reservations application is shown in Listing 8-12.

Listing 8-12. *The First Few Lines of hotels.xhtml*

```
<ui:composition xmlns=http://www.w3.org/1999/xhtml
    xmlns:ui="http://java.sun.com/jsf/facelets"
    xmlns:h="http://java.sun.com/jsf/html"
    xmlns:f="http://java.sun.com/jsf/core"
    xmlns:s="http://jboss.com/products/seam/taglib"
    template="template.xhtml">
```

Pay close attention to the last line, which is the line that selects the template. This line defines the template, so we are going to substitute this hard-coded line with a variable, as in Listing 8-13.

Listing 8-13. *The First Few Lines of hotels.xhtml with a Dynamic Template*

```
<ui:composition xmlns=http://www.w3.org/1999/xhtml
    xmlns:ui="http://java.sun.com/jsf/facelets"
    xmlns:h="http://java.sun.com/jsf/html"
    xmlns:f="http://java.sun.com/jsf/core"
    xmlns:s="http://jboss.com/products/seam/taglib"
    template="#{theme.template}">
```

As you can see, in the last line we substituted a dynamic call to the theme. The `theme` portion is the theme that has been selected (named `theme` by Seam), and the `template` part is the portion that was referenced in the properties file. You can then do something similar for the CSS and other template-driven dynamics on your pages. You will reference those just as you reference the `theme.template` in Listing 8-13.

Selecting Themes

You can select the theme dynamically or programmatically, just as you can the internationalization. Both ways use `themeSelector`, another Seam-embedded component. Allowing users to select themes can easily be done by using a select box and the `themeSelector`, as shown in Listing 8-14.

Listing 8-14. *The Code Used to Switch the Themes*

```
<h:selectOneMenu value="#{themeSelector.theme}">
    <f:selectItems value="#{themeSelector.themes}"/>
</h:selectOneMenu><br/>
<h:commandButton action="#{themeSelector.select}" value="Select Theme"/>
```

As you can see, changing a theme is just the action of using the select that sets the theme to be used. Similarly, if you wanted to switch themes programmatically, you would have to call the themeSelector component, set the name of the theme, and then call the action set by the commandButton to have it selected. Figure 8-5 presents a screen shot of the preceding selection in action.

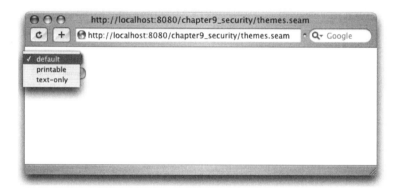

Figure 8-5. *The screen shot of the theme selection*

Web Services

Creating websites is the main function of Seam. However, it is not Seam's only use. In today's global market and especially at larger companies, reuse is the key. Often developers will write applications that take in fairly simple input, perform complex business processing to the input, and return a result. Depending on the company or the product, this can get quite complex.

If you have multiple presentation tiers that need to access a business process from different servers, there are a few ways to do it. One way would be, of course, to expose the EJB3 objects so that they could call them directly. However, this solution adds a security risk. In addition, accessing the server may not be possible (depending on the remoteness of the server).

This is where web services come into play. Web services provide a way of accessing the server through normal HTTP connections. Through web services, you send a request to the server, either XML or regular HTTP, and return to the user an XML document.

One of the most common examples of this is Amazon.com. When you go to Amazon.com, you can find books, music, other products, and just about anything these days. Well, these lookups and their mechanisms are fairly advanced, considering the sheer quantity and size. The responses bring back a variety of information to the user, including title, price, ranking, and so forth. Well, one thing Amazon.com relies on is having other websites advertise for them. In fact, some websites will pull back information from Amazon.com, and this occurs via web services. So the practical usage of web services in enterprise applications is priceless.

Types of Web Services

As I said, web services provide an ability to have computer-to-computer communication over a network. There are three ways this essentially happens: via Remote Procedure Call (RPC), document (Doc), or REpresentational State Transfer (REST). There are advantages and disadvantages to each.

The web services that you are probably most familiar with are the Simple Object Access Protocol (SOAP) calls via RPC or Doc. These have become a fairly standard industry tool. And most frameworks, such as Spring, have some integration support for them. SOAP calls can have the advantage of added security and are easier to implement than client interfaces for REST, which can be required for many companies. However, with those advantages there are negatives. SOAP calls require a heavier overhead and then become dependent on separate JARs. This has led some people to ask, "Why use SOAP?" SOAP provides added security, but is this necessarily needed?

Consider our Amazon.com example. This open site allows people to use web services to look up books and other items. What would be the most important thing for this site? Security? Not really, because Amazon allows the site to be open to all and has other mechanisms to stop denial-of-service and other types of attacks. The most important need for websites such as Amazon.com is throughput. Generally, many people access the site, so you would want to be able to react as fast as possible. This has led many to use RESTful web services.

REST is the preferred method for Amazon.com. I have used REST for internal applications that require many hits and need to minimize the processing time and memory used. If you are working on a presentation tier that does not need the security apparatus of web services, REST is definitely becoming the preferred method. I believe this is mainly because you will still be using regular servlet presentation tiers.

WEB SERVICES SUPPORTED IN SEAM

As of the writing of this book, Gavin King, creator of Seam, has said that SOAP web services will be implemented in Seam. This will most likely be in the 1.2 release. That being said, RESTful services are available. Now this may not be good for all, because some need the overhead of SOAP and some companies simply demand using SOAP. However if this does not describe you, you are in luck because RESTful services can be versatile.

REST in Seam

In all honesty, REST is a huge buzzword that is going around the industry, and with good reason. REST provides you with abilities that are similar (such as making a stateless request and receiving an XML response) to typical web services but with less overhead on the server than standard SOAP calls. This means that if you have a heavy load on the server, throughput can be faster. In addition, because REST behaves like a regular web request except that you are returning XML strings, implementing REST can be easier for non-SOAP-experienced developers.

Of course, all of this does have a cost. REST requires clients to do more work in receiving the XML because they have to parse it themselves. In contrast, SOAP has Web Services Description Language (WSDL) and XML Schema Definition (XSD) for strong typing to generate the client code.

My only gripe with RESTful services is that everyone seems to implement them slightly differently. There seems to be a textbook definition of how to use them; the URI has a hierarchy describing what it is you are looking for. The user can then use that hierarchy while sending over different types of requests (for example, `GET`, `DELETE`). Those requests will determine what the code does.

For example, you could send over `/address/123 Main St` with the `DELETE` request, and it would tell the server to delete the address 123 Main St. Then an XML response would be returned. In this example, the response would probably be some sort of confirmation. However, not many RESTful components seem to use this method of calling, and neither does Seam (at least not by default—I am sure you could customize your application to do this if you wanted).

What Seam does and what many RESTful services do is implement the fundamental basics of a REST request. The request should be a totally stateless request, and the URL you are sending over does not care about what was previously sent or any session. The URL is sent to the server, a request is made, and an XML response is returned. In all fairness, though, even I am guilty of implementing it this way. And it is not even because of being too lazy to implement it "properly"; it is mainly because except for your most basic application, your web services requests are often doing something more advanced than simple gets, sets, and deletes. Usually there is business logic and process built into it, and so those simple methods do not often work.

Thus implementing REST is going to be easy on your server. All you have to do is make sure your Seam components are stateless components that you want to call. You will then have to return XML, which should be easy because Facelets have automatic XML support.

Ajax

Ajax, Ajax, Ajax—what web application discussion would be complete without talking about one of the biggest buzzwords to hit Java development since HTML came out? It seems like almost everywhere you go, companies are asking for developers with Ajax experience, which by the way is about as abstract as asking for someone with XML experience. Many new conferences have come out specifically for Ajax, and Ajax has become a hot topic at Java conferences as well.

This is all for a good reason. Ajax gives the user the ability to have the page call the server asynchronously, pull back information from the page, and then update the page accordingly. This is all done without having to resubmit the entire page. Before Ajax, this type of functionality was available only through Java applets or Adobe Flash presentation tiers.

Ajax stands for *Asynchronous JavaScript and XML*, which oddly enough is not a 100 percent accurate definition. Although Ajax is usually asynchronous, and usually written in JavaScript, and often deals with transmission of XML, none of these items is a *must*. You can send Ajax messages synchronously, you do not have to use JavaScript to send them, and your response can be an XML file but can also be a regular string. Ajax was a term originally coined by Jesse James Garrett, but was first developed by Microsoft in an attempt to deal with remote scripting.

Seam Remoting

Our first adventure in Ajax is going to be with the components that come prepackaged with Seam, and these are referred to as *Seam remoting*. Seam remoting creates JavaScript asynchronous calls to Seam-defined components. This way, you have an easy way to call any Seam-defined component and receive the response to process it. The response of the Seam call will be sent over to a method for final processing, if necessary. Usually this will result in the processing of a string to change text someplace else, but it does not have to. You could just be sending over the information for temporary processing. Sometimes no processing is necessary if you are only sending data to the server without requiring a response. This often happens if a site wants to periodically save data that the user inputs.

Although Seam remoting does make asynchronous processing with Seam much easier, the one downside is that you cannot do any partial page updates. However, this is a common issue among Ajax frameworks such as the open source Dojo or OpenRico. If we want to do partial page updates, we will have to use Ajax4jsf, which incidentally is the other framework we are going to discuss.

Seam Remote Configuring

Because a complete Ajax call is both a client-side and server-side call, the configurations themselves will be on both the client and the server sides. Fortunately, the configurations are fairly straightforward. On the server side, we will be defining a special servlet for remoting. Then we will be referencing JavaScript on the client side.

For the first part, Seam adds a new servlet to web.xml called SeamRemotingServlet, as defined in Listing 8-15.

Listing 8-15. *Seam Remoting Servlet Defined in web.xml*

```
<servlet>
    <servlet-name>Seam Remoting</servlet-name>
    <servlet-class>org.jboss.seam.remoting.SeamRemotingServlet</servlet-class>
</servlet>

<servlet-mapping>
    <servlet-name>Seam Remoting</servlet-name>
    <url-pattern>/seam/remoting/*</url-pattern>
</servlet-mapping>
```

The servlet is part of the regular Seam JAR distribution, so no need to add a new JAR file. Just take note of the URL pattern; we will be using it when we define the JavaScript.

For the JavaScript portion, we are going to have to reference two JavaScript components. Listing 8-16 provides an example of the referenced components. Note that the URL pattern starts with seam/remoting/, which we had defined as the url-pattern in Listing 8-15.

Listing 8-16. *The Remoting JavaScript References Example in Our Page*

```
<script type="text/javascript" src="seam/remoting/resource/remote.js"></script>
<script type="text/javascript" src="seam/remoting/interface.js?testAction"></script>
```

The first line is fairly straightforward. In the second we are passing through a parameter name. As I said earlier, Seam remoting allows us to access Seam-defined components from the JSP page itself via JavaScript. The parameter names you pass through on the second JavaScript line are the Seam components you want to access on the page. And you will see us use these referenced components in the next example.

Basic Ajax Remoting Call

For our first Ajax example, we are going to start with the most basic of concepts. We are going to have a page with a button on it. When you click the button, the JavaScript makes an asynchronous call to the server and returns a string saying "Hello World!" This message will then be sent back to the page and displayed. Figure 8-6 shows the page before and after you click the button.

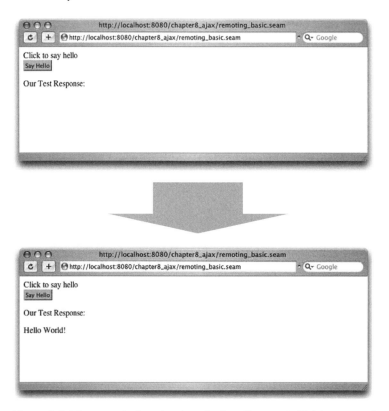

Figure 8-6. *The page before (top) and after (bottom) clicking to make our Ajax call*

Client-Side Code

For the first step, let's take a look at the code that generated the HTML page. For simplicity, I am going to break up this code by presenting it to you in two parts. For the first part, shown in Listing 8-17, I will display the code minus the JavaScript.

Listing 8-17. *The remoting_basic.jsp Code Used to Generate the Basic Ajax Example*

```
<%@ taglib uri="http://java.sun.com/jsf/html" prefix="h" %>
<%@ taglib uri="http://java.sun.com/jsf/core" prefix="f" %>
```

```
<f:view>
    Click to say hello<br/>
    <button onclick="javascript:sayHello()">Say Hello</button><br/>

    <p>
        Our Test Response: <br/>
        <div id="helloId">

        </div>
    </p>
</f:view>
```

This page is fairly simple and includes a button with a response that is blank. Note that the response is surrounded by a div tag. This is where we will be inserting the text dynamically after the Ajax call. The button calls the method sayHello(), which we have defined in Listing 8-18.

Listing 8-18. *The JavaScript for Our Remoting_basic.jsp*

```
<script type="text/javascript" src="seam/remoting/resource/remote.js"></script>
<script type="text/javascript" src="seam/remoting/interface.js?helloAction">
</script>

<script type="text/javascript">
    //<![CDATA[

    function sayHello() {
        Seam.Component.getInstance("helloAction").sayHello(callBackMethod);
    }

    // result is based on the STring that is returned from the sayHello method
    function callBackMethod(result) {
        var captionElement = document.getElementById("helloId");
        captionElement.innerHTML = result;
    }

    // ]]>
</script>
```

Now this is where the page starts to get more interesting. The first two lines are as we described in the configuration; they load up the JavaScript. Then we have the method that actually makes the call. The following line of code calls the Seam component with the name helloAction:

```
Seam.Component.getInstance("helloAction").sayHello(callBackMethod);
```

The method that the JavaScript calls is then `sayHello`. On the JavaScript, the method can take multiple parameters. The first parameters are those that match up to the method that is being called. The final parameter defines the callback method. In this case, the method `sayHello` does not have any parameters, so we have only one parameter: the callback method `callBackMethod`. You will see that method defined afterward. The method is what is called after the Seam component has been executed, and the parameter for that method is what is returned from the method (if any object is returned). In our case, we are going to return a string saying "Hello World!" The next few lines are standard JavaScript that will retrieve the element defined by the `div` tag, and change the text to what was returned.

Server-Side Code

Now let's jump over to the server side to see the code that we called. The code for the most part is untouched. The only thing that we will have to change is the interface for the `Session` object. Listing 8-19 shows the SLSB defined for the preceding call.

Listing 8-19. *HelloWorldAction.java to be Called by the JavaScript*

```java
@Stateless
@Name("helloAction")
public class HelloWorldAction implements HelloWorld {

    public String sayHello() {
        return "Hello World!";
    }
}
```

This looks like any typical SLSB. We have the parameterless `sayHello` that we called in the JavaScript, and the text being returned. Now let's take a look at the interface that is defined in Listing 8-20.

Listing 8-20. *The Interface for HelloWorldAction*

```java
@Local
public interface HelloWorld {
    @WebRemote
    String sayHello();
}
```

For the most part, the interface looks the same as well, except for the @WebRemote annotation. This annotation tells the Seam container that this method is visible by the client-side JavaScript.

So now you should have the necessary ability to create a basic component being called by a Seam application.

Ajax Remoting Call with Parameters

Now that we have the basics down, let's take it up a notch. We will add two different scenarios this time and will have them both pass a parameter. In the first example, the parameter will be a simple string. However, in the second example, we will have the JavaScript send an actual Java object over instead.

Let's take a first look at the web page that is created when we run this code. Figure 8-7 shows the before and after screens. In this example, unlike in Figure 8-6, we have an input box. I typed the names **John** and **Smith** into the input boxes.

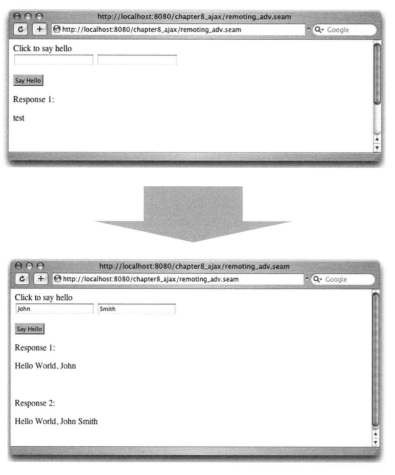

Figure 8-7. *The before (top) and after (bottom) pages for our second Ajax web call*

Client-Side Code

This is much like our previous Ajax call. In fact, much of what you will see will be similar. When looking at the JavaScript, you will notice two sets of calls. This is because we are calling the server twice—once by passing in a string, the other by passing in a JavaBean. Listing 8-21 shows the client-side JavaScript code.

Listing 8-21. *The JavaScript Code for the Two Remoting Calls*

```
<script type="text/javascript">
    //<![CDATA[

    function sayHello() {
        // First Call
        Seam.Component.getInstance("helloAction")
            .sayHelloWithName(document.form.firstName.value,callBackMethod);

        // Second Call
        var user = Seam.Remoting.createType("com.integrallis.ajax.domain.Person");
        user.setFirstName(document.form.firstName.value);
        user.lastName = document.form.lastName.value;
        Seam.Component.getInstance("helloAction")
          .sayHelloWithPerson(user, callBackMethod2);
    }

    function callBackMethod(result) {
        var captionElement = document.getElementById("helloId");
        captionElement.innerHTML = result;
    }
    function callBackMethod2(result) {
        var captionElement = document.getElementById("helloId2");
        captionElement.innerHTML = result;
    }
}
// ]]>
</script>
```

So the first call should look quite familiar. The only difference is this time we are passing a parameter through to it. The method, sayHelloWithName, takes the parameter and uses it to set "Hello World, John."

The second call is a bit more complex. The method requires a Person object. Here we introduce a new Seam call: Seam.Remoting.createType(). This will create a type based on the absolute path of the class. After that you can then use the methods to set the properties on the object. You will notice that we can set the object in two ways: either through the traditional Java setter way, or by setting the property directly. Either works well. In addition, if you wanted to create a component on the page by using its Seam component name, you would call `Seam.Component.newInstance("componentName")`.

Batch Remote Calls

In the preceding example, we made two separate physical calls to the server to get each of our individual responses. Now although in that example this really is not a big deal, you should think of the process in bigger terms. Each call had to make a connection to the server and wait for a response. If you were in a production environment and had to make multiple calls, this could prove to be quite expensive.

To overcome this, Seam remoting uses batch processing. It is quite simple: you have a start batch where you want to start the batch calls, and an execute batch where it ends. Look at the partial code in Listing 8-22.

Listing 8-22. *A Code Snippet of Using Batch Processing*

```
function sayHello() {
    // Run Both Components
    Seam.Remoting.startBatch();
    Seam.Component.getInstance(...)...
    ...
    Seam.Component.getInstance(...)...
    Seam.Remoting.executeBatch();
}
```

You use `startBatch()` to start the call. The method will not actually make the call to the server until `executeBatch()` is reached. In our example, I made the batch calls all in one method. However, in reality this could have been broken up by multiple JavaScript calls because we were doing different things. If that was the case and suddenly you wanted to programmatically decide to not make the batch call, you could call `Seam.Remoting.cancelBatch()` to cancel the present batch processing. You could then call `startBatch()` again and not have to worry about the other calls you initially put into the batch.

Here is where we stop the Ajax remoting examples. In the rest of this section, I will go over miscellaneous items related to Seam remoting.

Get Component Name

If you have a given component but do not know its name, you can obtain the name by using the command call `Seam.Component.getComponentName(variable)`. This command will return a string of the component's name. At first glance, you may wonder why you would want this, but think of this along the same lines as using `instanceof`. This will allow you to determine a specific component name if your method could return different components.

The Conversation ID

If you are working with the Page context, it may become necessary to get or set the conversation ID in the JavaScript. You can automatically get or set the conversation IDs by using the call `Seam.Remoting.getContext().getConversationId()` or `Seam.Remoting.getContext().setConversationId()`.

Data Types in JavaScript

Most Ajax frameworks that I have worked with have a crude framework to talk to the business logic tier. Usually it comes down to creating a normal request that you want. It really does not matter how you send the objects over, because they are all being sent over as strings anyway. However, as you have seen, using concrete data types with Seam is a much more direct connection to your business logic. As you have also seen, we pass over the objects directly, so we are going to need to be able to mimic actual Java objects inside the JavaScript. This of course is all built into Seam remoting.

The following are Java data types that you can use in Seam remoting:

String: You can use a regular JavaScript `var` object as a string.

Boolean: These are supported like regular JavaScript Boolean objects.

Enums: When using the Java enums, you can treat them just like strings. If you have to call an object that wants an enum as a method, just pass the name of it as a string.

Maps: Because JavaScript does not support maps, there is a Seam remoting object specifically used to create maps. Call `new Seam.Remoting.Map()` to create a JavaScript map object.

Date: You can use a JavaScript `Date` to represent any `java.util.Date` or `java.sql.Timestamp` object.

Hiding or Changing the Loading Message

Depending on how you like to read technical books, you may or may not have been running the examples as you go through this book. If you have been running the examples, you may have noticed a little "Please Wait…" message in the top-right screen of your web page when you ran the Ajax call. If you did not see it, rerun the Ajax application and check it out. If you are not following along with the code, then just take my word for it. This is a fairly common occurrence with Ajax frameworks.

If you do not like seeing the loading message or want the text to say something different or want an image displayed instead, you can custom configure that within Seam remoting.

To hide the display of the loading message, you have to override the method calls that create the loading message. This is achieved by the JavaScript in Listing 8-23.

Listing 8-23. *JavaScript to Suppress the Loading Message*

```
Seam.Remoting.displayLoadingMessage = function() {};
Seam.Remoting.hideLoadingMessage = function() {};
```

Changing the loading message's name is as simple as setting a JavaScript Seam variable. Listing 8-24 shows an example.

Listing 8-24. *An Example of Changing the Loading Message*

```
Seam.Remoting.loadingMessage = "Loading";
```

Similarly to hiding the message, you can also override the function calls to display a custom image or whatever else you want to do when the Seam loading occurs.

Debugging

What framework would be complete without the ability to debug it? Fortunately, that is not lost on Seam either. There are two ways you can turn on debugging: either by programming it within the JavaScript (as in Listing 8-25) or configuring it in `components.xml` (as in Listing 8-26).

Listing 8-25. *Call to Turn On Debugging from Within the JavaScript*

```
Seam.Remoting.setDebug(true);
```

Listing 8-26. *Call to Turn On Debugging from Within components.xml*

```
<component name="org.jboss.seam.remoting.remotingConfig">
    <property name="debug">true</property>
</component>
```

Excluding Objects on the Method Call

One obvious downside to Seam remoting is that you are essentially exposing EJB3 beans to the presentation tier by using JavaScript. By defining the methods that are allowed to be called, you can (if you know what you are doing) have JavaScript call methods. Fortunately, you can restrict what methods on the components the JavaScript have access to.

As you may recall, when you retrieve or create bean objects, there may be some methods there that you do not want exposed to the presentation tier. To prevent access to these methods, you can use the same annotation we used to allow access to methods: `@WebRemote`. This annotation can prevent the JavaScript from having access to the object. It is even so fine-grained that you could exclude individual objects on the collections. In Listing 8-27, our session has returned a `User` object. However, we do not want the presentation tier to have access to the password.

Listing 8-27. *Denying Access to Particular Fields*

```
@WebRemote(exclude = {"password"})
public User getUser()
```

In addition, you can supply a comma-separated list of properties to the `exclude` parameter. You can also specify the subproperties. This allows you to not only prevent exposure of data, but also prevent sending large objects and help with network latency.

Ajax4jsf in Seam

We have just gone over using Seam's built-in remoting to create Ajax calls. However, as I pointed out, even though this does allow us a good amount of flexibility in being able to call Seam components, it does not give us total flexibility. For example, we cannot perform partial page updates with this methodology.

Fortunately, there is already an alternative out there designed specifically for JSF: the open source project Ajax4jsf. By using Ajax4jsf, we can expand on the Ajax functionality we have with Seam remoting. I will not be going into detail about it because there is plenty of documentation on the Ajax4jsf website (`https://ajax4jsf.dev.java.net/nonav/ajax/ajax-jsf/`). The examples provided on the site will work just as easily with Seam-JSF as they will with regular JSF.

We will be using this project for our next few examples. I will walk you through downloading and configuring your application and then go through a few examples of writing an application with Ajax4jsf.

Download and Configure

Here we will download the necessary files, install the JARs, and configure them.
The Ajax4jsf binary distribution can be downloaded from `https://ajax4jsf.dev.java.net/`
`nonav/ajax/ajax-jsf/download.html#binary`. After you download it, expand the directory
and you will find a folder labeled `lib`. Simply take the two JARs from that directory,
`ajax4jsf.jar` and `oscache-2.3.2`, and put them into your `WEB-INF/lib` directory.

■Note At the time of writing this book, the distribution was labeled was 1.0.3. If the default distribution has changed, the preceding files may have different names.

Now that you have Ajax4jsf downloaded and the JARs installed, you can configure
your application to use Ajax4jsf. This configuration is not like the one we defined earlier
for remoting. The configuration for Ajax4jsf uses filters to intercept all the calls and perform any necessary processing. Listing 8-28 shows the code that needs to be inserted
into `web.xml`.

Listing 8-28. *The Ajax4jsf Defined in Our web.xml*

```
<filter>
    <display-name>Ajax4jsf Filter</display-name>
    <filter-name>ajax4jsf</filter-name>
    <filter-class>org.ajax4jsf.Filter</filter-class>
</filter>

<filter-mapping>
    <filter-name>ajax4jsf</filter-name>
    <url-pattern>*.seam</url-pattern>
</filter-mapping>
```

Here we define the Ajax4jsf filter. When you define your mapping, just make sure that
the mapping is defined for the URI you are using for your front-page calls. For the examples in this book, I always use `.seam` for all the Seam calls. However, some may use `.jsf` or
use just a directory structure instead.

Now you should have the server all ready to go, so let's start creating some usable
applications.

Dynamic Validation

Our first example uses Ajax4jsf to create some dynamic validations. In this example, we have a few input boxes on the page. This page, shown in Figure 8-8, is used to create a new user.

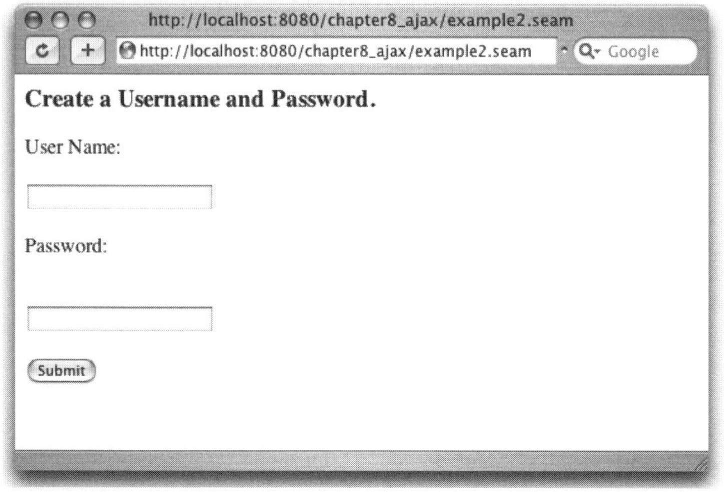

Figure 8-8. *The page to create a new user as you enter the page*

When the user accesses the page, they are supposed to enter a username and password. This example will use Ajax to make validation calls to the server to check whether the information entered is valid. It will do this on `onblur` events. This works by using Seam's interception of the Hibernate validation framework, by validating based on the Hibernate annotations for the `User` object. Listing 8-29 shows the `User` bean.

Listing 8-29. *The User Bean with Validation Annotations*

```
@Name("user")
public class User {

    private String name;
    private String password;

    @NotNull
    @Length(min=5, max=15)
    public String getName() {
        return name;
    }
```

```
public void setName(String name) {
    this.name = name;
}

@NotNull
public String getPassword() {
    return password;
}
public void setPassword(String password) {
    this.password = password;
}
}
```

As you can see, we have the name and password properties, both of which have validations associated with them. The name property is required, and the length must be between five and fifteen characters. The password property is also required. As I said, the validation occurs during an onblur event, which occurs when you leave the input box displayed onscreen. Let's pretend we input **jo** for the first box and then tab through twice and end up on the Submit button. The outcome of that situation is displayed in Figure 8-9.

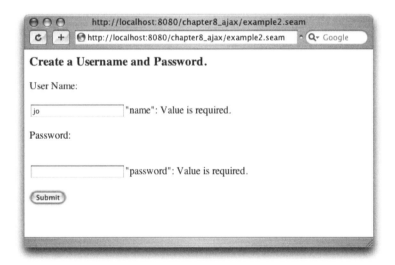

Figure 8-9. *The page after entering **jo** for the first tab and then tabbing through to the Submit button*

As you can see, this displays on the page two error messages that were not there before. This was done having an asynchronous call to the server, which means the validation occurs relatively quickly because the user doesn't have to complete the page before seeing that an error was made. This helps keep your users informed and hopefully less frustrated in the end.

So let's take a look at the code that created this. The code, shown in Listing 8-30, is a mixture of using JSF tags, Ajax4jsf tags, and Seam tags.

Listing 8-30. *The JSF Code to Display Our Ajax-Supported User Input Boxes*

```
<%@ taglib uri="http://java.sun.com/jsf/html" prefix="h" %>
<%@ taglib uri="http://java.sun.com/jsf/core" prefix="f" %>
<%@ taglib uri="http://jboss.com/products/seam/taglib" prefix="s" %>
<%@ taglib uri="https://ajax4jsf.dev.java.net/ajax" prefix="a" %>

<f:view>

<h:form>

<h3>Create a Username and Password.</h3>

<s:validateAll>
    <h:outputLabel for="name">User Name:</h:outputLabel></div>
    <div class="input">
        <s:decorate>
            <h:inputText id="name" value="#{user.name}" required-"true">
                <a:support event="onblur" reRender="userNameErrors"/>
            </h:inputText>
            <br/>
            <a:outputPanel id="userNameErrors">
                <s:message/>
            </a:outputPanel>
        </s:decorate>
    </div><br/>

    <h:outputLabel for="password">Password:</h:outputLabel></div>
    <div class="input">
        <s:decorate>
            <h:inputText id="password" value="#{user.password}" required="true">
                <a:support event="onblur" reRender="passwordErrors"/>
            </h:inputText>
            <br/>
            <a:outputPanel id="passwordErrors">
                <s:message/><br/>
            </a:outputPanel>
        </s:decorate>
    </div><br/>
</s:validateAll>
```

```
<input type="button" value="Submit"/>
</h:form>

</f:view>
```

There is quite a bit going on with this page, so let's take it step by step. First, `<s:validateAll>` will validate all the child (sub) properties of the tag by using the Hibernate validator. As I mentioned a bit earlier, we are validating against the domain objects that are annotated by Hibernate validators.

The next step is to create a label for the field. This field is marked with the `for` parameter. This parameter tells us what output label is associated with the input.

After this, we use the `<s:decorate>` tag to surround a mix of standard JSF tags, Seam tags, and Ajax4jsf tags. This can seem complicated, but it really is not that bad. The `<a:support>` tag can be applied to any of the input tags and merely tells us to apply Ajax support to this input.

The Ajax vent is triggered depending on what is defined by the `event` parameter. Then the `reRender` parameter tells what `<a:outPanel>` will be triggered by the Ajax event. The output panel for this case displays the message from Seam based on the validation.

So what is going to happen is that when an `onblur` event is reached, it will trigger the validation of the object. If the object is invalid, the error message will be displayed on the `outputPanel`.

JMS Messaging Using Ajax

Most of you probably have not thought of putting Ajax and JMS together before, although they are both asynchronous processes (normally—yes, I know they both *can* be synchronous). However, the combination definitely can be useful. Combining the two can allow your page to monitor JMS topics for new messages without having the extra overhead of going through a JavaBean.

Your first response may be, "Cool, but how would I use this?" There really are a variety of sites this could be used for, but the one that comes to mind is for intranet applications. More and more web applications are being used for internal-facing applications. Those ugly dumb terminals are finally being tossed away. And this would allow you to monitor a queue with, let's say, work tickets you have to use without having to constantly move off the page or using hard refreshes of the page.

Configuring JMS Listeners

The first step is to determine what it is you even want to listen to. In our example, we are going to listen to topics called `troubleTickets` and `emergencyRequests`. These topics must be registered in `seam.properties`, `web.xml`, or `components.xml`. This example places them into `components.xml`, as shown in Listing 8-31.

Listing 8-31. *Topics Being Listened to as Defined in components.xml*

```
<component name="org.jboss.seam.remoting.messaging.subscriptionRegistry">
    <property name="allowedTopics">troubleTickets, emergencyRequests</property>
</component>
```

Now obviously we are not putting a permanent hook into the topic when we are on the page. If we did, that would be quite insane. So what we do is listen to the topic at predefined intervals. This allows the JavaScript to monitor the topic without the user knowing. There are two variables used to monitor: one is the interval to check for any messages (pollInterval), and the other is the amount of time to wait on the server for a message (pollTimeOut). Both of these parameters are in seconds, which is different from most Java applications (which use milliseconds). This can be configured as in Listing 8-32.

Listing 8-32. *Defining the Poll Interval and Time-Out in components.xml*

```
<component name="org.jboss.seam.remoting.remotingConfig">
    <property name="pollTimeout">5</property>
    <property name="pollInterval">1</property>
</component>
```

You can define this not only at a global level, but also programmatically with JavaScript on the page. This will allow you to change the interval per page but also could allow your users to configure it with JavaScript if you want. The code in Listing 8-33 is an example of defining the interval programmatically.

Listing 8-33. *Defining the Poll Interval and Time-Out Using JavaScript*

```
<Script language="JavaScript">
    Seam.Remoting.pollInterval = 1;
    Seam.Remoting.pollTimeout = 5;
</Script>
```

■**Note** Remember that if you use a high pollTimeout value and you have many users, you could run the risk of running out of threads. So if you decide to use this, make sure to spend some time determining your maximum thread count and maximum number of users.

Using JMS Listeners

So now that you have your topics created and are listening to them, the next step is to actually do something with the topics. What we are going to do is something similar to what we did when we did straight Ajax remoting earlier, and that is to create a callback method expecting a response. Listing 8-34 uses `Seam.Remoting.subscribe()` to hook a JavaScript method with a particular topic.

Listing 8-34. *Linking a Topic with the Method processTroubleTickets*

```
<Script language="JavaScript">
    Seam.Remoting.subscribe("troubleTickets", processTroubleTickets);
</Script>
```

Now that we have the topic linked to the method, it is time to create the method. Although there are various types of payloads you can put into the topics, you have access to only two types in the JavaScript: `TextMessage` and `ObjectMessage`. You can either grab the message or the object, and then process it further. Listing 8-35 provides an example of processing both.

Listing 8-35. *The Implementation of the processTroubleTickets Method*

```
<Script language="JavaScript">
function processTroubleTickets(payload) {
    if (payload instanceof Seam.Remoting.TextMessage) {
        alert("Message Payload Containing - " + payload.getText());
    }
    else if (payload instanceof Seam.Remoting.ObjectMessage) {
        alert("Message Payload Containing - " + payload.getObject());
    }
}
</Script>
```

In the example, we used alerts to print out the payload. However, in a real application you would probably want to update some `<div>` tags or some input boxes.

■**Note** I have given what really is a brief tutorial on the different Ajax techniques to use with Seam applications. Any other framework that is JSF based should be compatible with Seam as well. I do believe the combination of Seam remoting and Ajax4jsf gives you a wide paintbrush, increasing Ajax-enabled pages without having to write much plumbing code of your own.

Security

Almost every application more than a few pages long requires security. In a large-scale corporate application, you are probably going to use one of the corporation's specific security methodologies. There are also custom authentication models you can use. You can easily have the site authenticate, save to a session, and then just check that session periodically. There is also a Seam-specific security model, and this is the model I am going to present in this section.

The Seam security model is quite simple. The user logs in, and a role is assigned to that user. Each user can have different roles assigned to them. The roles assigned are based on the user's login, usually from a back-end database. The roles can be as simple as having different permissions for a regular user and an administrator. Or the roles could be a culmination of a few permissions.

In this section, we are going to create a basic security example. We will define a security apparatus to capture a login. After the user is logged in, the user will be sent to a main page where they can choose to go to an admin page or a normal page depending on their permissions. By the end of this section, you should be able to set up your own authentication as well as set up roles for it.

■**Note** Authentication is not finalized in version 1.1.0 of Seam. In fact, in this version it is not 100 percent usable. Seam security is expected to be released in a production-ready version in 1.1.5, in early 2007. So some of this information in this section may not be complete. However, I wanted to include this section as a starter because of the importance of security for most web applications.

■**Note** You can refer to the source code at `http://www.integrallis.com` for a more up-to-date example of the security in Seam. The source code is also available at the Source Code/Download area of the Apress website (`http://www.apress.com`).

Security, and Seam security more specifically, is based on two concepts that are independent but work in conjunction: the ability to authenticate and the ability to check for permissions.

Implementing Authentication

Security implementation is fairly straightforward but requires a few moving parts. You are going to have to have a generic login page call `ProviderAuthentication`, which in turn has

AuthenticationProvider defined on it. I know the names are a bit confusing, but do not worry—implementing AuthenticationProvider is not too complicated. We will start by implementing these individual pieces.

Authentication Provider

Let's start with the authentication provider itself. This is where the authentication happens. Here you will have an authentication object passed in and you will use whatever mechanism you want in order to authenticate. More than likely this will be database driven, with the roles retrieved from the database as well. Listing 8-36 shows a simple username authentication, but in real life you would want to make this a bit more complicated.

Listing 8-36. *Our Implementation of AuthenticationProvider*

```
@Name("authenticatorAction")
public class AuthenticationAction implements AuthenticationProvider
{
    public Identity authenticate(Identity authentication)
      throws AuthenticationException
    {
        String user = authentication.getPrincipal().toString();
        String password = authentication.getCredentials().toString();
        Role[] roles = null;

        // generic login
        // database driven login would occur here to set the roles
        if (user.equals("admin")) {
            roles = new Role[] { new Role("access"), new Role("admin")};

        }
        else if (user.equals("user")) {
            roles = new Role[] { new Role("access")};
        }
        else {
            throw new AuthenticationException("Invalid username/password");
        }
        return new UsernamePasswordToken(authentication.getPrincipal(),
                    authentication.getCredentials(), roles);
    }
}
```

The important point is that you need to decide whether to authenticate. If the user's login has failed, you will throw an `AuthenticationException` exception. If the user's authentication has passed, you will want to set some roles, even if it is one generic `login` role. You also will notice that I have set multiple roles: a generic `access` role, indicating that the user should be able to access any secure pages, and a more advanced `admin` role, indicating that the page should be only for an admin user.

Provider Authentication

Defining the authentication provider is only the first part. As you may have noticed, Listing 8-36 also includes a Seam-defined component called `authenticatorAction`. We will need this when setting the `ProviderAuthenticator`, which is defined in `components.xml`, as shown in Listing 8-37.

Listing 8-37. *Defining ProviderAuthenticator in components.xml*

```
<component class="org.jboss.seam.security.authenticator.ProviderAuthenticator">
    <property name="providers">#{authenticatorAction}</property>
</component>
```

Here we are injecting our defined authentication provider into the provider authenticator. The `ProviderAuthenticator` is what we will be using on our login page to log the user in or out.

Creating the Login/Logout

Now that we have the login tools defined, we can create our pages to log the user in and out. The first part is the JSF page, which will look like any normal login-type JSP page. Listing 8-38 defines the `login.jsp` file.

Listing 8-38. *The login.jsp Page to Log In the User*

```
<f:view>
    <h:form>
        Login:<br/>
        User -
        <h:inputText id="name" value="#{user.username}" required="true"/><br/>
        Password -
        <h:inputText id="password" value="#{user.password}" required="true"/><br/>
```

```
<h:commandButton id="login" action="#{login.login}"
    value="Login" styleClass="button"/>
  </h:form>
</f:view>
```

This page will call the Seam component login, which is defined in Listing 8-39. Here you will see how easy it is to log in to the application.

Listing 8-39. *The Stateless LoginAction Class That Will Call the ProviderAuthentication*

```
@Stateless
@Name("login")
public class LoginAction implements Login
{
    @Logger
    Log log;

    @In(value = "user", required = false) @Out(required = false)
    User user;

    public String login()
    {
        try
        {
            Authenticator.instance().authenticate(user.getUsername(),
                user.getPassword());
            return "main";
        }
        catch (AuthenticationException ex)
        {
            FacesMessages.instance().add(ex.getMessage());
            return "login";
        }
    }

    public String logout()
    {
        Authenticator.instance().unauthenticateSession();
        Seam.invalidateSession();
        return "login";
    }
}
```

`LoginAction` defines two methods: one for logging in and one for logging out. Our login page set a `User` object, which we pass through the username and password to be authenticated. `Authenticator` is a built-in Seam component that will then call the `AuthenticationProvider` that we had initially created. If the login is successful, the user will then be forwarded to a main page.

The other method is the `logout()` method, which will invalidate the user and invalidate the session objects forwarding back to the login page.

So now that the basics are created and the site is able to log in and log out users, we will move on so you can see how to lock down individual components.

The Seam Security Manager

`SeamSecurityManager` is used to manage the authentication of permissions and rules for a user. The interesting thing about Seam security is that it uses the Drools rule engine to create rules for security. This adds overhead by having to add Drools JAR files and configurations to Seam, but also gives more flexibility in creating authentication rules.

Much of these rules are still part of the items in flux, so I will not discuss in detail how to create more-advanced rules. Instead I will present the more basic set of implementations. We will use the rules that the authentication login set previously for our upcoming examples.

Configuring SeamSecurityManager

To begin, we have to configure `SeamSecurityManager` and `SecurityConfiguration`. This will require setting the components in `components.xml`, as shown in Listing 8-40. Unlike many Seam components, these components are not instantiated by default with the application. This makes sense when you consider that in order to use them, you also have to have the Drools JARs deployed with your server, and that would hardly be a worthwhile prerequisite to have in order to use Seam.

Listing 8-40. *SeamSecurityManager and SeamConfiguration Set in components.xml*

```
<!-- Install a Security Configuration -->
<component class="org.jboss.seam.security.config.SecurityConfiguration"/>

<!-- Install the Seam Security Manager -->
<component class="org.jboss.seam.security.SeamSecurityManager"/>
```

You will also have to add a security rules file to the deployed EAR. This file is referenced by `SeamSecurityManager` as `security-rules.drl` located in the `META-INF` directory of the EAR. A small example of this file is in Listing 8-41. This file has no rules set on it.

Listing 8-41. *An Example of a security-rules.drl File*

```
package SeamSpacePermissions;

import org.jboss.seam.security.Identity;
import org.jboss.seam.security.rules.PermissionCheck;
import org.jboss.seam.example.seamspace.MemberImage;
```

After these configurations are complete, you will be able to call the permission-checking aspect of the components.

Component-Level Authentication

Security would be worthless if you could not lock down particular components. Built into Seam security are page-level annotations to lock down the individual pages in either a static or dynamic way. *Static permissions* are like those we defined in Listing 8-36, roles that are defined based on login to the site. *Dynamic permissions* are those that you define based on current inputs and states; they are as the word says, dynamic. For example, you do not want to allow someone to have access to page A if they have already completed a certain sequence of events.

Neither area is quite complete right now. There are three annotations so far that can be used: `@Restrict`, `@Permission`, and `@Permissions`. These will be used to set the permissions on Seam components.

Page-Level Authentication

Page-level authentication is performed by using function calls in the tag libraries as opposed to specific tag libraries. This gives you maximum flexibility when creating your page-based rules. When used in conjunction with JSTL tag libraries, the security functions are able to use the conditional JSTL tags with the Seam components.

The two functions that exist are `s:hasRole` and `s:hasPermission`, which check for roles or permissions, respectively. The first one is simpler. It takes in a string and will return a Boolean on whether the logged-in user has that particular role. The second one, `hasPermission`, will check for a permission based on name, action, and an array of arguments passed into it.

In our example in Listing 8-42, we will display data on the page only if the user has the `admin` role.

Listing 8-42. *An Example of a Page That Will Test for a User Having the admin Role*

```
<%@ taglib uri="http://jboss.com/products/seam/taglib" prefix="s" %>
<%@ taglib uri="http://java.sun.com/jsf/core" prefix="f" %>
<%@ taglib uri="http://java.sun.com/jsp/jstl/core" prefix="c" %>
```

```
<f:view>
    <c:if
        test="${s:hasRole('admin')}">
            This is an example of an admin page.
    </c:if>
</f:view>
```

As you can see, we are using the JSTL `if` tag, which will use the conditions defined on `test` to determine whether the `if` statement passes. In this case, we have the Seam-defined `hasRole` as a regular expression to define the condition.

Drools Support

Drools is a popular rules engine that is now part of JBoss Enterprise Middleware Suite (JEMS) projects. Like many rules engines, Drools allows you to apply declarative programming in the form of rules. In Drools, rules are simple `if-then` constructs that follow this pattern:

```
IF <condition> THEN <consequence>
```

In your application, you will have a collection of objects known as a *working memory* that your rules will act upon. The rules are evaluated against the working memory to determine whether one or more rules should be fired (executed). As rules are fired, they can change the state of the working memory and also produce side effects that can be used to generate application events.

Rules engines such as Drools are useful in domains where traditional procedural and object-oriented techniques result in code that is hard to maintain. Rules engines allow for a separation of business rules from your application code, and allow people with business knowledge (rather than programmers) to author and maintain these rules.

In addition, make sure you do not confuse the following terms when referring to Drools:

Working memory: Like a hash or bucket containing the facts (objects) and application data (other objects).

Facts: The objects that the rules are evaluated against. For example, object = car, rule = if car.color <> white, then fire rule increase_color_car_count. The color_car_count could be a fact (an object in the working memory that might affect the firing of a rule) or application data (the difference being that if you change application data, it can't trigger any rules to fire).

Application data: Any other object. The rules have access to these objects.

Rule: A construct in the form of if *this*, do *that*.

Rule base: A collection of rules. In Drools, rules are usually in an XML file, either in Java, Jython, or a domain-specific language (DSL).

Configuring Drools

There are a few things you need to do to configure rules to work in your Seam environment. The first step obviously is to create rules. In most environments, your rules are generated dynamically, so you will have to make the rules available to Seam. In future versions of Drools, there will be a rules server that you can use.

However, for testing purposes you can load up a static set of rules via a Seam component and store the rules in the Application context. To be able to define a rules file in `components.xml`, you can also define the DSL, as in Listing 8-43.

Listing 8-43. *Static Loading of Rules into Seam*

```
<component name="customRules"
        class="org.jboss.seam.drools.RuleBase">
    <property name="ruleFiles">ourStaticRules.drl</property>
    <property name="dslFile">policyPricing.dsl</property>
</component>
```

In the first line of the properties, the rules are defined, and in the second line the DSL is defined.

Finally, we need to make `org.drools.WorkingMemory` available to each Seam conversation. We do this by using a Seam-specific component that references our `customRules`. This has been defined in Listing 8-44.

Listing 8-44. *The WorkingMemory Component Created to Encapsulate Our Rules*

```
<component name="customWorkingMemory"
        class="org.jboss.seam.drools.ManagedWorkingMemory">
    <property name="ruleBase">#{customRules}</property>
</component>
```

Using Drools in a Seam Component

Now that the working memory has been defined, you can simply inject it and use it as you would any other component. Simply inject it by name or make the property the name defined as the component and you will be ready to use the rules to do assertions, or to fire any rules.

Using Drools in jBPM

In addition to providing jBPM integration as we showed in Chapter 7, Seam also provides Drools integration to jBPM. The Seam Drools integration allows you to create an `<assertObjects>` tag within your page flow or business process definition. The assertion can be in either a decision or a task node of the definitions. Listing 8-45 provides an example of using Drools within a decision.

Listing 8-45. *Drools Rules Built into a jBPM Decision*

```
<decision name="approval">

    <transition name="approved" to="ship">
        <action class="org.jboss.seam.drools.DroolsActionHandler">
            <workingMemoryName>customWorkingMemory</workingMemoryName>
            <assertObjects>
                <element>#{customer}</element>
                <element>#{order}</element>
                <element>#{order.lineItems}</element>
            </assertObjects>
        </action>
    </transition>

    <transition name="rejected" to="cancelled"/>
</decision>
```

Here you can see a regular jBPM transition tag, followed by an action tag specified by a Seam Drools handler. Inside the Drools handler you then define your assert objects as well as our working memory component that we had created earlier in `components.xml`.

As I mentioned, we can use Drools rules not only in transition but also in tasks, as defined in Listing 8-46.

Listing 8-46. *Drools Rules Built into a jBPM Task Node*

```
<task-node name="review">
    <task name="review" description="Review Order">
        <assignment handler="org.jboss.seam.drools.DroolsAssignmentHandler">
            <workingMemoryName>customWorkingMemory</workingMemoryName>
            <assertObjects>
                <element>#{actor}</element>
                <element>#{customer}</element>
                <element>#{order}</element>
                <element>#{order.lineItems}</element>
            </assertObjects>
        </assignment>
    </task>
    <transition name="rejected" to="cancelled"/>
    <transition name="approved" to="approved"/>
</task-node>
```

Just as we did in the decision tag, you have the same option to use the assignment handler on the task node. Hopefully this can help you get started if you want to use a combined Seam + Drools + jBPM project.

Summary

This chapter ends our discussion of the Seam programming concepts. By now you should have the knowledge needed to complete almost any web application task with Seam. This chapter covered a wide range of concepts: internationalization, themes, Ajax, web services, security, and Drools support. The purpose of this chapter was for you to start to understand some of the extras given with Seam. The next chapter will delve into configuring Seam for multiple situations, and although this configuration is not programmatically necessary, it can be quite useful.

CHAPTER 9

Advanced Configurations

We are now going to turn our efforts to looking at the different ways to configure Seam. Obviously, we have already gone over configuring and deploying Seam and by now have deployed quite a few applications. However, Seam has the ability to be leveraged in multiple environments under multiple conditions. To use Seam, you do not actually have to be in a Java EE environment or even be using EJB3 if you do not want to (it is preferred, though). Of course, you will have to use Java 5; there is no way around that.

In this chapter, I will show you some optional environments to run Seam in. These options include running Seam with an embedded EJB instead of a standard container, and running Seam with Hibernate instead of entity beans and with JavaBeans instead of session beans. After that, I will go over a few optional configuration changes in your XML files that we have not had to use yet. You may find some of these changes useful. Finally, I will end the chapter by discussing Seam's support for portlets.

Although on the surface you may feel this chapter is not totally necessary for your development and deployment of applications, the ability to use the embedded containers and the other environments may help you with testing and creating prototypes before having to write a full-fledged Seam-based application.

Optional Environmental Configurations

By default Seam is designed to be run in a Java EE environment, which by definition gives us Java 5 and EJB3 support as well as a host of other items (such as messaging). Just about all of our examples have used JSF with an EJB3 business logic tier. This is the configuration that Seam works best with and that it was initially designed for. However, that is not your *only* option when using Seam, because by its basic design Seam is a framework that can tie other frameworks together. Seam can be run with or without EJB3 objects and can even be run in a full-blown application server or in something simpler such as Tomcat.

In this section, I am going to present the various ways of using Seam with other environments and other configurations. I will start with a discussion of running Seam in an embedded container, and then move on to discussing the use of JavaBeans and Hibernate instead of EJB3 for our business logic tier.

Running Seam in the Embedded EJB3 Container

As I have said previously, under normal circumstances Seam is used to access EJB3 objects from your JSF presentation tier without the need for backing beans. In order to run EJB3 objects, obviously you will need an EJB container to run them in. This is almost always achieved by using an enterprise application server such as JBoss. However, this brings up two essential problems: first, not everyone has access to an enterprise-level server to deploy to; and second, it is hard to perform automated integration tests if you do not have an application server to readily deploy to.

Let's discuss the first of these problems. Having to have an application server may not seem like a huge problem to some of you. Obtaining an application server is easy—all you have to do is download JBoss, which is free. After it is downloaded, configuring it to run on your desktop takes only mere seconds. Just about anyone's desktop has the memory and resources available to run Java EE applications. However, this is not necessarily the case in a deployed production environment. When you have a production deployment, you are paying money for a server that is managed and monitored, usually with failover hard drives and maybe even entire servers to fail over or be replicated to. In this situation, running JBoss may not be entirely cost-effective and many developers do work on the side. Often if you are an individual person writing a small web application, or even a large application with a low number of users, you do not want to pay the extra money for JBoss services. It is much more cost-effective to use Tomcat instead in these situations. Running your server in containers such as JBoss enables you to leverage advantages such as pooling, session replication, and so forth. If you do not need these advantages, the alternative can be to use Tomcat. However, Tomcat is not a Java EE application server, so deploying EJB POJOs is not an option, unless of course you use an embedded EJB container, which is the solution I will be describing in this chapter.

The other reason for using an embedded server is for testing. In general, the more testing you do, the better. And the more advanced your testing, even better. Testing is even more important when you have a big team, especially a big team that is segregated geographically. There are multiple kinds of unit testing. However, in the end you should have some kind of integration testing. Integration testing can span a few different techniques. You can integrate by testing two applications working together or testing how your application works in a deployed environment. Although using POJOs for our business tiers makes it much easier to test the business logic, it does not give us the ability to test whether the presentation tier is speaking to that business logic correctly. Hence integration tests allow for just that, the testing of total communication. With frameworks such as Spring, this is achieved through mocking up HTTP GETs. However, when you are dealing with deployed EJBs, testing becomes a bit more difficult because you are not using the container itself (for example, Spring) but instead you are using a third-party container that you do not have direct control over, such as JBoss AS. This is where an embedded container can become handy. It can allow you to test how your system would react when exposed in an EJB container.

Using JBoss EJB3

JBoss obviously has an EJB3 container in its deployed application server; this is what allows us to deploy our applications. JBoss also allows the EJB3 container to be downloaded and used independently of the application server, and it actually segregates it out into a usable embedded container.

You can download the EJB3 and its embedded container from JBoss at `http://labs.jboss.com/portal/jbossejb3/`. The download contains two items: the full EJB3 container for an application server, and the EJB3 embedded container—which is what we are interested in. This is the container we are going to use as our embedded EJB container.

Now before you go to the site and start downloading this, please note I only pointed out where it is located and stored as a reference; you do not actually have to download it from that site. The JBoss Seam distribution contains all the necessary JAR files and configuration files that are needed for packaging your embedded container. I merely pointed out the location to let you know where all this came from.

Packaging Our New Container

Because the embedded container is going to be deployed or run in a nonapplication server, we will be creating a WAR file instead of an EAR file. This will require two main sets of changes to our existing application. First, we will have to change some configuration files and add some more default configuration files. Second, we will have to package it all up into a WAR. I know that sounds like quite a bit of work, but the good news is we do not have to change a single class file, which in the end was our goal.

Configuring the XML

If the embedded container required too many configuration changes in the XML, it would not be a valuable tool because you would have to create many custom XML files just for use. Although this would not matter if you were deploying exclusively to Tomcat, this would start to become a headache if you were using the embedded EJB container for testing or prototyping. If, though, you are using this as an actual production release, you could have issues if your development, testing, and production environments differ greatly. This practice may introduce significant extra maintenance, and users will need to weigh the risk. So there really are only two sets of configuration changes we need to make. One is in `components.xml` and the other is in `jboss-beans.xml`, a file that is not in a normal EAR deployment.

Configuring components.xml

The first file we will update is the `components.xml` file. The changes here are quite minimal and in fact you could make them by using a properties file and replacing it with your build script. In this case, we will just hard-code the changes. Listing 9-1 defines two of the components.

Listing 9-1. *The components.xml File with the Embedded EJB Turned On*

```
<components>
    <component name="org.jboss.seam.core.init">
        <property name="debug">true</property>
        <property name="myFacesLifecycleBug">true</property>
        <property name="jndiPattern">#{ejbName}/local</property>
    </component>

    <!-- Neccessary for Embedded EJB container -->
    <component class="org.jboss.seam.core.Ejb" installed="true"/>
</components>
```

The changes to this file are quite subtle. The first change is to `jndiPattern`. Before, we prefaced the `ejbName` with the EAR name. Because we no longer have an EAR and are using a local embedded container, we no longer need to define the EAR name first. So we delete the EAR name preface that is usually there.

The other change is to the embedded container option. Because we are using the embedded container, we set the `installed` property to `true`.

Configuring jboss-beans.xml

The other change to make is an addition of the `jboss-beans.xml` file. Under normal EJB3 persistence, we have the JBoss container (or whatever application server we are using) to create the data source and handle the pooling for it. However, because we are deploying to an environment that does not have data source pooling, we have to create the data source ourselves. (Keep in mind that different implementations of JDBC drivers and SQL databases may produce different test results.) To create the data source, we define a data source bean for our application, as shown in Listing 9-2.

Listing 9-2. *The jboss-beans.xml File Defining Our Database Persistence*

```
<?xml version="1.0" encoding="UTF-8"?>
<deployment xmlns:xsi="http://www.w3.org/2001/XMLSchema-instance"
xsi:schemaLocation="urn:jboss:bean-deployer bean-deployer_1_0.xsd"
xmlns="urn:jboss:bean-deployer">

<bean name="garageSaleDatasourceBootstrap"
        class="org.jboss.resource.adapter.jdbc.local.LocalTxDataSource">
    <property name="driverClass">com.mysql.jdbc.Driver</property>
    <property name="connectionURL">jdbc:mysql:.</property>
    <property name="userName">root</property>
    <property name="password">password</property>
```

```
        <property name="jndiName">java:/GarageSaleDS</property>
        <property name="minSize">0</property>
        <property name="maxSize">10</property>
        <property name="blockingTimeout">1000</property>
        <property name="idleTimeout">100000</property>
        <property name="transactionManager">
            <inject bean="TransactionManager"/>
        </property>
        <property name="cachedConnectionManager">
            <inject bean="CachedConnectionManager"/>
        </property>
        <property name="initialContextProperties">
            <inject bean="InitialContextProperties"/>
        </property>
    </bean>

    <bean name="garageSaleDatasource" class="java.lang.Object">
        <constructor factoryMethod="getDatasource">
            <factory bean="garageSaleDatasourceBootstrap"/>
        </constructor>
    </bean>

</deployment>
```

Here we define two beans to look up the data source that will be referenced by
`persistence.xml` via `jndiName`. You can use this as a template when creating your own
data source bean. The biggest thing to make sure of is that the `jndiName` property you
define here is the same as the one you have defined in `persistence.xml`.

Packaging the WAR

For the packaging of the WAR file, we are going to have to break up the changes into two
areas. The first part is the building of the embedded JAR, and the second part is the building of the WAR.

The Library Directory

The first step in creating our WAR is to create the embedded JAR. This is going to be
equivalent to creating the EJB3 JAR, except this time we are creating a JAR that we will
embed inside the `WEB-INF/lib` directory, as opposed to having the JAR at the root directory of the EAR. The JAR will contain four major items: the class files, `persistence.xml`,
`jboss-beans.xml`, and the `seam.properties` file. Figure 9-1 shows this JAR file and its partial
contents in relation to the other library files.

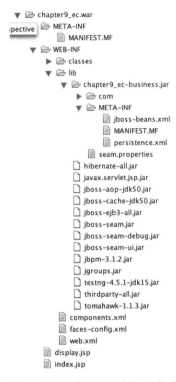

Figure 9-1. *The WAR file with the library directory highlighted*

Here you can see the embedded JAR as well as many other JAR files. These other JARs are necessary for the embedded container to work. Some of the files, such as `jboss-seam.jar`, you should be familiar with because we used them before for our other deployments. However, others such as `jboss-ejb3-all.jar` are not at all familiar. You can find these other JAR files in the `lib` directory of the Seam distribution.

The Embedded Configuration

The other set of contents to update outside of the normal configurations are the embedded configuration files. These embedded configuration files are included in the embedded EJB3 release; however, they are also in the Seam distribution. In the Seam distribution, the files are located under the `embedded-ejb/conf` directory. These embedded files will be stored in the `WEB-INF/classes` directory. Figure 9-2 shows the structure of the files.

As you can see, the configuration changes are necessary but minimal. These changes will allow you to create a WAR that contains EJBs that you can now deploy to Tomcat or run testing against. Please note that I have not gone over the actual changes to the build scripts that you will have to do. But as long as your build scripts mimic the directory structure and file locations I have outlined, you should be fine.

Figure 9-2. *The directory structure including the configuration files*

I will say the one downside to doing all this is that your deployed application becomes extremely big because it has to contain all the extra JARs. I am not sure how this will affect performance, but it is something to consider before actually using Seam with an embedded EJB3 container in a Tomcat production environment. Of course, as I stated at the beginning of this discussion, if this is a low-use application, then this may not pose a problem at all.

Running Seam with Hibernate

After reading the book thus far, you should be able to not only program with Seam, but also use JSF and EJB3 with it. I have even just discussed ways of getting around the need for a Java EE application server. However (and I think this is mainly due to EJB 2.*x*), EJB still has some negative and scary connotations. EJB in many ways is the boogey man of J2EE, and this negative connotation is one of the reasons application servers such as Spring have become so popular. It is not that EJB in its entirety was ever that scary; however, major parts of it—most noticeably entity beans and stateful session beans— were less than desired for many people. At any rate, depending on your level of comfort or the level of comfort of your employer, you may not want to take the plunge into EJB3 objects. However, there is another alternative, and one that many of you are probably fairly familiar with: Hibernate.

The examples in the book thus far were shown using EJB3 objects. The EJB3 objects for the most part serve two purposes, as a business logic tier and persistence tier. We can replace these two areas by using POJO JavaBeans for our business tier and using Hibernate for our persistence tier. This allows you to still use Seam to connect your front end to your middle tier, and to use the domain objects for your front end. And because everything you are creating is a POJO, the upgrade path is very mild if you later decide to upgrade to EJBs.

Example Using JavaBeans and Hibernate

To show you how to use Hibernate and JavaBeans with Seam, we will create a basic application for adding users and displaying those users on a web page. This application will consist of a JSF page, a JavaBean, and an entity bean. We will start with the entity bean in Listing 9-3.

Listing 9-3. *Our Entity Bean User Object*

```
@Entity
@Name("user")
public class User {

    @Id @GeneratedValue
    private long id;
    private String name;

    public long getId() {
        return id;
    }
    public void setId(long id) {
        this.id = id;
    }
    public String getName() {
        return name;
    }
    public void setName(String name) {
        this.name = name;
    }
}
```

As you can see, this entity bean looks just like our entity beans in our EJB3 containers, even down to the @Entity annotation. You can use all the annotations you normally use with entity beans, such as the validation and name attributes. So this obviously would require no change when upgrading to a full EJB3 environment.

However, we are not as lucky when it comes to the JavaBean. Still, even that change is not that obtrusive, as shown in Listing 9-4.

Listing 9-4. *Our Java Bean That Will Manage the Entity Bean*

```
@Scope(ScopeType.STATELESS)
@Name("userManager")
public class UserManagerAction implements UserManager {

    @In(create=true, value="userDatabase")
    private Session userDatabase;

    @In(required = false)
    User user;

    @DataModel
    private List<User> users;

    @Logger
    Log log;

    @Factory("users")
    @SuppressWarnings("unchecked")
    public void findUsers() {
        log.info("Find the Users");
        users = userDatabase.createQuery("From User u order by u.name").list();
    }

    public String saveUser() {
        log.info("Save user - #{user}");
        userDatabase.save(user);
        return "/index.jsp";
    }
}
```

The first obvious item to notice is that there is no annotation marking the class as @Stateless or @Stateful. This is simply because it is neither stateless nor stateful; it is a JavaBean. The rest of the page should look fairly familiar. For the most part, the code is the same as if you were using a full Seam + EJB3 class. In fact, the only noticeable difference (and this is a fairly big one) is the lack of using EntityManager. Instead, you are going to be using a Hibernate Session object. Although a Session object has different attributes, there are many similarities between the method signatures. Using a Session object makes it so the migration path from JavaBeans + Hibernate to EJB3 has a few bumps, but in the end is relatively smooth.

This is the code we will be using to deploy to the server. There are two setups we can use for deploying the code. The first is to deploy it as a WAR on our application server.

The other configuration, which will require a few more steps, is to deploy it as a WAR to a non–Java EE environment.

Inside the Java EE Container

For the first setup, we will configure the application server for deployment to a Java EE container such as JBoss. The setup in the end will build us a WAR. There is no reason to deploy an EAR, because we are not going to be using EJB3 objects. The configuration does require a few changes, because we are now using Hibernate and Hibernate transaction management instead of EJB3 transaction and domain persistence. In the next few steps, we will walk through the configuration file changes and how to deploy the WAR.

Configuration Changes

Our first step will be to change some configuration files around. Because this is a Hibernate application, we are going to need to add a Hibernate configuration file. We will then update the rest of our code to use this file and to implement Seam transactions because the container will no longer be managing them implicitly.

Configuring hibernate.cfg.xml

The Hibernate configuration file will be a standard one. You should be able to grab just about any that you have used before or use my example. There are only a few minor differences, including using `JBossTransactionalManagerLookup` for transaction management. In our Hibernate configuration file, we are defining the mapping for only one class, the `User` class. You can add more classes, depending on your application. Unlike normal Hibernate configurations, this one will not have lookups to mapping files for each table. You will not need it here because the configurations can be read from the annotations on the domain bean. Listing 9-5 defines the Hibernate configuration.

Listing 9-5. *The hibernate.cfg.xml File for Our Example*

```
<hibernate-configuration>
<session-factory name="java:/userDatabase">
    <property name="show_sql">false</property>
    <property name="connection.datasource">java:/hibernateDatasource</property>
    <property name="hbm2ddl.auto">create-drop</property>
    <property name="cache.provider_class">
        org.hibernate.cache.HashtableCacheProvider
    </property>
```

```
    <property name="transaction.flush_before_completion">true</property>
    <property name="connection.release_mode">after_statement</property>
    <property name="transaction.manager_lookup_class">
        org.hibernate.transaction.JBossTransactionManagerLookup
    </property>
    <property name="transaction.factory_class">
        org.hibernate.transaction.JTATransactionFactory
    </property>
    <mapping class="com.integrallis.hib.domain.User"/>
</session-factory>
</hibernate-configuration>
```

Configuring components.xml

Next, we need to define three things for our component piece—well, really two, but we will add the other one so it will make more sense when deploying to the non–Java EE container version. The first two are directly Hibernate related, and the third will define what type of container we are in. These configurations are defined in Listing 9-6. Take a look at them, and then I will go over what each one is for.

Listing 9-6. *The Additions to Our components.xml File*

```
<!-- Bootstrap Hibernate -->
<component name="userDatabase" class="org.jboss.seam.core.ManagedHibernateSession"/>
<component name="hibernateSessionFactory"
    class="org.jboss.seam.core.HibernateSessionFactory"/>
<component class="org.jboss.seam.core.Microcontainer" installed="false"/>
```

The first component we define is userDatabase, and the name should look familiar to you. This is the Session name we used in our previous JavaBean example in Listing 9-4, when we were creating the code. This component is used to inject the Session object into our JavaBean. The next one is a straightforward session factory definition, which (as you may know if you are familiar with Hibernate) is needed for Hibernate session management. The final one is used to mark whether the micro container is installed. We are defining it as not being installed because we are deploying to a Java EE environment.

Configuring faces-config.xml

Because we are using Hibernate for our database persistence, we are going to have to use a different phase listener to control the transactioning. Adjust the phase listener in faces-config.xml to TransactionalSeamPhaseListener, as in Listing 9-7.

Listing 9-7. *The Life Cycle Definition in faces-config.xml*

```
<lifecycle>
    <phase-listener>
        org.jboss.seam.jsf.TransactionalSeamPhaseListener
    </phase-listener>
</lifecycle>
```

Configuring web.xml

Finally, we have come to the end of our configurations and `web.xml`. This is a configuration change that you could use in any of the examples we have created thus far and is not distinctly unique to creating Hibernate applications, but it is definitely necessary when not running inside a Java EE transaction container. The code in Listing 9-8 is used as "a last line of defense" for transaction cleanup. This code will intercept all Seam calls and make sure that any uncommitted transactions are rolled back, thus not leaving any open transactions.

Listing 9-8. *The web.xml Addition to Add Transaction Cleanup*

```
<!-- Needed to ensure safe tx cleanup when using ®
<!-- Seam-managed sessions/persistence contexts -->
<filter>
    <filter-name>Seam Exception Filter</filter-name>
    <filter-class>org.jboss.seam.servlet.SeamExceptionFilter</filter-class>
</filter>

<filter-mapping>
    <filter-name>Seam Exception Filter</filter-name>
    <url-pattern>*.seam</url-pattern>
</filter-mapping>
```

Packaging the WAR

The packaging for the WAR will be much like the packaging we did earlier for the EJB embedded container. Here we have our classes again in an embedded JAR, although this time we have the `hibernate.cfg.xml` file in there as well. Figure 9-3 shows the directory structure minus the class files.

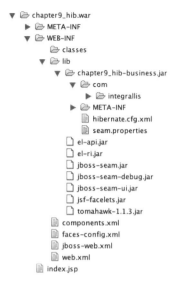

▼ 🗁 chapter9_hib.war
  ▶ 🗁 META-INF
  ▼ 🗁 WEB-INF
      🗁 classes
    ▼ 🗁 lib
      ▼ 🗁 chapter9_hib-business.jar
        ▼ 🗁 com
          ▶ 🗁 integrallis
        ▶ 🗁 META-INF
            📄 hibernate.cfg.xml
            📄 seam.properties
        📄 el-api.jar
        📄 el-ri.jar
        📄 jboss-seam.jar
        📄 jboss-seam-debug.jar
        📄 jboss-seam-ui.jar
        📄 jsf-facelets.jar
        📄 tomahawk-1.1.3.jar
      📄 components.xml
      📄 faces-config.xml
      📄 jboss-web.xml
      📄 web.xml
  📄 index.jsp

Figure 9-3. *The WAR file for our Java EE container deployment*

At this point, you should have your WAR created and be able to deploy it to JBoss for testing and use. As you will see, our web application behaves just like any other normal application would.

Outside the Java EE Container

Configuring outside the container is much like configuring inside the container except for a few distinct differences. There are four additional steps you will have to perform to configure outside the container:

1. Put the files from the Seam container directory `microcontainer/conf` into the class path of the deployed WAR.

2. Add `jboss-microcontainer.jar`, `jboss-jca.jar`, and `myfaces-*.jars` into the `lib` directory of the `WEB-INF` directory.

3. Add `jboss-beans.xml` to the application JAR.

4. Mark the microcontainer as `true` in the `components.xml`.

PARTING THOUGHTS ON HIBERNATE WITH SEAM

A few parting items to think about when using the Hibernate + Seam methodology: Although it is a rather impressive solution if you are planning an upgrade path from this to a full EJB3 environment, if you are not, this may not be the answer you are looking for. For one thing, you cannot use transactioning built into session beans, which is one of the big reasons for using session beans. So by default you are setting it to flush the session after your calls are complete. If your application requires anything but `required`, it could get more cumbersome to not only develop but to migrate to later on. Also, one of the big reasons for using Seam is to provide a more agile way of developing full Java EE–based applications. However, when using essentially a Hibernate + JSF environment, those advantages are not as great as when we use JSF + EJB. Although this solution will work perfectly, you may want to examine other more-agile solutions such as Codehaus'sTrails, which combines Hibernate and Tapestry in an agile way.

Optional Component Configurations

In Chapter 5, I started to explain how to create a Seam application, and even described some of the customizations you can do to your configuration files with Seam, such as the ability to turn debugging on or off. Because Seam is a framework unlike most, in that there is no direct coding of it, it instead sprinkles annotations and configurations throughout the code. Therefore, optional Seam configurations are equally spread out through the code.

In this section, I will go over additional configurations that you can include in your code and how to use it.

Additions to faces-config.xml

The `faces-config.xml` file is used by JSF to configure the Faces presentation tier. Likewise, it will be used by Seam on areas that need to be intercepted.

Phase Listeners

Earlier we defined for our sites `SeamPhaseListener`, which is used to manage the contexts between JSF and Seam, passing back and forth the various data. However, there are other contexts you should be aware of. One is `SeamExtendedManagedPersistencePhaseListener`, and the others are direct correlations of those for portlets:

`SeamPortletListener`: This is used to manage the Seam contexts when using a portlet server.

`SeamExtendedManagedPersistencePhaseListener`: This is to be used when you want your transactions to be Seam-managed transactions. Assuming that you have no errors, the transaction is committed when the application is complete or when `renderResponse()` or `responseComplete()` is called.

`SeamExtendedManagedPersistencePortletPhaseListener`: This is just like the preceding listener except that it is used in the portlet environment.

Managed Persistence Context

We have defined as part of our phase listener options two managed persistence phase listeners. If you decide to use these phase listeners, you will then also have to use a managed persistence context. Configuring your files to do this is relatively simple, but will require you to make a few changes.

The first thing we will do is create an entry in the `persistence.xml` file to define a name for the entity manager JNDI lookup. Listing 9-9 defines this example.

Listing 9-9. *The Entity Manager JNDI Defined in persistence.xml*

```
<property name="jboss.entity.manager.factory.jndi.name"
          value="java:/EntityManagerFactories/userData"/>
```

The next thing to do is to define the managed persistence context in `components.xml`. For this definition, we are going to use the JNDI name defined previously, as shown in Listing 9-10.

Listing 9-10. *The components.xml File with the Managed Persistence Context*

```
<component name="userDatabase"
          class="org.jboss.seam.core.ManagedPersistenceContext">
    <property name="persistenceUnitJndiName">
        java:/EntityManagerFactories/userData
    </property>
</component>
```

Now that you have the managed persistence context defined, you can use it in your EJB3 classes for `EntityManager`. All you have to do is either make sure `EntityManager` is named `userDatabase` or have defined the preceding name in your injection.

Setting the Expression Language Resolver

The next line will not be necessary if you are using the examples provided in this book because we are deploying to JBoss. However, sometimes you may want to use Sun's JSF 1.2 reference implementation. Mainly training classes will do this so as to not show bias toward an application server. In this case, you will need to add the code shown in Listing 9-11.

Listing 9-11. *Additional Code Needed for faces-config.xml*

```
<application>
    <el-resolver>org.jboss.seam.jsf.SeamELResolver</el-resolver>
</application>
```

Additions to web.xml

Finally, there is an extra option you can add to `web.xml` for managing Conversation contexts across redirects. This is necessary when you are using the long-running page conversations I described earlier and you are going to be using redirect. Without this option, the conversation ID would not be propagated across the redirect. This simply works by using filters to intercept all calls to Seam. Listing 9-12 provides an example, in which you assume the pattern of the URL requests is `*.seam`.

Listing 9-12. *Filter Addition for web.xml*

```
<filter>
    <filter-name>Seam Redirect Filter</filter-name>
    <filter-class>org.jboss.seam.servlet.SeamRedirectFilter</filter-class>
</filter>

<filter-mapping>
    <filter-name>Seam Redirect Filter</filter-name>
    <url-pattern>*.seam</url-pattern>
</filter-mapping>
```

Portlet Support

Portlets are not something many developers use, but they do have a purpose for certain types of web development. Portals are the front pages to a site, and each portal is designed to serve up many portlets. The site can then contain many portlet windows. Each of these windows is served by a separate portlet server. Websites are generally designed in this way when you want to bring together on one page components that are being designed by various groups and that may have various upgrade paths.

Configuration of your portlet environment is relatively simple. The only thing you have to worry about is setting the proper phase listener to either `PortletPhaseListener` or to `SeamExtendedManagedPersistencePortletPhaseListener`.

USING HTTP-SPECIFIC CODE IN YOUR SEAM COMPONENTS

When using portlets or when designing your applications in general with Seam, you need to keep in mind what they are injecting. Although portlet integration is relatively smooth, with Seam there is one big caveat: you need to make sure you are not using HTTP-specific information, such as the `HttpServletResponse` object. If you inject HTTP-specific information such as the `HttpSession` object directly into your Seam components, they will be compatible only for HTTP web requests. Therefore, you will want to use the Seam-specific contexts defined in Chapters 5 and 6 instead of HTTP-specific contexts.

Summary

The goal for this chapter was to familiarize you with the different deployment environments and configuration options for Seam. We went over the optional containers as well as optional configuration settings and ended with portlets. With the conclusion of this chapter, you should now know most of the areas of configuring and deploying Seam. We have now gone over all the main deployment environments, contexts, and configuration options.

The next chapter presents some tools to use that will help you develop Seam applications more effectively and more quickly.

CHAPTER 10

■■■

Seam Tools

This brings us to our final chapter in learning Seam. Although this chapter is the last, it is certainly not the least. This chapter covers two concepts: testing and tools.

In all fairness, I wish I could have gone over testing earlier. However, you bought this book to learn Seam, not to learn testing. So I purposefully kept the discussion until the very end. I find testing to be an intricate part of developing an application, and way too often developers sacrifice testing for time.

The other area this chapter covers are some tools you can use to help make your life easier when creating Seam applications. I will discuss the Hibernate tools that help auto-generate our Seam code, and another JBoss tool, JBoss jBPM Graphical Process Designer, that will be used to help create our business process code discussed in Chapter 7. The road map in Figure 10-1 shows that this chapter will take us through every tier.

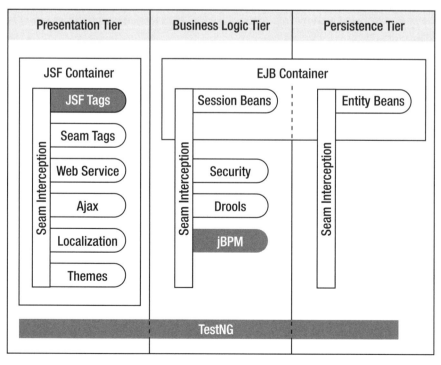

Figure 10-1. *Our road map shows that this chapter covers every tier.*

Testing

Testing is one of those areas that far too many people let fall by the wayside. Often in development, it is one of those areas that is still left until the end. This is starting to change as developers are beginning to use test-driven development. Test-driven development is based on the idea that test cases can help drive development.

In this section, I will present two basic areas of testing: unit testing and integration testing. I'll also provide details on the TestNG framework.

Unit Testing

If you have written any applications professionally, you probably have some experience with unit testing, or at least you should have. *Unit testing* tests individual Java files to make sure they meet your coding needs. By using unit testing, you can test your Java files under different use cases. Thus, one class file should often test multiple items, including positive and negative outcomes. This can be especially useful when it comes to performing testing on classes that deal with business logic.

The only limitation, of course, is that if your classes have parent classes in other packages or call different packages, those parent classes must be part of the import. This became exceptionally difficult when using EJB 2.1 to test your business logic. If you had your business logic wrapped inside the bean itself, it became fairly hard to write your testing units. You had to wrap J2EE EJB JARs into your testing packages. This made it hard to run quick unit tests and is one of the reasons that we now have POJO-based EJBs.

Having POJOs allows a much more simple approach to performing testing, because we can test our objects within the framework of the class itself. If this class calls a persistence tier, you can modify it accordingly. You can perform testing in a multitude of ways; most people end up using a testing framework. The two most popular Java frameworks out there are JUnit and TestNG. The examples in this chapter use TestNG.

TestNG

The TestNG component is starting to become a fairly popular testing tool. It is a simple testing tool that allows for annotations (which again is in keeping with our POJO model). If you were not using annotations, you would not be able to use TestNG. However, Seam requires us to use annotations and so we will not have that problem.

It is out of the scope of this book to provide a large-scale discussion about how to use TestNG. I will present some examples of using TestNG with EJB3.

For our first example, we are going to reference the `SalesManagerAction` class we used for the Garage Sale application in earlier chapters. For the most part, this example was untouched; I did have to perform a few modifications to it because in the application we did not provide setters for many of our class-level objects. Instead they were marked by annotations to be injected into the class. Listing 10-1 shows the modified SalesManagerAction class.

Listing 10-1. *The SalesManagerAction Class with Added Setters*

```
package com.integrallis.garagesale.business;

import javax.ejb.Remove;
import javax.ejb.Stateful;
import javax.persistence.EntityManager;
import javax.persistence.PersistenceContext;

import org.hibernate.validator.Valid;
import org.jboss.seam.annotations.Destroy;
import org.jboss.seam.annotations.In;
import org.jboss.seam.annotations.Name;
import org.jboss.seam.annotations.Out;
import org.jboss.seam.log.Log;

import com.integrallis.garagesale.domain.House;
import com.integrallis.garagesale.service.SaleManager;

public class SaleManagerAction implements SaleManager {

    private EntityManager em;

    private House house;

    public String addHouse() {
        em.persist(house);
        return "/homeSuccess.jsp";
    }

    @PersistenceContext
    public void setEntityManager(EntityManager em) {
        this.em = em;
    }

    @Remove @Destroy
    public void destroy() {
        System.out.println("SaleManagerAction.destroy()");
    }
```

```
    @Valid
    @In @Out
    public void setHouse(House h) {
        house = h;
    }
}
```

As you can see, the main functionality has not changed at all. We had to only make sure that the objects we originally were injecting now had setters on them instead. Although this may seem like somewhat of a hassle to go through, it is really a best-practice technique. Before, we were totally reliant on injecting items into our POJOs. This actually provides a much better methodology for creating classes.

For our test we are going to test the add functionality. This testing will require us to wrap the method call with a transaction, because this is initially run in a transaction as well. The test code will contain a variety of test methods. Some of the methods will be invoked before or after the set of test classes are run. Some methods will be used for the actual test methods. And finally, other methods will be used as regular unannotated methods that can be used to help out your setups, tear downs, or tests. I will explain how to mark what method does what after you take a look at the code for our test in Listing 10-2.

Listing 10-2. *Our TestNG Test of the Transaction*

```
package com.integrallis.garagesale.business;

import javax.persistence.EntityManager;
import javax.persistence.EntityManagerFactory;
import javax.persistence.Persistence;

import org.testng.annotations.Configuration;
import org.testng.annotations.Test;

import com.integrallis.garagesale.domain.House;

public class SaleManagerActionTest {

    @Test
    public void testAddingHouse() {
        EntityManager em = emf.createEntityManager();
        em.getTransaction().begin();
        House h = new House();
        h.setAddress("123 Main St");
```

```
        SaleManagerAction action = new SaleManagerAction();
        action.setHouse(h);
        action.setEntityManager(em);

        assert "success".equals(action.addHouse());

        em.getTransaction().rollback();
        em.close();
    }

    private EntityManagerFactory emf;

    @Configuration(beforeTestClass=true)
    public void init()
    {
        emf = Persistence.createEntityManagerFactory("userDatabase");
    }

    @Configuration(afterTestClass=true)
    public void destroy()
    {
        emf.close();
    }
}
```

First, let's start with a best-practice technique when creating test classes—and this goes for any test harness (whether JUnit or TestNG)—choosing the location of the test code. The test code should *not* go into the same directory structure of your classes. You do not want to package your test classes with your deployments in the same JAR file. However, that being said, it is a best practice to maintain the package structure of your test class and to even name the class similarly to the class you are testing. In this case, we ended the class name with the word Test.

Next let's take a look at a few of our configurations. Because EntityManager is a component used to contact the database, we have to create an object for it. This could be done by creating an actual object that connects to the database or by using a mock object. In this example, we choose to create EntityManagerFactory, which can be used to create EntityManager.

Now let's take a look at some of the common TestNG annotations used to create the test:

@Configuration: The first annotation to look at is the @Configuration annotation. If you are familiar with JUnit, using @Configuration is similar to using the setUp() and tearDown() methods. These methods can be set up to call before the test cases are run or after the test cases are run. If you pass through the argument beforeTestClass=true to the annotation, that method will be run at start-up. Conversely, if you pass afterTestClass=true, it will be run upon completion. Here you can set global objects such as EntityManagerFactory or a logger.

@Test: This annotation marks what classes you want to be run as a test. You can mark your assertions here. In our example, we mark that the class should return success. In addition, you would probably check that the actual values were entered into the database. Also you would want to test negative responses as well.

Note If you have any questions about using TestNG, refer to the documentation at http://testng.org/doc/.

Integration Testing

Integration testing is used to test the units together. Integration tests should test the interaction of units (that is, classes). In actuality, most integration tests will do mocks of your client calls so you will have a complete functionality test, from presentation to business logic to persistence tier.

These tests are extremely useful when you get further along in development and are changing back-end systems much more often. They allow you to know right away whether your change on the business logic tiers will cause any of your web pages to break. Of course, this is dependent on you making sure to update these tests if you update the JSF pages.

To perform integration testing, we are going to use a combination of TestNG and some base Seam classes to emulate a Faces request. Our example will build on the example we used previously with our unit test. The integration we are going to run will test adding a house. The code is in Listing 10-3.

Listing 10-3. *The TestNG Test That Tests for Adding a House*

```
public class HouseTest extends SeamTest {

    @Test
    public void testAddHouse() throws Exception
    {
```

```java
    new FacesRequest() {
        @Override
        protected void processValidations() throws Exception
        {
            validateValue("#{house.address}", "123 Main Street");
            validateValue("#{house.city}", "Columbus");
            validateValue("#{house.state}", "OH");
            assert !isValidationFailure();
        }

        @Override
        protected void updateModelValues() throws Exception
        {
            setValue("#{house.address}", "123 Main Street");
            setValue("#{house.city}", "Columbus");
            setValue("#{house.state}", "OH");
        }
        @Override
        protected void invokeApplication()
        {
            assert invokeMethod("#{salesManager.addHouse}").equals("success");
        }

        @Override
        protected void renderResponse()
        {
            assert getValue("#{house.address}").equals("123 Main Street");
            assert getValue("#{house.city}").equals("Columbus");
            assert getValue("#{house.state}").equals("OH");
        }
    }.run();
}
}
```

The first thing to notice is that the class extends SeamTest. The SeamTest class is part of the core Seam release. When extending the class, you can use two core operations to create a request. You can use the superclass to create a FacesRequest or a NonFacesRquest. These two classes are public inner classes on the SeamTest object. We will create implementations of these classes in our code by overriding method calls. Each of the method calls represents part of the JSF life cycle. This way you can intercept and test various parts of the request. Table 10-1 lists the method names and their descriptions.

Table 10-1. *The Method Names Available to Be Overridden for a JSF Request*

Method Name	Description
getViewId()	The JSF view ID of the page being submitted or the page name in a non-Faces request.
applyRequestValues()	This method is used for the apply request values phase that defines the interactions between the JSF and the components page.
processValidations()	This method is used during the process validation phase.
updateModelValues()	This method is used during the update model values phase.
invokeApplication()	This method is used during the invocation of the method and is definitely one you will need to override.
renderResponse()	This method is used during the render response that occurs between the JSF page and the component.

You are able to pick and choose which methods you need to override. In our example, we are validating and setting the values that we are passing to the business logic tier. We are setting the values on the House object, validating the items, and then submitting the House object to the database.

Testing can save valuable time in the long run. It helps in identifying errors and application behavior that you did not count on, especially in big applications when multiple people are changing code that affects your pieces. The precision that testing provides is directly proportional to the amount of time you spend coding your various use case scenarios.

Hibernate Console with Seam

One of the items packaged with the JBoss IDE for the Eclipse release is the Hibernate Console. If you are not familiar with this handy tool, it is mostly used to reverse engineer a database to create Hibernate objects. However, recently it has been upgraded to create Seam objects as well. This gives us an easy way to create Seam classes, especially if we have a rather large database.

This section shows how to reverse engineer the database step by step to create Seam objects. Although there are quite a few configuration options for the Hibernate Console, I am going to go over only what is necessary to reverse engineer the database.

Database in Question

To start, let's look at the database we are going to use for our reverse engineering. The database is based on the Travel Reservations application discussed throughout this book. However, I am going to shorten it for our example. This example uses only the Booking, Flight, and FlightBooked tables. Figure 10-2 shows the database diagram.

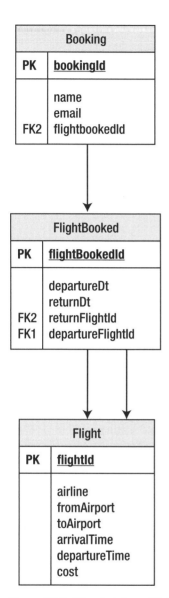

Figure 10-2. *The database flight-booking diagram we are using for reverse engineering*

So for our example, the reduced table layout will provide a complete line with dependencies.

Reverse Engineering the Database

To start, make sure that you have Eclipse open and then create a project named TicketingSystem. (You could name the project whatever you want, but TicketingSystem has to be the name if you want to follow this tutorial.)

Creating the hibernate.cfg.xml File

Now you're ready to create the Hibernate configuration file. You could do this manually or automatically through the configuration wizard. We are going to use the configuration wizard (although this is not the usual way I do it, because after you have one configuration created, you can easily cut and paste to create a new one).

Start by selecting File ➤ New ➤ Other, as shown in Figure 10-3.

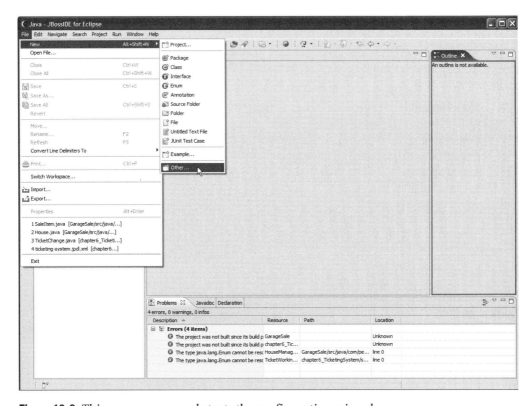

Figure 10-3. *This menu command starts the configuration wizard.*

The wizard opens. Expand the Hibernate directory and select Hibernate Configuration File, as shown in Figure 10-4.

On the next screen, select the parent folder where we are creating the hibernate.cfg.xml file. Because we are creating this in the TicketingSystem project, select TicketingSystem. Then click the Next button, as shown in Figure 10-5.

Figure 10-4. *In this window, select Hibernate Configuration File.*

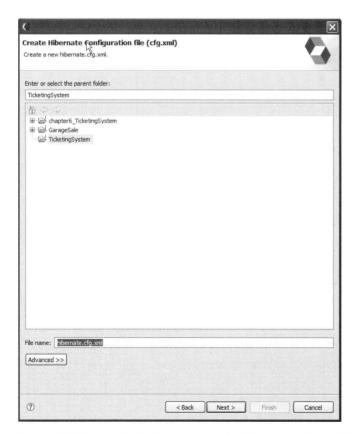

Figure 10-5. *Select the folder to create the hibernate.cfg.xml file in.*

After that is done, the final screen appears., as shown in Figure 10-6. On this screen, you configure the options for Hibernate.

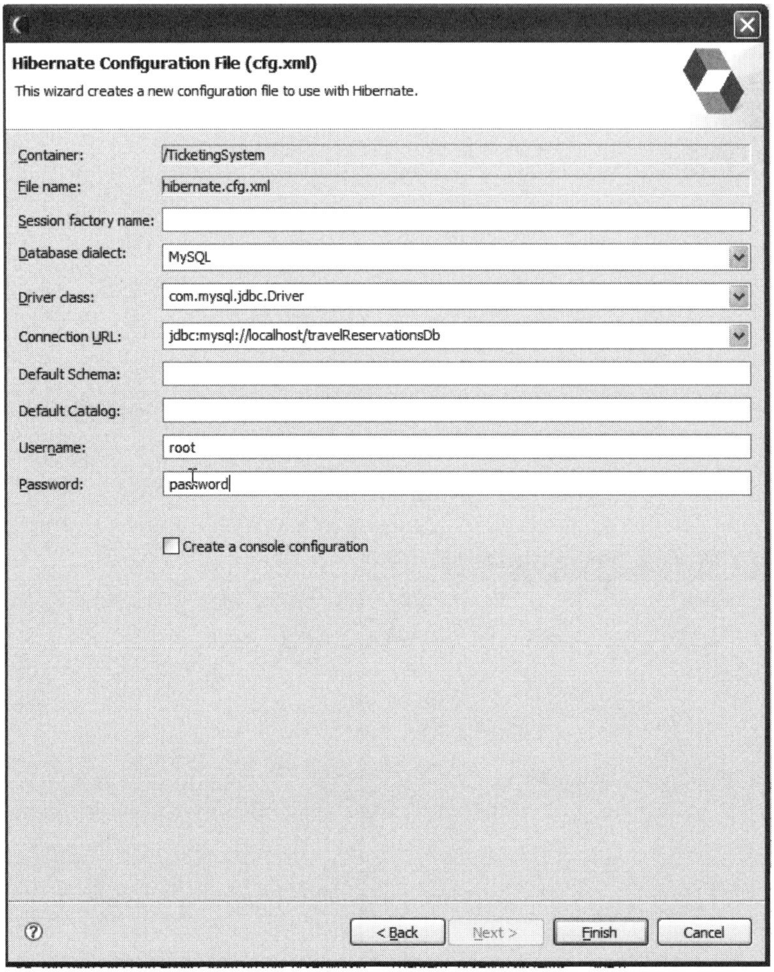

Figure 10-6. *The last page, which configures options for the hibernate.cfg.xml creation*

Here you select MySQL from the Database Dialect drop-down list because we are using MySQL for our example. The driver class is a standard MySQL driver class. For our connection URL, we are configuring to use a local database with the schema named travelReservationsDb. Type in the username and password for the database. After you click the Finish button, the wizard will create the hibernate.cfg.xml file, shown in Listing 10-4.

Listing 10-4. *Our hibernate.cfg.xml File Created by the Hibernate Configuration Wizard*

```
<?xml version="1.0" encoding="UTF-8"?>
<!DOCTYPE hibernate-configuration PUBLIC
    "-//Hibernate/Hibernate Configuration DTD 3.0//EN"
    "http://hibernate.sourceforge.net/hibernate-configuration-3.0.dtd">
<hibernate-configuration>
    <session-factory>
        <property name="hibernate.connection.driver_class">
            com.mysql.jdbc.Driver
        </property>
        <property name="hibernate.connection.password">password</property>
        <property name="hibernate.connection.url">
            jdbc:mysql://localhost/travelReservationsDb
        </property>
        <property name="hibernate.connection.username">root</property>
        <property name="hibernate.dialect">
            org.hibernate.dialect.MySQLDialect
        </property>
    </session-factory>
</hibernate-configuration>
```

Generating the Hibernate Code

Now that our `hibernate.cfg.xml` file has been created, we can generate the code. To do this, click Run ➤ Hibernate Code Generation ➤ Hibernate Code Generation, as shown in Figure 10-7.

This will take you to the code generation screen shown in Figure 10-8, where you will start a new code generation. Leave the output directory as `\TicketingSystem\`. Next, make sure that the rest of the check boxes are selected accordingly and set the package name. In this example, it is set to `com.integrallis.domain`.

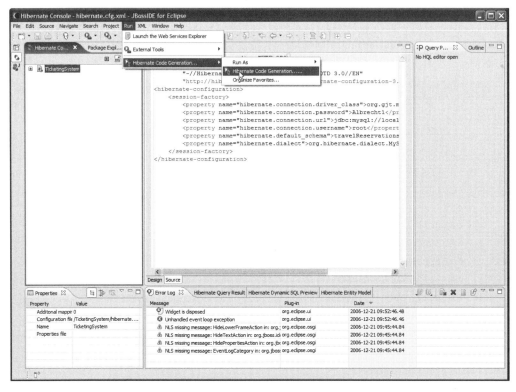

Figure 10-7. *The steps to start the Hibernate code generation*

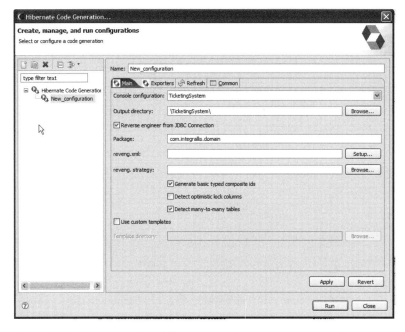

Figure 10-8. *The start of the Hibernate code generation console*

Finally, click the Exporters tab, shown in Figure 10-9. Here is where we can tell the code generator to generate Seam code. Make sure that the JBoss Seam Skeleton App is selected and click Run.

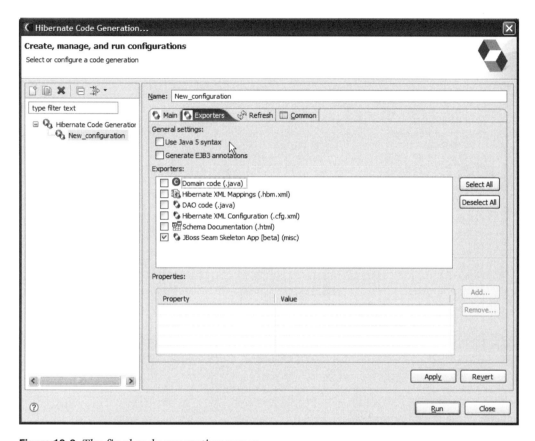

Figure 10-9. *The final code generation screen*

This will automatically generate all the code, including the Java objects, the JSP, build.xml, and so forth. The directory structure that will be created will look like the one in Figure 10-10.

Figure 10-10. *The directory structure created by the code generation*

Results of the Code Generation

The code generates not only the Java classes but also JSP pages for them. The types of classes generated are the EBs and some SFSBs that do some basic finder and edit methods. Although this works fairly well, you may notice one problem: the directory structure puts everything under the package you have defined. In general, this is not the best approach, to keep all your domain and DAO/business logic classes in the same directory. In addition, for some reason the domain objects such as `Booking`, `Flight`, and `FlightBooked` are not defined to be Seam objects (that is, the `@Name` annotation is not present).

That being said, this does provide a shortcut for creating some example files and could be extremely useful if you have your database written and are new to Seam.

jBPM Designer

The next tool we are going to use is the jBPM Graphical Process Designer, part of the JBoss IDE for Eclipse. In Chapter 7 you learned the hard way to create the jBPM XML files. Now you will learn the easy way. Both ways produce an XML result, but this way you can use a graphical interface, which will hopefully cut down on time and also help you to better visualize the components.

Starting the Process

You will start the creation the same way you started the Hibernate configuration creation: by clicking File ➤ New ➤ Other. This brings up the screen shown in Figure 10-11.

Figure 10-11. *Selecting the JBoss jBPM from the wizard*

Here you should select Process Definition or Process Project, depending on whether you want to create a process definition or a page flow. The next page, shown in Figure 10-12, has a text box for filling in the process name.

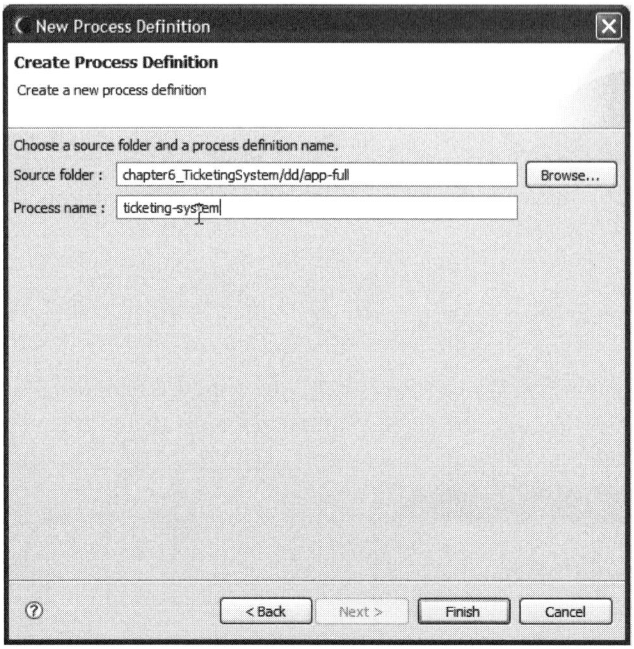

Figure 10-12. *Typing in the process name*

After you fill in the name and click the Finish button, the files will be generated and you can start creating your process definition or page flow. I will go over those screens in the next few pages. Alternatively, if you already have the XML created, you can skip this process and open the files, which will take you to the layouts for each.

Creating a Process Definition

Because we have already gone over the process definition concepts in Chapter 7, I will not bother doing it here as well. Instead, take a look at the example of a process definition shown in Figure 10-13.

This screen shows the process definition we defined earlier. As you can see, this graphical interface provides an easy way of creating forks, joins, nodes, and so forth. You also can reposition each of the diagrams as you choose.

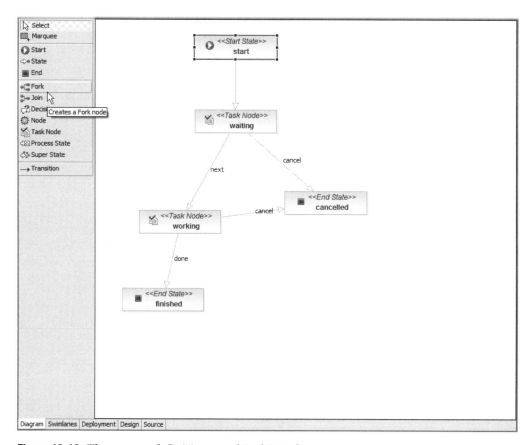

Figure 10-13. *The process definition graphical interface*

Creating a Page Flow

Next we will create a page flow. This again is the same page flow for billing we used in Chapter 7. The screen for this is shown in Figure 10-14.

Like the process definition page flow, this page flow tool provides a graphical interface for positioning your pages. You also can add pages, decisions, and so forth.

If you click on the Source tab for either of these page flows, you will then see the XML generated. The XML can look a bit out of order, but you can always change the order if you need to.

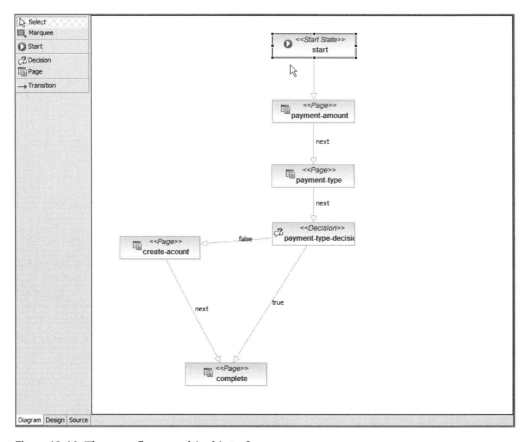

Figure 10-14. *The page flow graphical interface*

Summary

This was our final chapter in our look at JBoss Seam. You learned about using some tools to help with the creation of Seam and jBPM as well as unit testing. Unit testing, although it is the topic of this last chapter, is definitely a first-chapter concept when programming. It is something you want to start from the get-go of development to keep you on the right track.

The Seam generation tool and jBPM Graphical Process Designer can be equally valuable in cutting down coding time and again letting you worry about the more-difficult parts such as the layout of the JSF pages or the business logic.

APPENDIX A

■■■

JBoss AS

Because Seam was written by those at JBoss, naturally JBoss is the application server that Seam works best with. Seam, however, is not limited to working only with JBoss. You can use Seam on any application server that supports EJB3. (You can actually use it with pre-EJB3-supported servers, as I discuss in Chapter 9). This appendix focuses on JBoss 4.0.

What Is JBoss?

When people reference *JBoss*, they are usually referring to JBoss Application Server. However, there are multiple products from the JBoss group, Seam being one of them. JBoss as a company was started by Marc Fleury but was bought by Red Hat in early 2006. This is a good move for all of us in that it should help keep JBoss open source for at least the time being. And that *free* word is what makes it such a great application server for developers to learn on. You can download it locally without any restrictions on licensing.

Downloading JBoss

Before using JBoss, you obviously need to download and install it. You can download the latest JBoss production Application Server instance (4.0.*x*) from `http://labs.jboss.com/portal/jbossas/download`.

From this page, follow these steps:

1. Click the Downloads button. This takes you to the `labs.jboss.com` download page.

2. Choose the latest JBoss link labeled Run Installer for the latest production instance. The installer is necessary because without it you will not have EJB3 support on your application server.

Note At the time of this writing, the regular JBoss 4.0 was not compatible with Seam; the problem was with the EJB3 version bundled with it. A newer version had to be downloaded and installed afterward. However, to make life easier, there is a bundled download called the JEMS Installer that can be downloaded. The rest of the instructions on the installation are the same with either download.

Installing JBoss

Now that you have the installer downloaded, create the directory structure you want to install it to, and for the sake of ease just copy the downloaded file to that location. On the command line, type in the following:

```
java -jar <name_of_installer_jar>
```

Now, follow these steps:

1. The first screen asks you to select which language you want, as shown in Figure A-1. Select English (the default). Then click OK.

Figure A-1. *Language selection screen*

2. Click the OK button for this screen as well. Note that it may take some time for the installation to progress. Do not worry—it will be working.

3. The next page welcomes you to the install. Click Next.

4. Read the release notes and then click Next again.

5. The next page is the terms and conditions page, shown in Figure A-2. Click the radio button labeled I Accept The Terms of This License Agreement and then click Next.

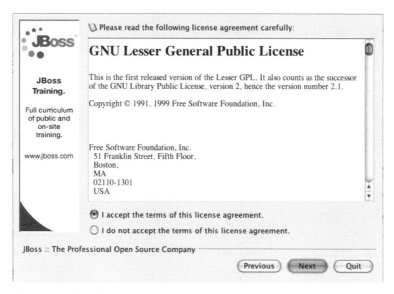

Figure A-2. *The license agreement screen*

6. Now select the path you want to install JBoss to and click Next.

7. The screen in Figure A-3 is one of the most important screens to pay attention to for our installation. On this screen you can choose whether to install EJB3. If you do not install EJB3, you will have `ClassNotFound` exceptions for the EJBs. Select the ejb3 option and click Next.

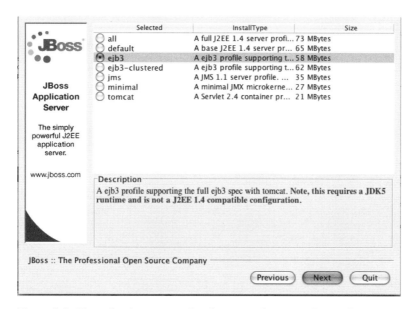

Figure A-3. *The selection screen for choosing the type of installation*

8. Now you are asked what packages you want to install. By default, all packages are selected. I suggest just keeping all of them installed. Then click Next.

9. The next screen asks you to choose a name. You can choose any name you want. However, if you choose anything but **default**, you will have to specify that name when you start up the server.

10. Next is the DataSource Configuration screen. Just keep HSQLDB selected and click Next.

11. The following screen deals with deployment isolation. Just keep the Enable Deployment Isolation/Call By Value check box unselected and click Next.

12. For the JMX security, you can type in a customized username and password if you like. The password is required, so type something in and write it down for future reference.

13. The final screen enables you to review everything you have chosen to install. Click Next to begin the actual installation. After the installation is complete, the screen progression window will indicate Finished, as in Figure A-4.

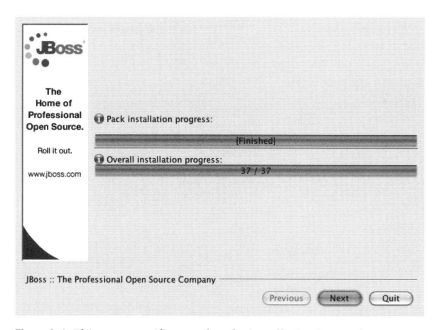

Figure A-4. *This screen notifies you that the installation is complete.*

14. Click Next again, and you will receive confirmation of installation and of the location of the uninstaller, as shown in Figure A-5.

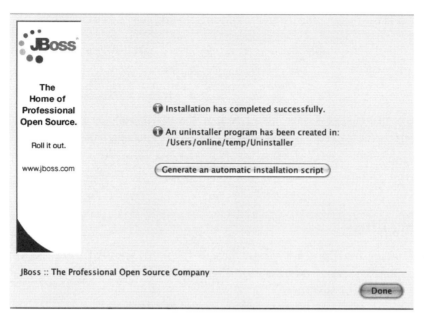

Figure A-5. *The final screen showing the location of the uninstaller*

Your JBoss Application Server should now be installed and ready to run. Make sure to remember where you installed it. In this book, I will refer to that path as `<JBoss_Path>`.

Using JBoss

Now that JBoss is installed, I will explain how to use it—including how to start it and where to locate some files that you may find useful. This section, however, is not intended to provide comprehensive coverage of JBoss. There is often more than one way to do something, and I will be covering what I feel is the easiest and simplest method.

■Note If you want to learn more about JBoss, check out `http://www.jboss.org`.

Running JBoss

Running JBoss is straightforward, and the program is ready to go after the installation. The location of the run files is `<JBoss_Path>/bin`. Note that the installer did not install based on whether the operating system was Microsoft Windows or Unix, so the run files exist for both in the `bin` directory:

- `run.bat` is the executable if you are running a Windows-based system.

- `run.sh` is the executable if you are running a Unix-based system (including Apple).

■**Note** If you decided during the setup to select anything other than **default**, you will have to run the start-up with the command switch `-c <name>`, where `<name>` is the name you chose.

Deploying JBoss

Deploying is also an easy process. All you have to do is copy your WAR, EAR, RAR, or SAR to the `<JBoss_Path>/server/<name>/deploy/` directory. I will refer to this directory as the *deployment directory* in the future.

Adding a Data Source

A data source gives you the ability to define a database connection outside the confines of the application. Not only does this define a source for the database, but it also runs in a pooled data source. Pooled data sources provide a better way to run a database, because they allow connections to be read and they maximize the number of connections going to the database. You can then access this data source via the Java Naming and Directory Interface (JNDI). Using the JNDI allows us to not have to hard-code anything in our code that relates directly to the database except the JNDI lookup name.

Creating the datasource.xml File

To set up the data source, create a data source XML file. The name of the file is unimportant; just make sure that the suffix is `.xml`. You will then place the file into the deployment directory, an example of this file is in Listing A-1.

Listing A-1. *An Example of a Data Source*

```xml
<?xml version="1.0" encoding="UTF-8"?>
<datasources>
 <local-tx-datasource>
  <jndi-name>GarageSaleDS</jndi-name>
    <connection-url>jdbc:mysql://localhost/garageSaleDb</connection-url>
    <driver-class>com.mysql.jdbc.Driver</driver-class>
    <user-name>root</user-name>
    <password>password</password>
    <min-pool-size>5</min-pool-size>
    <max-pool-size>20</max-pool-size>
    <idle-timeout-minutes>0</idle-timeout-minutes>
    <track-statements/>
 </local-tx-datasource>
</datasources>
```

Table A-1 explains the parameters defined in Listing A-1.

Table A-1. *Definitions of the JNDI Parameters*

Parameter Name	Definition
jndi-name	The name you are going to be using to reference the data source in your application configurations.
connection-url	The database-specific URL to the server. In this case, we are calling a server on the same box, with a database schema called garageSaleDb.
driver-class	The driver you are using for your database. In this case, we are using a MySQL driver.
user-name	The username that is defined to access this data source. In general, do not use the root username.
password	The password for the corresponding username.
min-pool-size	The starting pool size for the number of database connections to be allowed.
max-pool-size	The maximum number of database connections allowed by this pool.
idle-timeout-minutes	The amount of time before the connection times out.
track-statements	A Boolean (true/false) that has the data source monitor for unclosed Statements or ResultSets.

Adding the Library JAR File

So now that you have your data source connection defined, you need to add the necessary JAR file for it. In the preceding case we were using MySQL, so we had to add a MySQL JAR file. Copy the JAR file to `<JBoss_Path>/server/<name>/lib/`. In reality, you could use any database (including Hypersonic SQL Database, or HSQLDB), but for the examples in the book I have used MySQL. MySQL can be downloaded from `http://www.mysql.org/downloads/mysql/5.0.html#downloads`. It is a fairly straightforward installation. If you want further information, you can consult *Pro MySQL* by Michael Kruckenberg and Jay Pipes (Apress, 2005). After setting this up, restart JBoss and check the console for any visible errors. Your JBoss database should be configured.

Locating and Configuring Log Files

So by now you should have JBoss configured to use EJB3 and should have a data source added. You are ready to start running the system. However, first I want to give you some understanding of the log file and some of the configuration file locations.

The log files are located at `<JBoss_Path>/server/<name>/log/server.log`. The logger is set to rolling appending—so as the server is running, you will notice more files with a numerical appending. The logger in JBoss uses Log4J as its logger of choice. Consequently, these generated log files have a `log4j.xml` file associated with them. The `log4j.xml` file is located at `<JBoss_Path>/server/<name>/conf/log4j.xml`.

■**Note** If you need help understanding Log4J, consult the Log4J website at `http://logging.apache.org/log4j/docs/`.

There are multiple configuration files in the `<JBoss_Path>/server/<name>/conf` and `<JBoss_Path>/server/<name>/default` directories.

At this point, you should have JBoss Application Server installed and ready to use.

APPENDIX B

■ ■ ■

JBoss IDE

One of the keys to any development is an environment to develop in. Integrated development environments (IDEs) have been around for Java for a while now, and are much improved since the early days. There are a wide variety of IDEs to choose from: IntelliJ, NetBeans, and Eclipse.

Eclipse has become one of the standard IDEs for Java development. There are two main reasons for this. First, it's free. Second, it is easy to develop plug-ins for Eclipse and there is a large community of developers creating plug-ins for it. These plug-ins can be used to access Subversion version control, create Hibernate files, access databases, and more.

JBoss has created its own set of plug-ins for Eclipse. These plug-ins allow us to use Hibernate reverse engineering, jBPM creation, and other items. In fact, JBoss has an Eclipse + JBoss IDE download for Microsoft Windows.

This appendix covers how to download and install this IDE.

To download the JBoss IDE, go to `http://labs.jboss.com/portal/jbosside/download/index.html`. Then select the Beta-2-Bundle, as shown in Figure B-1.

After the download is complete, you will have a zip file to install. To extract the zip, right-click on the zip and select Extract All, as shown in Figure B-2.

That is all you will need. After the zip file is extracted into the Eclipse folder, you can double-click `eclipse.exe` to run Eclipse.

Note When extracting a zip file, often people will open the zip in Microsoft Windows Explorer and just drag and drop the contents. However, if you do that for this zip, the extraction will fail. So use the extractor.

I would suggest either using this installation or installing the plug-ins separately. Doing so makes various aspects of development easier in this book. We will use this installation for our development in Chapter 10.

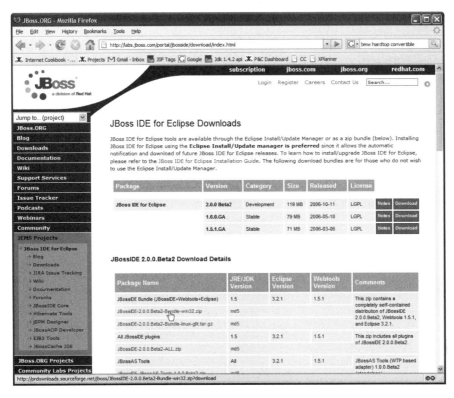

Figure B-1. *The website for downloading the JBoss IDE*

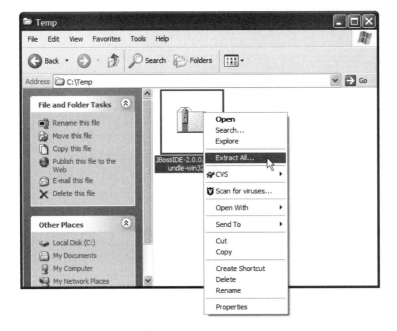

Figure B-2. *Extracting the JBoss IDE*

Final Thoughts

My goal with this book was far reaching from the get-go, and I hope it has set you on the right track in creating your Seam application. From the beginning, I realized that the target audience would range from the relatively new to the relatively experienced, so my hope was to create ever-increasing complex pages. Because JSF and EJB3 are relatively new to developers, and almost no developers have used them in a production environment, I definitely wanted to cover those two topics separately. If you still need more information, there are many books available to choose from.

When I first started using Seam, I have to admit I was a bit skeptical. I am a big Tapestry and Spring fan. I find the melding of the two very useful. However, the fact remains that standards are standards for a reason, and many major companies will stick to using JSF and EJB3 for that reason. Whether those two are the best tools for the job is debatable. Personally, I believe EJB3 has come a long way and I am happy with it. Although JSF is a bit more debatable, compared to frameworks we have had to use before, its strides are major. The question then comes to Seam. In my opinion Seam, is a *great* tool in the right hands, and could be disastrous in the wrong hands.

Let's start off by asking when you should use Seam. I would say most definitely if you ever are going to use EJB3 + JSF, Seam is a no-brainer. The next question then becomes, to what extent do you use Seam? Just the fact that I can manage my `HttpSession` objects with annotations and not have to worry about putting managed beans inside the `faces-config.xml` is a bonus in itself. After that, it is really up to the user and the needs of the project. Seam is labeled as an agile web application development application, and some try to compare it to Ruby. And if you look at all the initial effort in writing a Seam application, you may laugh at that—and quite frankly so do I to an extent. Ruby provides a flexible and fast way to put web applications on the Web. And if you need a simple CRUD application with some minor tweaks to the presentation tier, then something like Trails would be more along your scope. What Seam provides for is agile *enterprise*-level development. This is something that is sorely lacking. While developing these examples and writing this book, it was easy to identify many jobs I have been at where this would have saved me time in plumbing code.

My favorite TV series, Joss Whedon's *Buffy the Vampire Slayer*, always started out with, "In every generation a slayer is born." For us nerds I would say, "In every generation a framework is born." Clearly Struts was that framework for the start of this century, and Spring moved in for the next few years. What is going to be the framework of choice in 2007 and beyond? No one knows yet, but JSF and EJB3 with the backing of Sun and application vendors will definitely be hanging around. I believe Seam and its core idea to glue frameworks together seamlessly will be a concept that is going to be around and be abundantly useful for years to come.

Index

SYMBOLS

character, expression language, 74

A

a: tag prefix, Ajax4jsf, 254
ACID properties, transactions, 114
Action class, Struts, 27
   displaying dynamic data, 28
   HttpServletRequest attribute, 27
   HttpServletResponse attribute, 27
   listing and viewing pages, 37
   logging in, 34
   purpose of, 185
   requesting and saving data, 32
action component, jBPM page flow, 219
action events, JSF, 65
ActionForm object, Struts, 27
ActionMapping object, Struts, 27
activation, SFSB life cycle, 97, 99
actor assignment
   creating tasks, jBPM process
      definitions, 210–211
actor component, workflows, 194
actors, jBPM, 189, 210
add operation, entity manager, 111
Add page
   Garage Sale application, 79–81
   validation on JSF pages, 156
admin role
   testing for user having admin role, 263
Ajax (Asynchronous JavaScript and XML),
   240–257
   Ajax4jsf in Seam, 250–255
     defining Ajax4jsf filter, 251
     downloading and configuring
       Ajax4jsf, 251
     dynamic validations, 252
     tags creating dynamic validations,
       254
   JMS messaging using Ajax, 255–257
     configuring JMS listeners, 255–256
     using JMS listeners, 257

Seam remoting using Ajax, 240–250
   Ajax remoting call, 242–245
   Ajax remoting call with parameters,
     245–247
   batch remote calls, 247
   conversation ID, 248
   debugging, 249
   excluding objects on method call, 250
   getComponentName command, 247
   hiding/changing the loading
     message, 248
   Java data types for Seam remoting,
     248
   remote configuring of Seam, 241
aliases, JPQL, 113
annotations
   annotations on POJOs, 20
   collections, 107–110
   creating SLSBs, 95
   data model, 147
   ejb-jar.xml (EJB descriptors) and, 89
   entity bean annotations, 104–106
   Hibernate annotations, 154
   interceptors and, 135
   Java 5, 12, 14
   JSRs for Java 5 release, 12
   life cycle annotations, SLSBs, 96–97
   page-level annotations, 263
   reasons for using Seam, 6
   Seam architecture, 132
   starting/ending tasks, 207
   TestNG component, 288
   transforming complex objects into
     POJOs, 14
   XML configurations in EJB3, 88
annotations, list of
   @AssertFalse, Hibernate, 154
   @AssertTrue, Hibernate, 154
   @Begin, 170
   @BeginTask, 211
   @Column, 106
   @Configuration, 292

@Conversational, 169
@Create, 7
@CreateProcess, 203
@DataModel, 149
@DataModelSelection, 149
@EJB, 120
@Email, Hibernate, 154
@EmailChecks, 157
@End, 171
@EndTask, 209
@Entity, 102
@Factory, 149
@Future, Hibernate, 154
@GeneratedValue, 105
@Id, 105
@IfInvalid, 151, 155
@In, 128, 133, 134
@Interceptors, 127
@JndiName, 127
@JoinColumn, 108
@Length, Hibernate, 154
@Lob, 106
@Local, 95
@Logger, 144
@ManyToMany, 108
@ManyToOne, 107
@Max, Hibernate, 154
@MessageDriven, 101
@Min, Hibernate, 154
@Name, 7, 127
@NotNull, Hibernate, 154
@OneToMany, 108
@OneToOne, 108
@Out, 128, 133
@Past, Hibernate, 154
@Pattern, Hibernate, 154
@Permission, 263
@Permissions, 263
@PersitenceContext, 110
@PostConstruct, 96
@PreDestroy, 96
@Range, Hibernate, 154
@Remote, 95
@Remove, 100
@RequestParameter, 161
@Resource, 119
@Restrict, 263
@ResumeProcess, 204
@Role, 181

@Roles, 181
@Scope, 136, 148
@Size, Hibernate, 154
@StartTask, 209
@Stateful, 100
@Stateless, 8, 28
@SuppressWarnings, 113
@Table, 104
@Test, 292
@TransactionAttribute, 117
@TransactionManagement, 118
@Transient, 106
@UniqueConstraint, 105
@Valid, Hibernate, 151, 154
@WebRemote, 245
Ant (Apache Ant)
    configuration, packaging EAR file, 91
    creating WAR files for Faces, 57–58
API specification
    JSF background, 48
Application context, 164
    description, 138
    Seam contexts, 136
    Servlet context compared, 164
    stateful session beans, 164
application data, Drools rule engine, 264
application descriptors *see*
            application.xml file
application servers
    deploying web resources to, 57
    JBoss AS, 307–314
application.xml file
    configuring EJB3s for deployment,
        89–90
    configuring jBPM with Seam, 197
    modified with jBPM JAR file, 197
    packaging into EAR file, 91–92
    web configuration for, 147
applications
    Garage Sale application, 41
    invokeApplication method, 294
    ticketing system application, 44–45
    Travel Reservations application, 42–44
Apply Request Values phase, JSF, 70
applyRequestValues method, 294
architecture
    see also Seam architecture
    JSF, 59–68
    MVC, 9–11

three-tier architecture, 2–4
    Java EE architecture, 3, 4
arguments, varargs, 18
@AssertFalse annotation, Hibernate, 154
assertObjects tag
    using Drools in jBPM, 266
@AssertTrue annotation, Hibernate, 154
asynchronous processing
    Ajax, 240–257
    Ajax4jsf in Seam, 250–255
    JMS messaging using Ajax, 255–257
    message-driven beans and Seam, 101,
        184
    Seam remoting using Ajax, 240–250
atomicity, transactions, 115
authentication
    AuthenticationProvider class, 259–260
    authenticatorAction component, 260
    component-level, 263
    creating login/logout, 260–262
    implementing, 258–262
    logging in, 34
    page-level, 263
    ProviderAuthenticator component, 260
    SeamSecurityManager component, 262,
        263
    version 1.1.0 of Seam, 258
AuthenticationException exception, 260
AuthenticationProvider class, 259
Authenticator component, 262
authenticatorAction component, 260
AUTO generated value
    @GeneratedValue, 106
autoboxing, Java 5, 17
    JSRs for Java 5 release, 12

B

backing beans
    see also managed beans
    core areas of JSF, 63
    data model events, JSF, 65
    description, 50
    eliminating the need for, 162
    entity beans (EBs), 184
    event listener methods, 63
    faces-config.xml file, 50
    GarageSaleAction backing bean, 79
    Hello World example, 50
    JSF pages calling business logic, 121

reasons for using JSF, 5
    Seam replacement for, 63
    Update Model Values phase, JSF, 71
    uses of, JSF, 185
batch processing
    Seam remoting using Ajax, 247
BEA WebLogic
    JSF implementations, 49
bean-managed transactions see BMTs
beforeRedirect property, @EndTask, 209
@Begin annotation
    beginning long-running conversations,
        170
    join/nested parameters, type property,
        175
    multiple @Begin methods for
        conversation, 171
    starting page flow, 220
begin parameter, type property
    conversationPropagation tag, Seam, 174
@BeginTask annotation
    resuming tasks, 211
bijection
    annotation for Seam to perform, 127
    contexts injectable into POJOs, 183
    entity beans (EBs), 184
    interceptors and, 134
    message-driven beans (MDBs), 184
    Seam architecture, 132–134
    where to use, 133
    with stateless session beans, 134
Blob data type, @Lob, 106
BMTs (bean-managed transactions),
        117–119
    @Resource, 119
    @TransactionManagement, 118
    bean- or container-managed, 115
    commits, 119
    rollbacks, 118, 119
    setRollbackOnly method, 118
    UserTransaction interface, 118
Boolean data type
    Java data types for seam remoting, 248
browser settings
    selecting languages, 231
build
    checking Java version, 13
bundles
    defining multiple bundle names, 230

language bundles, 223, 224–231
message bundles, 228
resource bundles, 223, 230
business logic tier *see* business tier
business process, 187
business process code
jBPM Graphical Process Designer, 303–305
Business Process context, 136, 138, 187
business process tools
jBPM (JBoss Business Process Management), 188–221
components for creating process definitions, 192–196
page flow creation in Seam, 220–221
page flow definitions, 213–220
process definition creation in Seam, 197–213
process definitions, 189–196
purpose of, 187
business tier
benefits of using Seam framework, 2
calling validator from, 154–155
description, 3
MVC architecture, 9
reasons for using Seam, 6
Seam integration with EJB3, 140
stateful session beans, 97–101
stateless session beans, 93–97
three-tier architecture, 2–4
using transactions inside EJBs, 115
why use SBs for business tier, 92
Button component, JSF, 73

C

c: tag prefix, 264
see also JSTL tag libraries
calendar component, JSF, 51
callback method
Ajax remoting call, 244
using JMS listeners, 257
casting
find method signature, 112
Java Persistence Query Language, 113
casting errors, generics, 15
changeProcessDefinition method, 213
Check box component, JSF, 73
Check box list component, JSF, 73

classes
contents of WAR files, 58
creating test classes, 291
classes tag
creating WAR file for Faces via Ant, 58
click events
action events, JSF, 65
Clob data type, @Lob, 106
CMTs (container-managed transactions), 116–117
@TransactionAttribute, 117
bean- or container-managed, 115
commits, 116, 117
EJB3 types of transactions, 116
rollbacks, 116, 117
setRollbackOnly method, 117
Codehaus's Trails, 282
collections
annotations, 107–110
iterating through collections, 15
@Column annotation
entity beans, 106
column tag, html, 72
commandLink tag, JSF, 173, 174
commits
bean-managed transactions, 119
container-managed transactions, 116, 117
compiled classes
contents of WAR files, 58
Component label component, JSF, 73
Component object
Seam integration with EJB3, 140
component-level authentication, 263
components
configuring faces-config.xml file, 56
configuring web.xml file for Faces, 53
getComponentName command, 247
jBPM Business Process component, 189–213
jBPM page flow component, 213–221
Process Validations phase, JSF, 70
components, JSF, 71–74
component layout, 72–73
standard JSF components, 73–74
components, Seam, 141–157
actors, 210
Authenticator component, 262
authenticatorAction component, 260

component-level authentication, 263
data model, 147–151
  JSF presentation tier, 150–151
  POJO, 148–150
debug mode, 144–147
logging, 143–144
login component, 261
optional component configurations, 282–284
  additions to faces-config.xml, 282–284
  additions to web.xml file, 284
page-level authentication, 263
ProviderAuthenticator component, 260
Seam configuration options, 141–143
  JNDI name, 142
  Seam interceptor, 142
SeamSecurityManager component, 262
SecurityConfiguration component, 262
switching process definitions, 211
using Drools in Seam components, 265
using HTTP specific code in, 285
using for internationalization, 234
validation, 151–157
  calling validator from business tier, 154–155
  schema generation, 157
  validation mechanism in Seam, 152
  validation on domain model, 153–154
  validation on JSF pages, 155–156
WorkingMemory Drools component, 265
components.xml file
  configuring Drools, 265
  configuring jBPM with Seam, 198
  configuring JMS listeners, 255
  configuring page flow with Seam, 220
  configuring ProviderAuthenticator, 260
  configuring SeamSecurityManager, 262
  configuring SecurityConfiguration, 262
  configuring XML in EJB3 container, 271–272
  creating themes, 234
  defining language bundles with Seam, 230
  jBPM process definition XML defined in, 198
  managed persistence context, 283
  reference to resource bundle in, 230

running Seam inside Java EE container, 279
turning on debugging, 249
Concurrency Utilities
  JSRs for Java 5 release, 12
conditional statements
  JSF expression language (EL), 75
configuration
  Ajax4jsf, 251
  creating Hibernate configuration file, 296–299
  Drools rule engine, 265
  configuring log files, JBoss AS, 314
@Configuration annotation
  using TestNG component, 292
configuration, Seam, 123–126
  adding JAR files, 125
  adding properties file, 126
  configuration options, 141–143
    JNDI name, 142
    Seam interceptor, 142
  configuring server for Seam, 20
  embedded configuration files, 274
  finalizing setup, 126
  optional component configurations, 282–284
    additions to faces-config.xml, 282–284
    additions to web.xml file, 284
  optional environmental configurations, 269–282
    running Seam in embedded EJB3 container, 270–275
    running Seam with Hibernate, 275–282
  remote configuring of Seam, 241
  running Seam with Hibernate inside Java EE container, 278–280
  updating XML files, 124–125
connection scripts
  entity beans and database persistence, 89
connection-url parameter
  creating datasource.xml file, 313
consistency, transactions, 115
container-managed transactions *see* CMTs
context demarcation, entity beans, 184

context parameters
    adding to web.xml file for state saving,
        124
    configuring web.xml file for Faces, 53,
        54
    turning on Seam debugging, 146
contexts
    see also Seam contexts
    @Role annotation, 181
    @Roles annotation, 181
    accessing contexts, 182
    Business Process context, 187
    contexts injectable into POJOs, 183
    conversation ID, 248
    inaccessible contexts, 183
    message-driven beans and, 184
    POJOs, 181
    priority order for looking up contexts,
        183
    servlet contexts, 24–25
        HttpSession context, 24
        Servlet context, 24
        ServletRequest context, 24
    where contexts live, 182
    which business object to use with, 184
Contexts class, 182
Continue link
    using Session context, 163
controller, MVC architecture, 9
controller classes, Tapestry, 10
Conversation context, 166–180
    additional configuration, 172
    benefits of, 167
    description, 137
    entity beans (EBs), 184
    how it works, 167–172
    JSF integration with conversations,
        172–180
        links with long-running
            conversations, 173–175
        performing workspace management,
            175–179
        redirecting long-running
            conversation, 179
    multiple sessions, 166
    Seam contexts, 136
    Seam debugging, 180
    stateful session beans (SFSBs), 185
    Travel Reservations application, 166

conversation ID
    Seam remoting using Ajax, 248
@Conversational annotation
    ConversationInterceptor, 169
    creating long-running conversations,
        169
ConversationEntry objects
    properties, 177
conversationId parameter, JSF param tag
    links with long-running conversations,
        173
ConversationInterceptor
    @Conversational annotation, 169
    middle of long-running conversations,
        171
conversationList component, Seam, 177
conversationList.xhtml file, 176
conversationPropagation tag, Seam
    links with long-running conversations,
        174
    type property, 174
conversations
    @Begin annotation, 170
    @End annotation, 171
    adding conversationId to URL of
        requests made, 172
    description, 168
    end conversation component, jBPM
        page flows, 220
    GET requests, 168
    JSF integration with conversations,
        172–180
        links with long-running
            conversations, 173–175
        performing workspace management,
            175–179
        redirecting long-running
            conversation, 179
    long-running conversations, 168,
        169–172
        creating, 169
        normal propagation of conversation,
            173–174
        other propagations of conversation,
            174–175
    maintaining long-running
        conversation, 172
    nested conversations, 168
    purpose of, 169

Seam debugging, 180
short-term conversations, 168
starting page flow, 220
starting/ending tasks, 209
switching workspaces, 178
temporary conversations, 168
viewing lists of conversations, 175–178
workspaces, 172
convertDateTime converter, 63
convertDateTime tag, JSF, 63
converters, JSF, 63
cookieEnabled property, ThemeSelector
    object, 235
cookies
    setting Seam to remember locale via,
        231
core objects
    reference to resource bundle in
        components.xml, 230
core taglib references, 72
    Ajax4jsf creating dynamic validations,
        254
    commandLink tag, JSF, 173, 174
    convertDateTime tag, JSF, 63
    facet tag, JSF, 72, 73
    validateLongRange tag, JSF, 62, 71
    view tag, JSF, 72, 80, 82
country code
    Locale object, java.util, 224
    setting up language bundles, 225
@Create annotation
    Hello World example, 7
create parameter, @In, 134
@CreateProcess annotation, 203
createType method
    Ajax remoting call with parameters, 246
CRUD-based examples
    Garage Sale application, 41
CSS (cascading style sheets)
    themes, 234
currency
    setting up language bundles, 225
current property
    ConversationEntry object, 178

D
data
    displaying dynamic data, 26, 28–30
    requesting and saving data, 26, 30–34

data model, Seam components, 147–151
    JSF presentation tier, 150–151
    POJO, 148–150
data model events, JSF, 65
data source
    adding JBoss data source, 312–314
    configuring jboss-beans.xml file, 272
data source descriptor *see* persistence.xml
        file
Data table component, JSF, 73
data tier
    entity beans (EBs), 102–110
    Hibernate, 102
    Java Data Objects (JDO), 102
data types
    Java data types for Seam remoting, 248
database diagram
    ticketing system application, 44
    Travel Reservations application, 42
databases
    Hibernate Console reverse engineering
        database, 294
    persistence.xml (data source
        descriptor), 88
    transaction processing, 115–119
@DataModel annotation
    retrieving/editing list using SFSB, 149
DataModel object
    Page context, 166
    retrieving/editing list using SFSB, 148
@DataModelSelection annotation
    retrieving/editing list using SFSB, 149
DataModelSelection object
    retrieving/editing list using SFSB, 148
DataSource Configuration screen
    installing JBoss AS, 310
datasource.xml file
    creating JBoss data source, 312–313
dataTable tag, html, 72
    displaying list of addresses, 150
    List page, Garage Sale application, 82
    viewing lists of conversations, 177
    viewing tasks, 204
date components, JSF, 51
Date data type
    Java data types for Seam remoting, 248
dates
    converting into displayable items, 63
    determining style for dates, 63
    inputDate tag, Tomahawk, 81

dateStyle
    determining style for dates, 63
debug method, 144
debug mode, Seam components, 144–147
debugging
    logging with Seam, 143, 144
    Seam debugging conversations, 180
    Seam remoting using Ajax, 249
    web.xml code turning on, 146
Decimal Arithmetic Enhancement
    JSRs for Java 5 release, 11
decision component, jBPM page flows,
        219
decision component, workflows, 195
decisions
    Drools rules built into jBPM decision,
        266
decorate tag, Seam
    Ajax4jsf creating dynamic validations,
        255
default theme
    creating themes, 235
delegated implementation
    renderer, JSF, 62
Delete action
    deleting item from list using SFSB, 149
delete operation
    operations on entity manager, 111
dependency injection
    see also bijection
    IoC (inversion of control), 132
deployment directory, JBoss, 312
deployment isolation
    installing JBoss AS, 310
description property
    ConversationEntry object, 178
design
    jBPM Graphical Process Designer,
        303–305
development
    integration testing, 292–294
    JBoss IDE, 315
    testing, 288–294
        TestNG component, 288–292
    unit testing, 288
direct implementation
    renderer, JSF, 62
directory structure
    file structure of EAR, EJB3, and WAR
        directories, 126

dirty reads, 115
display page
    Session context object, 163
displayable select property
    ConversationEntry object, 178
displaying dynamic data
    presentation implementation patterns,
        26, 28–30
Doc (document)
    types of web services, 238
domain model
    validation on, 153–154
downloads
    Ajax4jsf, 251
    EJB3 (Enterprise JavaBeans 3), 271
    Java 5, 12–13
    JBoss AS, 307
    JBoss IDE, 315
    MyFaces, 51
    MySQL, 314
    Seam, 123
    Tomahawk JAR files, 52
driver-class parameter
    creating datasource.xml file, 313
Drools files
    security-rules.drl file, 262
Drools rule engine, 264–267
    application data, 264
    configuring Drools, 265
    facts, 264
    if-then constructs, 264
    rule, 265
    rule base, 265
    Seam security model, 262
    using Drools in jBPM, 266
    using Drools in Seam components, 265
    working memory, 264, 265
    WorkingMemory component, 265
Drop-down list component, JSF, 73
durability, transactions, 115
DynaForm, Struts
    requesting and saving data, 32
dynamic data, displaying, 26, 28–30
dynamic permissions
    page-level annotations, security, 263
dynamic validations
    Ajax4jsf in Seam, 252

E

EAR (Enterprise ARchive) file
  adding security rules file to deployed
    EAR, 262
  application descriptors
    (application.xml), 90
  description, 88, 89
  file structure of EAR directory, 126
ear tag
  packaging EAR file, 92
EB domain objects
  reasons for using Seam, 6
EBs *see* entity beans
Eclipse, 315
Edit action
  retrieving/editing list using SFSB, 148
edit method
  action events, 65
EJB 2 (Enterprise JavaBeans 2)
  history of EJB3, 86
  Java Naming and Directory Interface, 88
@EJB annotation
  calling EJBs, 120
EJB descriptors *see* ejb-jar.xml file
EJB model
  history of EJB3, 86
ejb-jar.xml file
  adding jboss-seam.jar file, 125
  configuring EJB3s for deployment, 89
  creating JAR package for EJB, 91
  with SeamInterceptor object, 142
EJB2 (Enterprise JavaBeans 2)
  concerns addressed in EJB3, 1
EJB3 (Enterprise JavaBeans 3), 85–120
  calling EJBs, 119–120
  configuring EJB3s for deployment,
    88–92
    application descriptors
      (application.xml), 89–90
    creating JAR package for EJB, 91
    creating XML files, 88–90
    data source descriptor
      (persistence.xml), 88–89
    EJB descriptors (ejb-jar.xml), 89
    packaging, 90–92
    packaging EAR file, 91–92
  downloading, 271
  entity beans (EBs), 102–110
    basics of, 102–104

    collections annotations, 107–110
    entity bean annotations, 104–106
  EntityManager object, 110–114
    Java Persistence Query Language,
      113–114
    operations on entity manager,
      111–113
    persistence context, 110–111
  file structure of EJB3 directory, 126
  history of, 86–88
  installing JBoss AS, 309
  Java Persistence Query Language,
    113–114
  message-driven beans, 101–102
  reasons for JBoss Seam, 2
  reasons for using, 5
  reasons for using Seam, 5
  Seam environment requirements, 6
  Seam integration with EJB3, 140
  session beans, 92–101
    stateful session beans, 97–101
    stateless session beans, 93–97
  testing EJBs, 120
  transactions, 114–119
    bean-managed transactions, 117–119
    container-managed transactions,
      116–117
    transaction processing, 115–119
    types of transactions, 116, 117
  using TestNG component, 288
  validation, 151
EJB3 container
  configuring XML in, 271–273
    components.xml file, 271–272
    jboss-beans.xml file, 272–273
  packaging WAR files, 273–275
    embedded configuration files, 274
    library directory, 273
  running Seam in embedded EJB3
    container, 270–275
    packaging new container, 271–275
    using JBoss EJB3, 271
  why use SBs for business tier, 92
EJB3 JAR
  creating JAR package for EJB, 91
  packaging into EAR file, 91–92
  packaging WAR files, 273

EJBs
    calling, 119–120
    creating JAR package for EJB, 91
    using term EJB generically, 86
    using transactions inside EJBs, 115
EL *see* JSF expression language
@Email annotation, Hibernate, 154
@EmailChecks annotation
    schema generation, 157
embedded configuration files
    packaging WAR files, 274
embedded server
    running Seam in embedded EJB3
        container, 270
@End annotation
    ending long-running conversations, 171
    multiple @End methods for
        conversation, 171
end conversation component, jBPM page
        flows, 220
end parameter, type property
    conversationPropagation tag, Seam, 174
end state component, workflows
    components for creating process
        definitions, 196
    creating workflows, jBPM, 192
@EndTask annotation, 209
enhanced for loop, Java 5, 16
Enterprise ARchive file *see* EAR file
Enterprise JavaBeans 3 *see* EJB3
@Entity annotation
    entity beans, 102
    using JavaBeans and Hibernate, 276
entity beans (EBs), 102–110
    adding fields to entity beans, 111
    annotations, 104–106
    backing beans, 184
    basics of entity beans, 102–104
    collections annotations, 107–110
    Conversation context and, 168
    database persistence, 88
    default binding, 184
    entity bean annotations, 104–106
    entity bean with NotNull validations,
        153
    Hibernate and, 102
    history of EJB3, 87
    negative connotations with EJB2, 1
    persistence, 184

POJOs, 184
    referencing other EBs, 107–110
    removing fields from entity beans, 111
    stateless session bean example, 128
    updating fields on entity beans, 112
    uses of, 184
    using JavaBeans and Hibernate, 276
    where to use bijection, 133
Entity Manager *see* EntityManager object
EntityManager object, 110–114
    @PersitenceContext annotation, 110
    changing persistence context, 150
    description, 102
    factories creating, 110
    injecting entity managers into SBs, 110
    Java Persistence Query Language,
        113–114
    managed persistence context, 283
    method-level modifications on SLSBs,
        128
    operations on entity manager, 111–113
        add, 111
        delete, 111
        update, 112
    persistence context, 110–111
    using JavaBeans and Hibernate, 277
    using TestNG component, 291
enumerated types, Java 5, 17
enumerations
    JSRs for Java 5 release, 12
Enums data type
    Java data types for Seam remoting, 248
enums, Java 5, 17
environments, JBoss IDE, 315
environments, Seam
    environment requirements, 6
    optional environmental configurations,
        269–282
    running Seam in embedded EJB3
        container, 270–275
    running Seam with Hibernate, 275–282
Event context, 165
    description, 137
    JavaBeans, 185
    Seam contexts, 135
event listener methods
    backing beans, 63

event parameter
Ajax4jsf creating dynamic validations, 255
events, JSF, 64–66
action events, 65
data model events, 65
major difference between Seam and JSF, 64
phase events, 66
value-change events, 65
examples
sample applications, 40–45
expression language *see* JSF expression language
externalizing data
internationalization, 223

F
f: tag prefix, 72
see also core taglib references
<f:view> component
Hello World example, 8
facelets
conversationList.xhtml file, 176
using themes, 236
XML support for, 240
Faces *see* JSF (JavaServer Faces)
faces-config.xml file
action events, 65
adding setting of state-saving method, 125
additions to, 282–284
after adding Seam phase listener, 124
configuring XML files for Faces, 54–56
description, 50
Hello World example, 50
JSF pages calling business logic, 121
navigation rules, 76
running Seam inside Java EE container, 279
selecting languages using locale definitions from, 233
setting expression language resolver, 284
facet tag, JSF, 72, 73
@Factory annotation
retrieving/editing list using SFSB, 149
facts, Drools rule engine, 264

fileset tag
creating WAR file for Faces via Ant, 58
filters
configuring web.xml file for Faces, 53
defining Ajax4jsf filter, 251
filter addition for web.xml file, 284
find method
method signature, 112
flights.xhtml page
viewing lists of conversations, 176
flushMode parameter, @StartTask, 209
for loop, Java 5, 16–17
for loops, Java 5
JSRs for Java 5 release, 12
foreign keys
@ManyToMany annotation, 108
@ManyToOne annotation, 107
@OneToMany annotation, 108
@OneToOne annotation, 108
fork component, workflows, 195
form tag, html
Add page, Garage Sale application, 80
Formatted output component, JSF, 73
frameworks
see also Seam framework
JSF (JavaServer Faces), 11
MVC architecture, 10–11
servlets and frameworks, 25
Spring MVC, 10
Struts, 10
Tapestry, 10
web services, 238
from-action tag, navigation rules, 78
from-view-id tag, navigation rules, 76, 78
front controller
configuring web.xml file for Faces, 54
full value
determining style for dates, 64
@Future annotation, Hibernate, 154

G
Garage Sale application, 41
Add page, 79–81
validation on JSF pages, 156
JSF (JavaServer Faces), 78–83
creation of pages and backing beans, 79
List page, 81–83
Seam debugging, 146
using TestNG component, 288

garageSale bean, 79
GarageSaleAction backing bean, 79
garbage collection
    @PreDestroy annotation, 96
@GeneratedValue annotation
    entity beans (EBs), 105
Generic Types
    JSRs for Java 5 release, 11
generics, Java 5, 15–16
    find method signature, 112
GET requests
    conversations, 168
    MVC architecture, 9
getComponentName command
    Seam remoting using Ajax, 247
getOutputText method
    Hello World example, 7
getProcessDefinitions method
    switching process definitions, 213
getServletContext method
    Servlet object, 24
getSession method
    creating HttpSession objects, 24
getters
    @Transient annotation, 106
getViewId method, 294
global navigation rules, 76
GNU licence agreement screen
    installing JBoss AS, 309
graphical process design
    jBPM Graphical Process Designer,
        303–305
greetings
    referencing components inside
        properties file, 228
    setting up language bundles, 225
Grid panel component, JSF, 73
Group panel component, JSF, 73

H

h: tag prefix, 72
    see also html taglib references
hasPermision function, 263
hasRole function, 263
Hello World example
    backing bean for, 50
    faces-config.xml file, 50
    JBoss Seam, 7–8
    JSF (JavaServer Faces), 49–51
    JSF Page with Hello World output, 50

Hibernate
    @Valid annotation, 151
    creating configuration file, 296–299
    entity beans and, 102
    entity beans and database persistence,
        89
    generating Hibernate code, 299
    Hibernate Console with Seam, 294–302
    history of EJB3, 87
    Java Persistence Query Language, 113
    JBoss plug-ins for Eclipse, 315
    running Seam with Hibernate, 275–282
        configuration changes, 278–280
        configuring components.xml, 279
        configuring faces-config.xml, 279
        configuring hibernate.cfg.xml, 278
        configuring web.xml, 280
        inside Java EE container, 278–281
        outside Java EE container, 281
        packaging WAR file, 280
        using JavaBeans and Hibernate,
            276–278
    session, 161
Hibernate annotations, 154
    Ajax4jsf creating dynamic validations,
        252
Hibernate Code Generation window, 299
Hibernate validator
    Ajax4jsf creating dynamic validations,
        252, 255
    calling from business tier, 154
    validation mechanism in Seam, 151
hibernate.cfg.xml file
    creating, 296–299
    generating Hibernate code, 299
    jBPM specific configuration files, 198
    running Seam inside Java EE container,
        278
Hidden field component, JSF, 74
href output
    links with long-running conversations,
        173
HTML files
    contents of WAR files, 58
html taglib references, 72
    Ajax4jsf creating dynamic validations,
        254
    column tag, 72
    dataTable tag, 72, 82
    form tag, 80

messages tag, 156
outputLink tag, 173
outputText tag, 73
panelGrid tag, 80
HtmlDataTable
List page, Garage Sale application, 81
HTTP-specific contexts
using in Seam components, 285
HttpServlet object
implementation of Servlet interface, 24
Session context, 159
HttpServletRequest attribute
Action class, Struts, 27
HttpServletRequest class
HttpServlet object and, 24
web frameworks and, 10
HttpServletResponse attribute
Action class, Struts, 27
HttpServletResponse class
HttpServlet object and, 24
web frameworks and, 10
HttpSession context, 24
invalidate method, 25
HttpSession data
destroying, 25
life cycle of SFSBs, 100
HttpSession interface
HttpSession context, 24
HttpSession objects
HttpServlet object and, 24
logging in, 34, 36
long-running conversations, 168
stateful session beans, 185
Hyperlink component, JSF, 74

I

IBM WebSphere
JSF implementations, 49
@Id annotation
entity beans (EBs), 105
IDENTITY generated value
@GeneratedValue annotation, 106
IDEs
Eclipse, 315
JBoss IDE, 315
idle-timeout-minutes parameter
creating datasource.xml file, 313
if tag, JSTL, 264
if-then constructs
Drools rule engine, 264

@IfInvalid annotation, 151, 155
ifNotBegunOutcome property
redirecting long-running conversation, 180
ifOutcome property, @EndTask, 209
Image component, JSF, 74
immediate property, UIComponent
Apply Request Values phase, JSF, 70
implementation patterns, 25–40
displaying dynamic data, 28–30
listing and viewing pages, 37–40
logging in, 34–37
presentation implementation patterns, 26
requesting and saving data, 30–34
Seam, 28
Struts, 27
imports
static imports, Java 5, 19
@In annotation
accessing contexts, 182
actor assignment, 211
bijection with stateless session beans, 134
method-level modifications on SLSBs, 128
parameters, 134
where to use bijection, 133
index.xhtml page
redirecting long-running conversation, 180
initial parameters
configuring web.xml file for Faces, 53
injection, dependency, 132, 133
see also bijection
Inline message component, JSF, 74
inputCalendar component
using Tomahawk for JSF components, 52
inputDate component
using Tomahawk for JSF components, 52
inputDate tag, Tomahawk
Add page, Garage Sale application, 81
installed property
configuring components.xml file, 272
installing JBoss AS, 308–311
instantiation of objects
why use SBs for business tier, 92
integration testing, 292–294

interceptor classes
 wrapping calls to interceptor, 135
interceptors
 annotations and, 135
 bijection and, 134
 Seam architecture, 134
 Seam configuration options, 142
 Seam integration with EJB3, 140
@Interceptors annotation
 example of SLSB class, 127
 Seam configuration options, 141, 142
internationalization, 223–234
 language bundles, 223, 224–231
  using with Seam, 226–231
 page-level lookup of
   internationalization files, 226
 selecting languages, 231–234
  manually selecting language, 231
  using locale definitions from faces-
    config.xml, 233
 using Seam components for, 234
 with JSF alone, 226–227
 with JSF and Seam, 228–231
invalidate method
 destroying HttpSession data, 25
inversion of control (IoC), 132
 see also bijection
Invoke Application phase, JSF, 71
invoke application phase, Page context,
  166
invokeApplication method, 294
IoC (inversion of control), 132
 see also bijection
isDebugEnabled property
 logging with Seam, 143
isolation
 ACID properties of transactions, 115
 deployment isolation, JBoss AS, 310

J
JAR (Java ARchive) files
 adding library JAR file, 314
 adding Seam JAR files, 125
 configuration of web frameworks, 51
 configuring jBPM with Seam, 197
 creating JAR package for EJB, 91
 installing Tomahawk JAR files, 52
 module tag, 90
 packaging into EAR file, 91–92

 packaging WAR files, 273
 Seam debugging, 146
Java 1.5.0 see Java 5
Java 5, 11–20
 annotations (metadata), 14
 autoboxing, 17
 downloading, 12–13
 enhancements, 14–20
 enums, 17
 for loop, 16–17
 generics, 15–16
 JSRs for Java 5 release, 11
 language features, 14–20
 Seam environment requirements, 6
 static imports, 19
 varargs, 18–19
Java 5 Software Development Kit, 13
Java API for XML Processing (JAXP), 12
Java ARchive files see JAR files
Java community
 JSF specification, 2
Java Community Process see JCP
Java Data Objects (JDO), 102
Java EE (Java Enterprise Edition)
 running Seam with Hibernate
  inside Java EE container, 278–281
  outside Java EE container, 281
 three-tier Java EE architecture, 3
Java Management Extensions see JMX
Java Memory Model and Thread
  Specification, 12
Java Message Service see JMS
Java Naming and Directory Interface see
  JNDI
Java objects
 POJOs (plain old Java objects), 20
Java Persistence Query Language see JPQL
Java Platform Profiling Architecture, 12
Java SASL specification, 12
Java Specification Request (JSR), 11
Java Transaction API (JTA)
 referencing non-JTA data, 89
Java web applications see web
  applications
JavaBeans
 Conversation context and, 168
 default binding, 185
 running Seam with Hibernate using,
  276–278

Stateless context, 161
uses of, 185
Javadoc tag, annotations, 14
JavaScript
    excluding objects on method call, 250
    Java data types for Seam remoting, 248
    remote configuring of Seam, 241
    turning on debugging, 249
JavaServer Faces *see* JSF
javax.persistence.* package, 104
javax.servlet package, 23
JAXP (Java API for XML Processing), 12
JBoss, 307, 311
JBoss AS (JBoss Application Server),
        307–314
    adding data source, 312–314
        creating datasource.xml file, 312–313
    adding library JAR file, 314
    deploying JBoss, 312
    downloading, 307
    installing, 308–311
    locating and configuring log files, 314
    running JBoss, 311
JBoss IDE, 315
JBoss Seam *see* Seam
JBoss Seam framework *see* Seam
        framework
jboss-beans.xml file
    configuring XML in EJB3 container,
        272–273
jBPM (JBoss Business Process
        Management), 188–221
    actors requirement, 189
    components for creating process
        definitions, 192–196
    configuring with Seam, 197–202
    description, 188, 189
    Drools rules built into jBPM decision,
        266
    Drools rules built into jBPM task node,
        267
    how jBPM works, 190
    jBPM specific configuration files, 198
        hibernate.cfg.xml file, 198
    jBPM tokens, 206
    page flow creation in Seam, 220–221
        configuring page flow with Seam, 220
        starting page flow, 220
    page flow definitions, 213–220

brief description, 188
        components for creating page flow,
            217–220
    process definition creation in Seam,
            197–213
        configuring jBPM with Seam,
            197–202
        creating process definition, 203–204
        creating tasks, 207–211
        resuming tasks, 211
        switching process definitions,
            211–213
        viewing tasks, 204–207
    process definitions, 189–196
        brief description, 188
        components for creating, 192–196
    running with Seam or EJB3, 187
    tasks requirement, 189
    using Drools in jBPM, 266
    using jBPM for ticketing system,
            190–192
    when to use, 189
    workflow requirement, 189
    workflows, creating, 191–192
jBPM Graphical Process Designer,
            303–305
    page flow graphical interface, 306
    process definition graphical interface,
            304
jbpm.cfg.xml file, 202
JCP (Java Community Process)
    JSF background, 48
    reasons for using JSF, 2, 4
    servlet specification, 23
JDBC Rowset Implementations, 12
JDK 5.0 (Java 5 Software Development Kit)
    downloading Java 5, 13
JDO (Java Data Objects)
    creating data tier, 102
JEMS (JBoss Enterprise Middleware Suite)
    Drools rules engine, 264
JMS (Java Message Service)
    configuring JMS listeners, 255–256
    JMS messaging using Ajax, 255–257
    message-driven beans, 101
    using JMS listeners, 257
JMX (Java Management Extensions)
    JSRs for Java 5 release, 11, 12
    security, installing JBoss AS, 310

JNDI (Java Naming and Directory
    Interface)
  creating datasource.xml file, 313
  EJB 2.x specification, 88
  entity beans and database persistence,
    89
  parameters, 313
JNDI name
  Seam configuration options, 142
  specifying JNDI name, 127
jndi-name parameter
  creating datasource.xml file, 313
@JndiName annotation
  example of SLSB class, 127
  Seam configuration options, 141, 142
jndiName property
  configuring jboss-beans.xml file, 273
jndiPattern, JBoss
  configuring components.xml file, 272
  Seam configuration options, 142
join component, workflows, 196
join parameter, type property
  conversationPropagation tag, Seam,
    174, 175
@JoinColumn annotation
  @ManyToOne annotation, 108
JPQL (Java Persistence Query Language),
    113–114
  @SuppressWarnings annotation, 113
  parameter to EntityManager object, 113
JSF (JavaServer Faces), 47–83
  Ajax4jsf in Seam, 250–255
  architecture, 59–68
  background, 48–49
  backing beans, 50, 63
  components, 71–74
    component layout, 72–73
    date/calendar components, 51
    standard components, 73–74
    UI component and renderer, 61–62
    using Tomahawk, 51–52
  configuring XML files, 52–56
    faces-config.xml file, 54–56
    web.xml file, 53–54
  converters, 63
  converting dates/numbers into
    displayable items, 63
  core taglib references, 72
  creating WAR (Web ARchive) files, 57–58

description, 11
events, 64–66
expression language see JSF expression
    language
<f:view> component, 8
Faces form component, 73
faces-config.xml file, 50
Garage Sale application, 78–83
  creation of pages and backing beans,
    79
Hello World example, 49–51
html taglib references, 72
implementations, 49
integration with conversations, 172–180
  links with long-running
    conversations, 173–175
  performing workspace management,
    175–179
  redirecting long-running
    conversation, 179
internationalization with JSF alone,
    226–227
internationalization with JSF and Seam,
    228–231
Java community and, 2
JSP pages, 59
life cycle see JSF life cycle
listeners, 64–66
maintaining long-running
    conversation, 172
managed beans, 67–68
messages, 66
MyFaces, 10
navigation, 67
  Invoke Application phase, 71
  page flow, JSF, 76
need to include JSF files in
    deployments, 51
page flow, 76–78
pages see JSF pages
POJOs (plain old Java objects), 59
presentation tier, 150–151
rapid application development for, 59
reasons for JBoss Seam, 2
reasons for using, 4
reasons for using Seam, 5
Seam environment requirements, 6
tag library, 62
tags, 254

UI component and renderer, 61–62
using in non JSF server environment, 51
validator, 62
web frameworks and, 10
JSF expression language (EL), 74–75
    conditional statements, 75
    defining objects inside tag libraries, 74
    indicating start of expression language, 74
    setting expression language resolver, 284
JSF life cycle, 68–71
    Apply Request Values phase, 70
    Invoke Application phase, 71
    phase events, JSF, 66
    Process Validations phase, 70
    Render Response phase, 71
    Restore View phase, 69
    Update Model Values phase, 71
JSF pages
    @IfInvalid annotation, 151, 155
    calling business logic, 121
    expression language, 74
    Hello World example, 7
    Hello World output, 50
    referencing component or bean, 127
    Seam architecture, 141
    stateless session bean example, 130
    validation on JSF pages, 155–156
JSP pages
    Add page, Garage Sale application, 79–81
    displaying list of addresses, 150
    JSF architecture, 59
    List page, Garage Sale application, 81–83
    login.jsp file, 260
    Restore View phase, JSF, 69
    validation on JSF pages, 155
JSP tag library, 147
JSR (Java Specification Request), 11
JSTL tag library
    see also Seam tag library
    if tag, 264
    page-level authentication, 263
JTA (Java Transaction API)
    referencing non-JTA data, 89
JVM (Java Virtual Machine)
    Monitoring and Management
        Specification for, 12

L
language bundles, 224–231
    defining multiple bundle names, 230
    internationalization, 223
        with JSF alone, 226–227
        with JSF and Seam, 229
    language files, 226
    properties file, 225
    setting up, 225
    using with Seam, 226–231
language code
    Locale object, java.util, 224
    setting up language bundles, 225
language files
    using language bundles, 226
Language selection screen
    installing JBoss AS, 308
languages, selecting, 231–234
    manually selecting, 231
    using locale definitions, faces-config.xml, 233
large object data types, @Lob, 106
lastDatetime property
    ConversationEntry object, 178
@Length annotation, Hibernate, 154
    Ajax4jsf creating dynamic validations, 252
lib tag
    creating WAR file for Faces via Ant, 58
library directory
    packaging WAR files, 273
library files
    adding library JAR file, 314
    contents of WAR files, 58
licence agreement screen, JBoss AS, 309
Lifecyle class
    Seam integration with MVC, 139
Link action component, JSF, 74
link tag, Seam
    links with long-running conversations, 173
links
    links with long-running conversations, 173–175
List box component, JSF, 74
List page
    Garage Sale application, 81–83
ListDataModel
    data model events, JSF, 66

listeners
  adding to servlet request life cycle in
      web.xml, 125
  backing beans, 5
  configuring JMS listeners, 255–256
  configuring web.xml file for Faces, 53,
      54
  description, 64
  JSF, 64–66
  Seam integration with MVC, 139
  SeamExtendedManagedPersistence
      PhaseListener, 283
  SeamExtendedManagedPersistence
      PortletPhaseListener, 283
  SeamPhaseListener, 282
  SeamPortletListener, 283
  using JMS listeners, 257
listing and viewing pages
  presentation implementation patterns,
      26, 37–40
lists, generics, 15
loading message
  hiding/changing, 248
@Lob annotation
  entity beans (EBs), 106
@Local annotation
  creating SLSBs, 95
Locale object, java.util, 224
  country code, 224
  internationalization with JSF alone, 227
  language code, 224
  variant code, 224
locales
  internationalization with JSF and Seam,
      228
  setting Seam to remember locale via
      cookie, 231
LocaleSelector
  selecting languages, 231
localization
  converting dates/numbers into
      displayable items, 63
log4j.xml file
  locating and configuring log files, 314
LogFactory
  logging by using LogFactory, 143
@Logger annotation
  logging with Seam, 144

logging
  locating and configuring log files, 314
  logging using LogFactory, 143
  Seam components, 143–144
  using Session context, 163
  which logger to use, 143
logging in
  presentation implementation patterns,
      26, 34–37
login component
  implementing authentication, 260–262
login method, LoginAction class
  implementing authentication, 262
login.jsp file
  creating login/logout, 260
LoginAction class
  calling ProviderAuthentication, 261
LoginAction code, 210
logout method, LoginAction class
  implementing authentication, 262
long value
  determining style for dates, 64
long-running conversations, 168, 169–172
  beginning, 169
  creating, 169
  creating links with, 173–175
  ending, 171
  middle of, 170
  normal propagation of conversation,
      173–174
  other propagations of conversation,
      174–175
  redirecting, 179
loops
  enhanced for loop, 16

M

managed beans
  see also backing beans
  configuring faces-config.xml, 56
  JSF architecture, 67–68
managed persistence context, 283
MANDATORY transaction, EJB3, 116
@ManyToMany annotation
  entity beans (EBs), 108
@ManyToOne annotation
  entity beans (EBs), 107
mappedBy property, @OneToMany, 108
Maps data type
  Java data types for seam remoting, 248

@Max annotation, Hibernate, 154
max-pool-size parameter
    creating datasource.xml file, 313
MDBs *see* message-driven beans
medium value
    determining style for dates, 64
message bundles
    defining language bundles with Seam, 230
    internationalization with JSF alone, 227
Message list component, JSF, 74
message-driven beans (MDBs), 101–102
    contexts and, 184
    uses of, 184
@MessageDriven annotation, 101
messages
    hiding/changing the loading message, 248
    interval to check for any messages, 256
    wait time on server for messages, 256
messages tag, html
    validation on JSF pages, 156
messages, JSF, 66
metadata *see* annotations
Metadata Facility
    JSRs for Java 5 release, 12
method signatures
    find method, 112
    varargs, 18
methods, JavaScript
    excluding objects on method call, 250
    linking topics with methods, 257
@Min annotation, Hibernate, 154
model
    MVC architecture, 9
    updateModelValues method, 294
module tags, EAR file, 90
modules, EAR file, 89
monetary display
    setting up language bundles, 225
Monitoring and Management
        Specification for JVM, 12
Multiline text area component, JSF, 74
Multiselect list box component, JSF, 74
MVC (Model-View-Controller)
        architecture, 9–11
    controller, 9
    frameworks, 10–11
    JSF framework, 11

    model, 9
    MyFaces, 10
    Seam integration with MVC, 139
    Spring MVC, 10
    Struts, 10
    Tapestry, 10
    view, 9
MyFaces
    date/calendar components for JSF, 52
    downloading, 51
    JSF framework, 10
    JSF implementations, 49
MySQL, downloading, 314

N
@Name annotation
    example of SLSB class, 127
    Hello World example, 7
    where to use bijection, 133
name property
    Ajax4jsf creating dynamic validations, 253
name/value pairs
    property files, 224
namespaces
    XML namespaces, 230
        defining themes with, 235
navigation diagram
    ticketing system application, 45
navigation rules
    faces-config.xml file, 76
        configuring, 56
    from action tag, 78
    from-view-id tag, 76, 78
    global navigation rules, 76
    same name returns, 77
navigation, JSF *see under* JSF
nested conversations, 168
nested parameter, type property
    conversationPropagation tag, Seam, 174, 175
Network Transfer Format for Java
        Archives, 12
NEVER transaction, EJB3, 116
no-conversation-id property
    redirecting long-running conversation, 179

nodes
  bringing nodes back together, 196
  deciding which task nodes to go to, 195
  joining two states together, 196
  task node component, workflows, 193
  tasks component, workflows, 193
non-jta-data-source configuration option, 89
none parameter, type property
  conversationPropagation tag, Seam, 174
@NotNull annotation, Hibernate, 154
  Ajax4jsf creating dynamic validations, 252
NotNull validations
  entity bean with, 153
NOT_SUPPORTED transaction, EJB3, 116
numbers
  converting into displayable items, 63

O

object instantiation
  why use SBs for business tier, 92
OGNL (Object-Graph Navigation Language)
  reasons for using Seam, 11
onblur event
  Ajax4jsf creating dynamic validations, 252, 255
onChange events
  value-change events, JSF, 65
@OneToMany annotation
  entity beans (EBs), 108
@OneToOne annotation
  entity beans (EBs), 108
operations on entity manager, 111–113
  add, 111
  delete, 111
  update, 112
@Out annotation
  bijection with stateless session beans, 134
  customizing property name, 163
  defining context scope, 136
  method-level modifications on SLSBs, 128
  parameters, 133
  where to use bijection, 133
outjection see bijection

outPanel tag, Ajax
  Ajax4jsf creating dynamic validations, 255
Output text component, JSF, 74
outputLink tag, html
  links with long-running conversations, 173
outputText method
  Hello World example, 8
outputText tag, html, 73

P

packages
  javax.servlet package, 23
packaging
  configuring EJB3s for deployment, 90–92
  creating JAR package for EJB, 91
  packaging EAR file, 91–92
page component, jBPM page flows, 218
Page context, 165–166
  conversation ID, 248
  description, 137
  invoke application phase, 166
  scoping objects, 166
  Seam contexts, 135
  state, 165
  stateful session beans, 185
page flow definitions, jBPM, 213–220
  components for creating page flow, 217–220
    action, 219
    decision, 219
    end conversation, 220
    page, 218
    redirect, 219
    start page, 218
    start state, 217
  configuring page flow with Seam, 220
  description, 188
  page flow creation in Seam, 220–221
  purpose of, 213
  starting page flow, 220
  when not to use, 214
  when to use, 213
page flow graphical interface
  jBPM Graphical Process Designer, 306
page flow, JSF, 76–78
  navigation, JSF, 76

page-level annotations, Seam security, 263
page-level authentication, 263
pageflow parameter, @Begin
    starting page flow, 220
pages
    display page of Session context object,
        163
    hiding/changing the loading message,
        248
    internationalization, 223–234
    listing and viewing pages, 26, 37–40
    navigation, JSF, 67
    page component, page flows, 218
    page-level lookup of
        internationalization files, 226
    performing partial page updates, 250
    start page component, page flows, 218
    themes, 234
pages.xml file
    redirecting long-running conversation,
        179
    viewing lists of conversations, 175
panelGrid tag, html
    Add page, Garage Sale application, 80
passivation, SFSB life cycle, 97, 98
password parameter
    creating datasource.xml file, 313
password property
    Ajax4jsf creating dynamic validations,
        253
passwords
    excluding objects on method call, 250
@Past annotation, Hibernate, 154
@Pattern annotation, Hibernate, 154
patterns
    implementation patterns used in Seam,
        25–40
    presentation implementation patterns,
        26
@Permission annotation, 263
permissions
    authentication of permissions/rules for
        users, 262
    dynamic permissions, 263
    hasPermision function, 263
    static permissions, 263
@Permissions annotation, 263

persistence
    @Transient annotation, 106
    adding record to database, 111
    changing persistence context, 149
    configuring jboss-beans.xml file, 272
    entity beans, 184
    EntityManager object, 110–111
    jBPM specific configuration files, 202
    managed persistence context, 283
    removing records from SLSB, 111
    setting context for binding instance of
        POJO, 148
    SFSB life cycle, 97
    stateful session beans, 185
    updating fields on entity beans, 112
    when to use Session context, 164
persistence tier, 3
    benefits of using Seam framework, 2
    three-tier architecture, 2–4
persistence.xml (data source descriptor)
    configuring EJB3s for deployment,
        88–89
    configuring jboss-beans.xml file, 273
    creating JAR package for EJB, 91
    managed persistence context, 283
@PersitenceContext annotation
    changing persistence context, 149
    EntityManager object, 110
phase events, JSF, 66
phase listeners, Seam
    faces-config.xml file after adding, 124
    managed persistence context, 283
    SeamExtendedManagedPersistence
        PhaseListener object, 283
    SeamExtendedManagedPersistence
        PortletPhaseListener object, 283
    SeamPhaseListener object, 282
    SeamPortletListener object, 283
plain old Java objects see POJOs
plug-ins
    JBoss plug-ins for Eclipse, 315
plumbing code
    Seam eliminating, 122
POJOs (plain old Java objects), 20
    annotated as Session context, 164
    annotations (metadata), 14, 20
    contexts, 181
    contexts injectable into POJOs, 183
    entity beans, 102, 184

JSF architecture, 59
JSF background, 49
message-driven beans, 102
running Seam with Hibernate, 275
Seam architecture, 132
Seam components data model, 148–150
Seam integration with EJB3, 140
setting context for binding instance of, 148
three-tier Java EE architecture with Seam, 4
transforming complex objects into, 14
why use SBs for business tier, 92
pollInterval variable, JMS listeners, 256
pollTimeOut variable, JMS listeners, 256
pooledTaskInstanceList token, jBPM, 206
pooling
    displaying pooled tasks, 205
    SFSB life cycle, 97
    SLSB life cycle, 93
        life cycle annotations, 96
    why use SBs for business tier, 92
portals, 284
portlet support, Seam, 284
PortletPhaseListener
    configuring portlet environment, 285
portlets, 285
POST requests, MVC architecture, 9
post-then-redirect, JSF
    maintaining long-running
        conversation, 172
postbacks
    Restore View phase, JSF, 70
@PostConstruct annotation
    SLSB life cycle, 96
@PreDestroy annotation
    SLSB life cycle, 96
presentation implementation patterns, 26
    displaying dynamic data, 26, 28–30
    listing and viewing pages, 26, 37–40
    logging in, 26, 34–37
    requesting and saving data, 26, 30–34
presentation tier
    benefits of using Seam framework, 2
    description, 3
    Hello World example, 8
    JSF fundamentals, 47–83
    JSF presentation tier, 150–151
    MVC architecture, 9

reasons for using JSF, 4
reasons for using Seam, 6
three-tier architecture, 2–4
UI component and renderer, JSF, 61
why use SBs for business tier, 92
primary keys, @Id annotation, 105
primitives, autoboxing, 17
printable theme
    creating themes, 235
process definition graphical interface
    jBPM Graphical Process Designer, 304
process definitions, jBPM, 189–196
    changeProcessDefinition method, 213
    components for creating, 192–196
        actors, 194
        decision, 195
        end state, 196
        fork, 195
        join, 196
        start state, 192
        state, 195
        task nodes, 193
        tasks, 193
        transitions, 193
    configuring jBPM with Seam, 197–202
    creating tasks, 207–211
        actor assignment, 210–211
        description, 188
    getProcessDefinitions method, 213
        jBPM requirement for workflow, 189
    process definition creation in Seam, 197–213
        creating process definition, 203–204
    resuming tasks, 211
    switching process definitions, 211–213
    tokens, 188
    viewing tasks, 204–207
process design
    jBPM Graphical Process Designer, 303–305
Process Validations phase, JSF, 70
processes
    creating workflows, jBPM, 192
    dynamic switching of processes, 188
    waiting for come back from external system, 195
processTroubleTickets method, 257
processValidations method, 294

properties file
    adding Seam.properties file, 126
    configuring JMS listeners, 255
    internationalization with JSF alone, 226,
        227
    referencing components inside, 228
    setting up language bundles, 225
property files
    creating themes, 234
    internationalization with JSF alone, 227
    resource and language bundles, 224
    setting up language bundles, 225
ProviderAuthenticator component
    implementing authentication, 260
    LoginAction class calling, 261

Q
queries
    Java Persistence Query Language,
        113–114

R
RAD (rapid application development)
    JSF (JavaServer Faces), 59
Radio button list component, JSF, 74
@Range annotation, Hibernate, 154
redirect component, jBPM page flows, 219
relationships
    @ManyToMany annotation, 108
    @ManyToOne annotation, 107
    @OneToMany annotation, 108
    @OneToOne annotation, 108
@Remote annotation
    creating SLSBs, 95
remoting see Seam remoting using Ajax
@Remove annotation
    life cycle of SFSBs, 100
@Remove annotation
    ending long-running conversations, 171
Render Response phase, JSF, 71
renderer, JSF, 61–62
    delegated/direct implementations, 62
renderers
    configuring faces-config.xml file, 56
renderResponse method, 294
request cycle, Event context, 165
requesting and saving data
    presentation implementation patterns,
        26, 30–34

@RequestParameter annotation
    stateless JavaBean, 161
requests
    adding conversationId to URL of, 172
    applyRequestValues method, 294
    HttpServletRequest class, 24
    JSF background, 49
    requesting and saving data, 26, 30–34
required parameter, @In, 133
required parameter, @Out, 133
REQUIRED transaction, EJB3, 116, 117
REQUIRES_NEW transaction, EJB3, 116
reRender parameter
    Ajax4jsf creating dynamic validations,
        255
@Resource annotation
    bean-managed transactions, 119
resource bundles, 224
    externalizing content, 223
    reference to resource bundle in
        components.xml, 230
responses
    HttpServletResponse class, 24
    renderResponse method, 294
REST (REpresentational State Transfer)
    REST in Seam, 239
    types of web services, 238
Restore View phase, JSF, 69
@Restrict annotation, 263
@ResumeProcess annotation, 204
reverse engineering database
    Hibernate Console, 294
        JBoss plug-ins for Eclipse, 315
RMI (Remote Method Invocation)
    Event context objects, 165
@Role annotation
    using contexts for POJOs, 181
roles
    hasRole function, 263
    implementing authentication, 260
    Seam security model, 258
    testing for user having admin role, 263
@Roles annotation
    using contexts for POJOs, 181
rollbacks
    bean-managed transactions, 118, 119
    container-managed transactions, 116,
        117

RPC (Remote Procedure Call)
    types of web services, 238
rule base, Drools rule engine, 265
rules, 262
rules engines, Drools, 264–267
run files
    running JBoss, 311

S

s: tag prefix, 150
SalesManagerAction class
    using TestNG component, 288
same name returns
    navigation rules, 77
sample applications, 40–45
    Garage Sale application, 41
    ticketing system application, 44–45
    Travel Reservations application, 42–44
SASL specification, Java, 12
saving data
    requesting and saving data, 26, 30–34
SBs *see* session beans
schema generation
    validation, Seam components, 157
scope
    @Role annotation, 181
    @Roles annotation, 181
    defining context scope, 136
    Page context, 166
@Scope annotation
    defining context scope, 136
    retrieving/editing list using SFSB, 148
    using contexts for POJOs, 181
scope parameter, @In, 133
scope parameter, @Out, 133
Seam, 121–157
    Ajax4jsf in Seam, 250–255
    architecture *see* Seam architecture
    components *see* components, Seam
    configuring Seam *see* configuration,
        Seam
    contexts *see* Seam contexts
    description, 1, 122
    downloading, 123
    eliminating plumbing code, 122
    environment *see* environments, Seam
    example of SLSB class, 127
    full life-cycle call with Seam, 139
    framework *see* Seam framework

Hello World example, 7–8
Hibernate Console with Seam, 294–302
implementation patterns *see*
        implementation patterns
interceptor *see* interceptors
JBoss AS (Application Server), 307–314
jBPM (JBoss Business Process
        Management), 188–221
jBPM Graphical Process Designer,
        303–305
JMS messaging using Ajax, 255–257
language bundles, using with Seam,
        226–231
    internationalization with JSF and
        Seam, 228–231
method-level modifications on SLSBs,
        128
performing partial page updates, 250
phase listeners *see* phase listeners,
        Seam
portlet support, 284
reasons for using Seam, 5
remoting *see* Seam remoting using Ajax
REST in Seam, 239
running Seam in embedded EJB3
        container, 270–275
    packaging new container, 271–275
    using JBoss EJB3, 271
running Seam with Hibernate, 275–282
    inside Java EE container, 278–281
    outside Java EE container, 281
    using JavaBeans and Hibernate,
        276–278
security *see* Seam security
setting Seam to remember locale via
        cookie, 231
stateless session bean example, 126–131
tag library *see* Seam tag library
testing, 288–294
    integration testing, 292–294
    TestNG component, 288–292
    unit testing, 288
web services supported, 239
web.xml turning on debugging, 146
wrapping calls to interceptor, 135
Seam architecture, 131–141
    annotations, 132
    bijection, 132–134
    interceptors, 134

inversion of control (IoC), 132
JSF pages, 141
POJOs, 132
Seam integration with EJB3, 140
Seam integration with MVC, 139
three-tier architecture, 138–140
Seam contexts, 135–138
    Application context, 136, 138, 164
    Business Process context, 136, 138, 187
    Conversation context, 136, 137, 166–180
    defining context scope, 136
    Event context, 135, 137, 165
    Page context, 135, 137, 165–166
    Seam integration with MVC, 139
    Session context, 136, 138, 161–164
    Stateless context, 135, 137, 160–161
Seam framework
    @Stateless annotation, 28
    benefits of using Seam framework, 2
    displaying dynamic data, 30
    event listeners difference to JSF, 64
    listing and viewing pages, 39
    logging in, 36
    message-driven beans and, 101
    requesting and saving data, 33
    three-tier architecture with Seam, 3
    three-tier Java EE architecture with
        Seam, 4
    web frameworks, 28
Seam remoting using Ajax, 240–250
    Ajax remoting call, 242–245
    Ajax remoting call with parameters,
        245–247
    batch remote calls, 247
    conversation ID, 248
    debugging, 249
    excluding objects on method call, 250
    getComponentName command, 247
    hiding/changing the loading message,
        248
    Java data types for Seam remoting, 248
    remote configuring of Seam, 241
Seam security, 258–264
    adding security rules file to deployed
        EAR, 262
    authentication in version 1.1.0 of Seam,
        258
    Drools rule engine, 262
    excluding objects on method call, 250

implementing authentication, 258–262
    AuthenticationProvider class,
        259–260
    Authenticator component, 262
    authenticatorAction component, 260
    component-level authentication, 263
    creating login/logout, 260–262
    login component, 261
    page-level annotations, 263
    page-level authentication, 263
    ProviderAuthenticator component,
        260
    roles, 258
    SeamSecurityManager component, 262,
        263
    SecurityConfiguration component, 262
Seam tag library
    Ajax4jsf creating dynamic validations,
        254
    conversationId tag, 173
    conversationPropagation tag, 174
    hasPermision function, 263
    hasRole function, 263
    link tag, 173
    page-level authentication, 263
    using to display list of addresses, 150
    validateAll tag, 156
SeamExtendedManagedPersistencePhase
        Listener, 283
SeamExtendedManagedPersistencePortlet
        PhaseListener, 283, 285
SeamInterceptor object
    Seam configuration options, 142
    Seam integration with EJB3, 140
SeamListener object
    adding listeners to servlet request life
        cycle, 125
    Seam integration with MVC, 139
SeamPhaseListener object
    phase listeners, 282
    Seam integration with MVC, 139
SeamPortletListener object
    phase listeners, 283
SeamRemotingServlet object
    remote configuring of Seam, 241
SeamSecurityManager component, 262,
        263
SeamSpacePermissions package
    example of security-rules.drl file, 263

SeamTest class
    integration testing, 293
Secret field component, JSF, 74
security *see* Seam security
security-rules.drl file
    adding security rules file to deployed
        EAR, 262
SEQUENCE generated value
    @GeneratedValue annotation, 105, 106
serializable objects
    contexts in servlets, 24–25
servers
    configuring server for Seam, 20
    JBoss AS, 307–314
Servlet class file, 23
Servlet context, 24
    Application context compared, 164
    ServletContext interface, 24
Servlet interface
    implementation of, 23
servlet mapping
    configuring web.xml file for Faces, 53
Servlet object, 23
    getServletContext method, 24
Servlet specification
    JSF background, 48
    web frameworks and, 10
ServletContext interface, 24
ServletContext objects
    HttpServlet object and, 24
ServletRequest context, 24
ServletRequest interface
servlets, 23–25
    adding listeners to servlet request life
        cycle, 125
    configuring web.xml file for Faces, 53
    contexts in servlets, 24–25
        HttpSession context, 24
        Servlet context, 24
        ServletRequest context, 24
    frameworks and, 25
    JCP servlet specification, 23
    SeamRemotingServlet, 241
    web applications and, 23
session beans (SBs), 92–101
    @Local annotation, 95
    @PostConstruct annotation, 96
    @PreDestroy annotation, 96
    @Remote annotation, 95

@Remove annotation, 100
@Stateful annotation, 100
@Stateless annotation, 95
    bean- or container-managed, 115
    injecting entity managers into SBs, 110
    stateful session beans, 97–101
    stateless session beans, 93–97
    why use SBs for business tier, 92
Session context, 161–164
    description, 138
    display page of Session context object,
        163
    HttpServlet object, 159
    Seam contexts, 136
    setting context for binding instance of
        POJO, 148
    Stateless class with, 162
    when to use, 164
Session object
    Ajax remoting call, 244
    using JavaBeans and Hibernate, 277
sessions, 161
    Conversation context, 166
setRollbackOnly method
    bean-managed transactions, 118
    container-managed transactions, 117
SFSBs *see* stateful session beans
shopping cart
    life cycle of SFSBs, 99
        @Stateful annotation, 100
short value
    determining style for dates, 64
short-term conversations, 168
@Size annotation, Hibernate, 154
SLSBs *see* stateless session beans
SOAP (Simple Object Access Protocol)
    types of web services, 238
specifications
    JSRs for Java 5 release, 11
Spring
    history of EJB3, 87
Spring framework
    web services, 238
Spring MVC, 10
start page component, jBPM page flows,
    218
start state component, jBPM page flows,
    217
start state component, workflows, 192

startDatetime property
    ConversationEntry object, 178
@StartTask annotation, 209
state
    adding context parameters to web.xml
        file, 124
    adding setting of state-saving method,
        125
    end state component, workflows, 196
    Page context, 165
    start state component, page flows, 217
    start state component, workflows, 192
state component, workflows, 195
@Stateful annotation
    life cycle of SFSBs, 100
    retrieving/editing list using SFSB, 148
stateful session beans (SFSBs), 97–101
    @PersitenceContext annotation, 111
    activation, 97, 99
    Application context, 164
    changing persistence context, 149
    default binding, 185
    Delete action, 149
    Edit action, 148
    how Conversation context works, 168
    HttpSession objects, 185
    life cycle of SFSBs, 97–101
    long-running conversations, 172
    negative connotations with EJB2, 1
    passivation, 97, 98
    retrieving/editing list, 148
    uses of, 185
@Stateless annotation
    creating SLSBs, 95
    making JavaBean an EJB3 object, 8
    Seam framework, 28
Stateless class
    with Session context object, 162
Stateless context, 160–161
    description, 137
    entity beans, 184
    JavaBean, 161
    Seam contexts, 135
    stateless session beans, 184
stateless session beans (SLSBs), 93–97
    @PersitenceContext annotation, 110
    @Stateless annotation, 28
    bijection with SLSBs, 134
    calling validator from business tier, 155

creating SLSBs, 95
default binding, 184
example of SLSB class, 127
life cycle annotations, 96–97
life cycle of SLSBs, 93
method-level modifications by Seam,
    128
removing records from SLSB, 111
Seam example, 126–131
Session context, 162
uses of, 184
static imports, Java 5, 19
    JSRs for Java 5 release, 12
static permissions
    page-level annotations, security, 263
String data type
    Java data types for seam remoting, 248
Struts, 27
    Action class, 27
        displaying dynamic data, 28
        listing and viewing pages, 37
        logging in, 34
        requesting and saving data, 32
    ActionForm object, 27
    ActionMapping object, 27
    component layout, 72
    description, 10
    DynaForm, requesting and saving data,
        32
    JSF background, 49
    web frameworks and, 10
subscribe method, Seam.Remoting
    using JMS listeners, 257
Sun Microsystems
    history of EJB3, 86
support tag, Ajax
    Ajax4jsf creating dynamic validations,
        255
SUPPORTS transaction, EJB3, 116
@SuppressWarnings annotation
    Java Persistence Query Language, 113
Switcher object, 178
switching workspaces, 178

T
t: tag prefix, 81
    see also tomahawk taglib references
@Table annotation
    entity beans, 104

TABLE generated value
  @GeneratedValue annotation, 106
tag libraries
  EL defining objects inside tag libraries,
    74
  Hello World example, 8
  JSF (JavaServer Faces), 62
  JSF pages, 5
  page-level authentication, 263
tag library (taglib) inputs, 72
tag library, JSP, 147
tag library, Seam *see* Seam tag library
tag library URIs
  configuring web.xml file for Faces, 53
tags
  Ajax4jsf creating dynamic validations,
    254
  classes tag, 58
  column tag, html, 72
  commandLink tag, JSF, 173, 174
  conversationId tag, Seam, 173
  conversationPropagation tag, Seam, 174
  convertDateTime tag, JSF, 63
  dataTable tag, html, 72, 82
  ear tag, 92
  f: prefixed tags *see* core taglib references
  facet tag, JSF, 72, 73
  fileset tag, 58
  form tag, html, 80
  from-view-id tag, 76
  h: prefixed tags *see* html taglib
    references
  inputDate tag, Tomahawk, 81
  lib tag, 58
  link tag, Seam, 173
  messages tag, html, 156
  module tags, 90
  outputLink tag, html, 173
  outputText tag, html, 73
  panelGrid tag, html, 80
  t: prefixed tags *see* tomahawk taglib
    references
  validateAll tag, Seam, 156
  validateLongRange tag, JSF, 62, 71
  view tag, JSF, 72, 80, 82
  webinf tag, 58
Tapestry, 10
targetEntity property, @OneToMany, 108

task nodes
  creating workflows, jBPM, 192
  Drools rules built into jBPM task node,
    267
task nodes component, workflows, 193
taskIdParameter parameter, @StartTask,
    209
taskInstanceList token, jBPM, 206
taskInstanceListForType token, jBPM, 206
tasks
  annotations starting/ending tasks, 207
  creating tasks, 207–211
    actor assignment, 210–211
  description, 189
  displaying pooled tasks, 205
  how jBPM works, 190
  jBPM requirement for, 189
  resuming tasks, 211
  viewing tasks, 204–207
    pooledTaskInstanceList token, 206
    taskInstanceList token, 206
    taskInstanceListForType token, 206
  workflows and, 189
tasks component, workflows
  components for creating process
    definitions, 193
  defining actors for tasks using actor ID,
    194
  defining actors for tasks using pooled
    actors, 194
templates
  hotels.xhtml with dynamic template,
    236
  themes, 234, 236
temporary conversations, 168
@Test annotation
  using TestNG component, 292
testing, 288–294
  creating test classes, 291
  integration testing, 292–294
  running Seam in embedded EJB3
    container, 270
  testing EJBs, 120
  TestNG component, 288–292
  unit testing, 288
TestNG component, 288–292
  integration testing, 292
Text field component, JSF, 74
text-only theme, 235

themes, 234–237
  creating themes, 234–235
  default theme, 234
  defining themes with XML namespaces, 235
  printable theme, 235
  selecting themes, 236
  text-only theme, 235
  using themes, 236
themeSelector component, 236
ThemeSelector object, 234
three-tier architecture, 2–4
  Java EE architecture, 3, 4
  Seam architecture, 138–140
  Seam integration with EJB3, 140
  Seam integration with MVC, 139
  with Seam, 3, 4
ticketing system application, 44–45
  configuring jBPM with Seam, 197
  creating process definition, 203
  displaying pooled tasks, 205
  generating Hibernate code, 299
  Hibernate Console reverse engineering database, 295
  processTroubleTickets method, 257
  switching process definitions, 211–213
  using jBPM for ticketing system, 190–192
  viewing tasks, 204
tokens, jBPM, 206
  pooledTaskInstanceList token, 206
  process definitions, 188
  taskInstanceList token, 206
  taskInstanceListForType token, 206
tokens, workflows
  creating process definition, 203
  creating workflows, jBPM, 192
  task node component, 193
  tasks component, 193
Tomahawk, 52
tomahawk taglib references
  inputDate tag, tomahawk, 81
Tomcat
  running Seam in embedded EJB3 container, 270
tools
  Hibernate Console, 294–302
  jBPM Graphical Process Designer, 303–305

topics
  configuring JMS listeners, 255
  linking topics with methods, 257
  using JMS listeners, 257
@TransactionAttribute annotation
  container-managed transactions, 117
@TransactionManagement annotation
  bean-managed transactions, 118
transactions, 114–119
  ACID properties, 114
  atomicity, 115
  bean-managed, 117–119
  container-managed, 116–117
  consistency, 115
  description, 114
  dirty reads, 115
  durability, 115
  EJB3 types of, 116
    default type, 117
    MANDATORY, 116
    NEVER, 116
    NOT_SUPPORTED, 116
    REQUIRED, 116, 117
    REQUIRES_NEW, 116
    SUPPORTS, 116
  isolation, 115
  transaction processing, 115–119
  using TestNG component, 290
  using transactions inside EJBs, 115
  why use SBs for business tier, 92
@Transient annotation
  entity beans, 106
transition property, @EndTask, 209
transitions
  Drools rules built into jBPM decision, 266
transitions component, workflows, 193
Travel Reservations application, 42–44
  Conversation context, 166
  Hibernate Console reverse engineering database, 294
  using themes, 236
try ... catch
  bean-managed transactions, 119
type property
  conversationPropagation tag, Seam, 174
type safety
  typesafe enums, 17

Find it faster at http://superindex.apress.com/

U

UI component, JSF, 61–62
UIComponent objects
  Apply Request Values phase, JSF, 70
UIViewRoot component
  Restore View phase, JSF, 70
Unicode Supplementary Character
    Support, 12
uninstaller, JBoss AS, 310
@UniqueConstraint annotation
  entity beans, 105
unit testing, 288
Update Model Values phase, JSF, 71
update operation, entity manager, 112
updateModelValues method, 294
URLs (uniform resource locators)
  adding conversationId for requests
      made, 172
  configuring web.xml file for Faces, 54
  connection-url parameter, 313
user flow diagram
  Travel Reservations application, 44
user-name parameter
  creating datasource.xml file, 313
UserTransaction interface
  bean-managed transactions, 118

V

@Valid annotation, Hibernate, 154
  calling validator from business tier, 155
  validation mechanism in Seam, 151
validateAll tag, Seam
  Ajax4jsf creating dynamic validations,
      255
  validation on JSF pages, 156
validateLongRange tag, JSF, 62, 71
validations
  @IfInvalid annotation, 151, 155
  Ajax4jsf creating dynamic validations,
      252
  annotation for Seam to perform, 127
  entity bean with NotNull validations,
      153
  entity beans, 184
  Hibernate validation framework, 151
  Process Validations phase, JSF, 70
  processValidations method, 294

Seam components, 151–157
  calling validator from business tier,
      154–155
  schema generation, 157
  validation mechanism in Seam, 152
  validation on domain model, 153–154
  validation on JSF pages, 155–156
validator, JSF, 62
  calling validator from business tier,
      154–155
value parameter, @In, 134
value parameter, @Out, 134
value-change events, JSF, 65
varargs, Java 5, 18–19
variables
  static imports, 19
variant code
  Locale object, java.util, 224
versions
  checking Java version, 12
view tag, JSF
  Add page, Garage Sale application, 80
  core taglib references, 72
  List page, Garage Sale application, 82
viewing pages
  listing and viewing pages, 26, 37–40
views
  getViewId method, 294
  MVC architecture, 9
  Restore View phase, JSF, 69

W

WAR (Web ARchive) files
  contents of, 58
  creating for Faces, 57–58
    compiling via Ant, 57–58
  defining different name, 90
  file structure of WAR directory, 126
  packaging EJB3 container, 271, 273–275
  packaging into EAR file, 91–92
  Seam with Hibernate inside Java EE
      container, 278, 280
  WAR file example, 57
web application design
  MVC architecture, 9–11
web applications
  fundamental component of, 23
  implementation patterns used in Seam,
      25–40

message-driven beans, 184
presentation implementation patterns,
        26
rapid application development, 59
sample applications, 40–45
    Garage Sale application, 41
    ticketing system application, 44–45
    Travel Reservations application,
        42–44
servlets, 23–25
Web ARchive files *see* WAR (Web ARchive)
    files
web contexts
    module tag, 90
web frameworks
    configuration of, 51
    description, 10
    JavaServer Faces, 11
    message-driven beans, 101
    MVC architecture, 10–11
    Seam, 28
    Spring MVC, 10
    Struts, 10, 27
    Tapestry, 10
    validator, 62
web pages *see* pages
web request
    sessions, 161
web resources
    deploying to application servers, 57
web services, 237–240
    REST in Seam, 239
    SOAP, 238
    types of, 238
WEB-INF directory
    configuring XML files for Faces, 53
    creating WAR file for Faces via Ant, 58
    creating WAR files for Faces, 57
web.xml file
    adding context parameter for state
        saving, 124
    adding listener to servlet request life
        cycle, 125
    additions to, 284
    Ajax4jsf configuration, 251
    configuration for, 147
    configuring JMS listeners, 255
    configuring XML files for Faces, 53–54
    creating WAR file for Faces via Ant, 58

creating WAR files for Faces, 57
filter addition for, 284
maintaining long-running
    conversation, 172
running Seam inside Java EE container,
    280
SeamRemotingServlet, 241
turning on Seam debugging, 146
webinf tag
    creating WAR file for Faces via Ant, 58
WebLogic, BEA
    JSF implementations, 49
@WebRemote annotation
    Ajax remoting call, 245
    excluding objects on method call, 250
websites
    multiple sessions, 166
WebSphere, IBM
    JSF implementations, 49
workflows, jBPM
    components for creating process
        definitions, 192–196
        actors, 194
        decision, 195
        end state, 196
        fork, 195
        join, 196
        start state, 192
        state, 195
        task nodes, 193
        tasks, 193
        transitions, 193
    creating, 191–192
    how jBPM works, 190
    jBPM requirement for, 189
    switching process definitions, 211–213
    tasks and, 189
working memory, Drools rule engine, 264,
    265
workspaces, 172
    JSF integration with conversations,
        175–179
    switching workspaces, 178
    viewing lists of conversations, 175–178

X

XML files/configuration files
    ActionForm object, Struts, 27
    annotations (metadata), 14

Find it faster at http://superindex.apress.com/

configuring EJB3s for deployment,
        88–90
    application descriptors
        (application.xml), 89–90
    data source descriptor
        (persistence.xml), 88–89
    EJB descriptors (ejb-jar.xml), 89
configuring XML files for Faces, 52, 56
    faces-config.xml, 54–56
    web.xml, 53–54
configuring XML in EJB3 container,
        271–273
    components.xml, 271–272
    jboss-beans.xml, 272–273
contents of WAR files, 58
creating datasource.xml, 312–313
creating WAR file for Faces via Ant, 58
creating workflows, jBPM, 191–192
EJB3 annotations, 88
jBPM Graphical Process Designer, 303
jbpm.cfg.xml, 202
log4j.xml, 314
pages.xml file, 175, 179
reference to resource bundle in
        components.xml, 230
running Seam inside Java EE container
    configuring components.xml, 279
    configuring faces-config.xml, 279
    configuring hibernate.cfg.xml, 278
    configuring web.xml, 280
switching process definitions, 212
updating, Seam configuration, 124–125
XML namespaces, 230
defining themes with namespaces, 235
XML response
    REST in Seam, 239
xmlns tag
    core objects, 230
    XML namespaces, 230

You Need the Companion eBook

Your purchase of this book entitles you to buy the companion PDF-version eBook for only $10. Take the weightless companion with you anywhere.

We believe this Apress title will prove so indispensable that you'll want to carry it with you everywhere, which is why we are offering the companion eBook (in PDF format) for $10 to customers who purchase this book now. Convenient and fully searchable, the PDF version of any content-rich, page-heavy Apress book makes a valuable addition to your programming library. You can easily find and copy code — or perform examples by quickly toggling between instructions and the application. Even simultaneously tackling a donut, diet soda, and complex code becomes simplified with hands-free eBooks!

Once you purchase your book, getting the $10 companion eBook is simple:

❶ Visit **www.apress.com/promo/tendollars/**.

❷ Complete a basic registration form to receive a randomly generated question about this title.

❸ Answer the question correctly in 60 seconds, and you will receive a promotional code to redeem for the $10.00 eBook.

2560 Ninth Street • Suite 219 • Berkeley, CA 94710

Offer valid through 9/07.